# How to Get
# What You Want
## *and Want What*
## *You Have*

# JOHN GRAY,
### Ph.D.

# How to Get
# What You Want
# *and Want What*
# *You Have*

A PRACTICAL AND SPIRITUAL
GUIDE TO PERSONAL SUCCESS

*HarperCollinsPublishers*

HarperCollins books may be purchased for educational, business, or sales promotional use. For information please write: Special Markets Department, HarperCollins Publishers, Inc., 10 East 53rd Street, New York, NY 10022.

FIRST EDITION

*Designed by Alma Orenstein*

Library of Congress Cataloging-in-Publication Data

Gray, John
    How to get what you want and want what you have : a practical spiritual guide to personal success / John Gray. — 1st ed.
        p.  cm
    ISBN 0-06-019409-X
    1. Success—Psychological aspects.  I. Title.
BF637.S8G693  1999
158'.1—dc21                                                    98-53436

99 00 01 02 03  RRD/❖  10 9 8 7 6 5 4 3 2 1

*This book is dedicated with greatest love and affection to my wife, Bonnie Gray. Her love, joy, wisdom, and light have not only graced my life but shine in every line of this book.*

# CONTENTS

# ACKNOWLEDGMENTS

I THANK MY WIFE, Bonnie, and our three daughters, Shannon, Juliet, and Lauren, for their continuous love and support.

I thank Oprah Winfrey and the entire wonderful staff of Harpo Studios for participating in a personal success workshop and then inviting me to present it on TV over six successive Wednesdays. That experience helped crystallize many of the ideas of this book.

I thank Diane Reverand at HarperCollins for her brilliant feedback and advice. I also thank Laura Leonard, my dream publicist; and Carl Raymond, Janet Dery, Anne Gaudinier, and the other incredible staff at HarperCollins.

I thank my agent Patti Breitman for believing in my message and recognizing the value of *Men Are from Mars, Women Are from Venus* nine years ago. I thank my international agent

Linda Michaels for getting my books published in more than forty languages.

I thank my staff: Helen Drake, Bart and Merril Berens, Ian and Ellie Coren, Bob Beaudry, Martin and Josie Brown, Pollyanna Jacobs, Sandra Weinstein, Michael Najarian, Donna Doiron, Jim Puzan, and Rhonda Coallier for their consistent support and hard work.

I thank my many friends and family members for their support and helpful suggestions: my brother Robert Gray, my sister Virginia Gray, Clifford McGuire, Jim Kennedy, Alan Garber, Renee Swisco, Robert and Karen Josephson, and Rami El Bratwari.

I thank the hundreds of workshop facilitators who teach Mars-Venus Workshops throughout the world and the thousands of individuals and couples who have participated in these workshops during the past fifteen years. I also thank the Mars-Venus counselors who continue to use these principles in their counseling practices.

I thank my mother and father, Virginia and David Gray, for all their love and support as they gently guided me on my own journey toward personal success. And thanks to Lucile Brixey, who was like a second mother to guide me and love me.

I thank Maharishi Mahesh Yogi, who was like a second father for nine years, my first role model and mentor to guide me to achieve both inner and outer success. Many of the ideas today regarding how I meditate I learned directly from him twenty-eight years ago.

I thank my dear friend Kaleshwar, who directly assisted me in writing various sections of this book. It clearly would not have happened without his help.

I give thanks to God for the incredible energy, clarity, and support I received in bringing forth this book.

*John Gray*
NOVEMBER 1, 1998

# How to Get
# What You Want
## *and Want What*
## *You Have*

# INTRODUCTION

THE REAL CHALLENGE in life is not just getting what you want, but continuing to want what you have. Many people have learned how to get what they want, but then they no longer enjoy it. Whatever they get is never enough; they always feel as if they are missing something. They are not happy with themselves, their relationships, their health, or their work. There is always one more thing to disturb their peace of mind.

At the other end of the spectrum, there are those who are much more content with who they are, what they do, and how much they have, though they do not know how to get more of what they want. Their hearts are open to life, yet they are still not making their dreams come true. They do their best, but wonder why others have more. Most people fit somewhere between these two extremes.

Personal success is the middle ground, the place from which you get what you want and continue to want what you have. Personal success is not measured by who you are, how much you possess, or what you have accomplished. Instead, personal success is measured by how good you *feel* about who you are, what you have done, and what you have. Personal success is within our grasp, but we must clearly know what it is and set our intention to have it.

---

**Personal success is getting what you want and continuing to want what you have.**

---

Personal success, however, is not just about feeling good or happy with your life. It also involves feeling confident that you can get what you want and motivated to do what it takes. Personal success requires a clear understanding of how to create the life you want. For some, finding personal success is learning how to get more; for others, it's understanding how to be happier; and for many, it is learning both of these important skills.

Achieving personal success does not have to be left to chance, destiny, luck, or good fortune. Although some people are born with the ability, for most, the skills must be learned and practiced before personal success can be achieved. The good news is that you *can* learn how to achieve personal success, and you are probably much closer to it than you could ever imagine. For most people, it is just a matter of making a few small but significant changes in the way they think, feel, or act to create the fulfilling life they want.

---

**A few small but significant changes in the way we think can pave the way to greater personal success.**

---

Applying one or two new insights to your life can literally change everything overnight. Although circumstances may temporarily be the same, the way you look at your life can change in an instant. When the glare of life is too much, putting on dark glasses enables you to begin to relax and to see clearly again in an instant. Likewise, by making a few adjustments you will suddenly not only be happier with what you have, but also be confident that you are on the road to getting what you want.

## Four Steps to Personal Success

There are four steps to achieving greater success in your life. Throughout *How to Get What You Want and Want What You Have,* we will explore each of these steps in greater detail. They are:

**Step One: Set your intention.** Recognize where you are now and clearly see where you need to go to achieve the right balance of inner and outer success for you. No matter how hard you try, if you are going in the wrong direction, all you will meet in life is resistance, and you will never reach where you want to go. By acting in harmony with your soul's desire, and not just the desires of your mind, heart, and senses, you will be well prepared for both inner and outer successes.

**Step Two: Get what you need.** Learn how to get what you need to be true to yourself. It is not enough to say, "I want to be me." To know yourself and be true to yourself, you must understand the ten different kinds of love and support that every person needs. With an understanding of what you are missing and how to get it, you will begin automatically to experience inner success. A car may work fine, but if you don't fill it up with gas it won't run. Likewise, if you are not getting certain love needs fulfilled, you cannot find your true self.

**Step Three: Get what you want.** Understand the secrets of creating outer success without having to give up being true to yourself, and you will begin to get everything you want in the outer world. Realize the importance of strong desires, positive beliefs, and passionate feelings in creating and attracting what you want. Learn how to strengthen the power of your desires by acknowledging and transforming negative feelings and emotions.

**Step Four: Remove the blocks to personal success.** Become aware of the twelve common blocks that could be holding you back from having what you want, and begin to clear the way for both inner and outer success. Learn to release any of the twelve blocks that may be holding you back: blame, depression, anxiety, indifference, judgment, indecision, procrastination, perfectionism, resentment, self-pity, confusion, and guilt. With this new ability, you will begin to experience that nothing outside yourself is holding you back.

## Deborah Finds a Husband

When Deborah first started learning personal success, she was struggling to achieve greater outer success and desperate to get married. By resetting her intention toward finding peace and happiness within, she was able to let go of struggle. To make this shift, she realized she wasn't getting the support she needed. She wasn't giving herself the support to relax and do what she wanted to do. As she started to feel better about herself and her life, she was able to start attracting and creating what she wanted.

Not only did she find a great job, but she finally met the man of her dreams and got married. To move on into her new life and get married, she had to remove three of the blocks to personal success. In the past, when it came to making a commitment, she would become confused, judgmental, and indecisive. By removing these blocks, she was able to continue to want the man who loved her. By following the four steps to personal success, Deborah started making her dreams come true.

## Tom Starts a Bakery

Tom had always wanted to have his own bakery, but had settled for working at a television station. He didn't want to be doing his job and occasionally resented and judged the people with whom he worked. The first step for Tom to begin achieving personal success was to set his intention to be happy regardless of his circumstances. He began practicing meditation and experienced as a result increased inner fulfillment and happiness.

His job was no longer a major source of dissatisfaction for him. By getting the support he needed in meditation, he began visualizing what he wanted. He started getting little things right away. It seemed his life was filled with little miracles. He would want a travel assignment and get it. Or he would want to be praised and acknowledged, and it would happen. His confidence that he could attract and create what he wanted grew.

This confidence freed him to follow his dreams. He left his job and started a bakery. To make this shift, he first had to let go of his blocks. At his job, he often had to deal with resentment and judgments. Gradually, as these blocks dropped off, he let go of his procrastination and indecision and made the move toward starting his new business, which is now a great success.

## Robert Reconnects with His Children

Robert was already a multimillionaire when we began applying the principles and practices of personal success. He had achieved outer success, but he was miserable. He had been divorced three times, and he wasn't on speaking terms with his children. From the outside, he had it all, and no one except his counselor and his ex-wives knew how unhappy he was. People who don't have a lot of money often can't imagine that with millions of dollars a person might have difficulty being happy. Yet it is very common.

Robert learned to look within to find his happiness. He wanted to attract someone in his life to share his great wealth, but first he had to enjoy it himself. He always had to have a beautiful woman by his side to feel good. He learned to be happy without a partner for one year. He took time off to travel the world.

As he finally learned that he could be happy on his own, he took time to heal his relationships with his children. As he started giving and receiving the love he needed, his dependence on outer success decreased. He was glad he had it, but realized how it had kept him from finding real peace and happiness.

To resolve issues with his children and to find a partner to share his life, he had to move through many blocks. He had to let go of his blame, judgments, and indifference toward his ex-wives, and understand why his children resented him. By releasing these blocks, he was grateful to reconnect with his kids and feel peace and joy in his life.

## Facing Life's Challenges

As you achieve personal success, life ceases to be a struggle; what was difficult becomes easier. Life will still have its problems, but you will be more successful in solving them. Doors that seemed locked before will begin to open. You will feel relieved and free to be yourself and to do what you are here to do. You will be better equipped to meet life head on. Life's inevitable challenges will become opportunities to make you more powerful.

In whatever way you don't already experience your inner goodness and greatness, the radiant light of your true self will begin to shine and light your way. With the dawning of this inner light, your journey through darkness will be over. Not only will you begin to clearly sense what you are here in this world to do, but you will realize that you are not alone. The truth that you are loved and supported in this world will become a living, tangible experience.

---

**With the dawning of the inner light
of self-love, your journey
through darkness will be over.**

---

Personal success is not an imaginary state of grace devoid of conflict, disappointment, or frustration. A big part of mastering personal success is learning how to transform negative feelings into positive feelings and negative experiences into lessons learned. Being true to yourself is a growing process involving much change, which includes experiencing life's ups and downs. Achieving personal success means that when you fall down, you will know exactly how to get back up.

Those who take the risk to be themselves and to follow their hearts will occasionally fall down. Mistakes, setbacks, and adjustments are a part of life, an important part of how we learn and grow.

---

**The main difference between those who
succeed in life and those who fail is the
knowledge of how to get back up.**

---

Personal success is different for everyone. For some, it is a roller-coaster ride, and they love it. For others, it is a gentle ride on a big Ferris wheel. Though there is a lot of starting and stopping, they enjoy a great view with good conversation. Most of the time, they get to enjoy going around without any interruption. Certainly everyone's ride in life is unique, but in every case there will be ups and downs, twists and turns, starts and stops.

As you achieve greater personal success, you will still feel negative emotions, but they will always lead you back to increasing waves of joy, love, confidence, and peace. Once you learn how to move though negative emotions, you will realize how important they are, and you wouldn't want to live your life without them. If you are looking to experience a life without the flow of negative and positive emotions, visit a graveyard and rest in peace.

Being alive means movement. The secret of personal success is staying in touch with your inner peace, joy, love, and confidence. When you feel confident that you know how to begin to get what you want, you are less restless, you accept that life is a process, and you understand that it sometimes takes time to get what you want. When your heart is open and you are being true to yourself, you are able to enjoy and appreciate every step of your unique journey. The expectation for life to be perfect drops away as you discover that what you attract and create in your life is perfect for you.

You hold the power and the key to your future; you can do it, and only you can do it for you. With these new insights, you will gain the ability to find answers to all the questions you may have had about creating success. You will gain a new perspective that will help you make sense of your experiences in life. You will know with confidence how to get to where you want to go. These four steps provide a practical and spiritual road map for you to create the life you are meant to live.

# CHAPTER 1

# *Money Can't Buy Happiness*

MANY PEOPLE HAVE achieved a lot in their lives, but they lack peace. The world is filled with unhappy millionaires who cannot sustain loving relationships. Yet they and those who emulate them continue to think that more money or more of "something" will finally help them feel good about themselves and their lives.

As we all know, money does not buy happiness or love. Even though this maxim is familiar, it is still easy to get caught in the web of illusion that outer success can make us happy. The more we think that money is capable of making us happy, the more we give away our power to be happy without it.

As you read this, some part of you is probably thinking, "Yeah, I know that money can't really make me happy, but it sure can help." Although this thought is reasonable, it is important to recognize that it is a misconception that robs you of your power. To reset your direction in life, to make sure you are moving in the direction of personal success, you must recognize that money can't make you happy. The experience that money makes you or others happy is an illusion.

## The Nature of Illusion

Let's explore for a moment the nature of illusion. When you experience the sun moving across the sky each day, another part of you knows that the sun isn't really moving. Although your senses register the movement, your mind knows that the sun is not moving. Though you feel stationary, you know the earth is spinning on its axis. Your mind knows that movement of the sun is an illusion, and that in truth you are moving.

Comprehension of this illusion requires abstract thinking. A young child cannot figure it out. Schoolteachers notice a shift from concrete thinking to abstract thinking in a child's development. In most cases, the shift happens practically overnight. One day, the student can't even begin to understand an algebra equation, and then suddenly, when the brain is ready, the student gets it. If the brain is not yet ready, no amount of instruction will help a student understand.

---

**To comprehend or recognize an illusion, the brain must reach a certain level of development.**

---

This shift in children from concrete thinking (the world is what you see) to abstract thinking (concepts are real as well) generally happens around puberty. As a child reaches twelve or thirteen, the brain has developed enough to comprehend concepts adults assume are obvious. Just as a child develops, the brain capacity of mankind develops over time as well. Ideas that challenged the greatest minds in history are now comprehended by fourteen-year-old science students.

## The Making of Common Sense

Just five hundred years ago, everyone thought the earth was flat and the sun moved across the sky. They were not ready to comprehend this simple illusion. Their brains were not yet ready to comprehend the abstract thoughts necessary to recognize that the earth was moving and the sun was stationary. When Copernicus described the phenomenon in 1543, many could not accept the challenge to their beliefs. He was perceived as a threat by the church and imprisoned in his home for the rest of his life.

After relatively a few years, his discovery became accepted. Mankind had taken a leap. What was impossible for most to comprehend became fact. Right now mankind is taking part in another leap forward to understand the secrets of personal success. All the great teachings and religions have led mankind to this point. Yet as we venture forward, these important traditions will continue to be a strong foundation. The algebra student will always depend on basic "concrete thinking" math skills to progress.

At this exciting time in history, many illusions are being recognized as such—for example, the illusions about relationships between men and women. I am always asked, "Why didn't someone write *Men Are from Mars, Women Are from Venus* before? It is all so obvious. It just seems like common sense."

## An Idea Whose Time Has Come

The simple answer to this question is that it is an idea whose time had come. It would not have been so popular fifty years ago or even twenty years ago. When I started teaching *Men Are from Mars, Women Are from Venus* in the early eighties, some people were still getting upset with me, misinterpreting and misunderstanding what I had to say. They just could not comprehend the notion that men and women were different *and* that both were equally good. In their minds, if men and women were different, one had to be superior. Since I am a man, people assumed I was saying men were better than women. Gradually, during the course of fifteen years, the ideas in *Men Are from Mars, Women Are from Venus* have been accepted as common sense not only in America, but around the world. This shift in comprehension is global.

The common sense of one generation was always a new discovery to previous generations. Just fifty years ago, the theme of the women's movement was that we are all equal because we are the same; women are not different from men. To earn equality, women had to prove that they were the same as men. At least society was letting go of the notion that one sex was better than the other. Now, once again, it is common knowledge that men and women are different, but we realize that being different doesn't mean one is "better" than the other.

---

**The common sense of one generation
was always a new discovery to
previous generations.**

---

We are on the threshold of recognizing the equality of the sexes without mistakenly assuming that one sex is in any way intrinsically better than the other. This same insight is gradually awakening us and preparing us to release racial discrimination as well. In a similar way, more and more people are recognizing and appreciating the value of all religious teachings. It is becoming accepted that God does not discriminate because of one's religion. God's grace is available to all regardless of whether you are agnostic, atheist, Christian, Jewish, Hindu, Muslim, whatever. God loves us regardless of what we believe. As the world becomes a smaller place, we have the opportunity to experience firsthand the goodness in various people of different faiths. This recognition of the goodness in all people regardless of their faith has freed many to release their limited beliefs from the past.

People are beginning to accept as common sense that all major religions can teach the truth and be different. And thank goodness; millions of lives have been lost because people have been unable to comprehend that spiritual messages could be different but equal. As we enter the new millennium, it is now becoming common sense that "the paths are many, but they all lead to the same place." We are seeing through the illusions that there is only one way, or one superior people, or one superior teaching or religion, for all people. As we see the wisdom in all religions, we are able to appreciate the truths in our personal paths even better.

## A New Door Is Being Opened

With all these advances in common sense, a new door is being opened for mankind. We are now capable of debunking other illusions: the illusion that the outer world is responsible for how we feel; the illusion that outer success has the power to make us happy.

Even though it may seem that the outer world is responsible for how we feel, in truth we are fully responsible. When the outer world gives us more of what we want and "makes us happy," the happiness is fleeting, because we continue to think that we need more to be happy. As we believe that we are dependent on the outer world, our inner connection becomes weaker. Just as happiness disappears with the belief that we can't be happy without more, joy begins to last when we believe and regularly experience that our happiness is not dependent on outer circumstances. Let's take money as an example to explore.

Joy begins to last when we experience that
our happiness is not dependent on
outer circumstances.

It is not money that makes us happy, but our inner belief, feeling, and desire. When we get more money, we are happy because we believe that we are now able to be ourselves. The permission to be ourselves actually makes us happy and not the money. For a brief moment we believe, "Now I have the power to be me and do what I want."

We have depended on money for this belief because we have been unable to turn within to discover that we have always had that power. Right now you have the power to begin turning inside to experience your inner goodness and greatness. With a little instruction and practice, you can begin to experience the truth of this important insight.

Right now you have the power to begin
turning inside to experience your inner
goodness and greatness.

In every case, money makes us happy because we believe that money allows us to be, do, have, or experience what we want. We are deficient in our ability to experience that who we are is already happy, loving, peaceful, and confident.

This experience, however, is within the reach of every person. In the past, only a few could attain this realization, and even then it would sometimes take a lifetime to achieve. Now the experience is immediately available by taking a few steps in a new direction. What was once attainable only to the recluse who left society to find inner peace is now available to all without having to give up a normal lifestyle.

When Jim came in for counseling, he was depressed. He

was about forty-two, and he was not pleased with how his life had turned out. When he saw people drive by with expensive cars, he would feel bad inside, as if he had failed somehow. He had not measured up and was not good enough.

He resented that others had more than he. He had done all the right things. He had gone to school. He had worked hard and gone to church. Why was he not getting the fun toys? Why was he missing out? Jim was resentful and judgmental of the wealthy and felt sorry for himself.

After a personal success workshop, his whole attitude about money changed. He realized that he had never really cared that much about money, and that's why he didn't have much. Although he wanted more, he realized that he had actually done okay in life. He also began to see how he was holding himself back by rejecting money.

His new challenge was to continue being happy with less, but to want more. When he would see expensive cars, he would say, "That's for me." As he started letting go of his resentments and judgments about money, he gave himself permission to want more. He forgave himself for his setbacks and mistakes in life and was even grateful for the lessons he learned.

He learned that he had both the power to have more and to be completely happy with what he had. He clearly experienced that he didn't need more to make him happy. As he let go of his attachment to money, he also started to make more. He learned the secret of getting what you want. He was able to want more while also appreciating what he had.

---

**What was once available only to a few who choose to leave the stress of society to find inner peace is now available to all.**

---

When I began teaching many of the principles of personal success more than twenty-five years ago, the results were good, but nothing approaching what they are today. The principles have certainly worked for me, but it has taken most of my life to achieve. What people can gain from a two-day weekend workshop took me more than twenty years to achieve. The difference between now and then is like night and day, and even then the results were impressive.

Although a teacher likes to take a little credit for the success of his students, I am very aware that the time is right. Mankind is taking a wonderful step. We have all been born at this special time to take this step together. When the student's brain is ready, as in algebra, new insight and understanding becomes attainable with a little instruction and practice.

As a teacher for more than twenty-five years, I have witnessed this shift. The capacity to comprehend how we alone are responsible for our feelings is now within everyone's reach. With this one simple but important insight, the secrets of creating personal success finally can be comprehended and applied by all and not just by a few fortunate ones.

# CHAPTER 2

# *Outer Success Magnifies Our Feelings*

M ONEY, RECOGNITION, marriage, children, a great job, terrific clothes, winning a lottery, or any other form of outer success is like a magnifying glass that is turned on your inner feelings. If you are already peaceful, you will feel more peaceful. If you are already happy and loving, you will be happier and more loving. If you are already confident, you will be more confident.

On the other hand, to the degree that you are not happy, the joy, love, confidence, or peace in your life will diminish. Without your first achieving personal success, "having more" will just complicate your life and create more problems. If you are not happy first, getting rich will not make you any happier.

If you are already happy and you know that you are not dependent on more money to be happy, greater wealth can make you happier. There is nothing wrong with wanting more money. The quest for more money limits us only when we forget the real source of happiness is within.

17

The secret of getting what you want and wanting what you have is first to learn how to be happy, loving, confident, and peaceful regardless of outer conditioning. Then, as you achieve more worldly success, you can become happier. By first learning to be happy with what you already have, material success will follow in an appropriate manner according to what you really want in life.

## The Illusion of External Success

The inherent promise of all external success is an illusion. When we are unhappy, we think a new car, a better job, or a loving partner will make us happier. Yet with each acquisition, the opposite effect is achieved.

When we are unhappy, we commonly think "having more" will take away our inner pain. But it doesn't. There is never enough. As we continue to feel unhappy "because we don't have more," the illusion of outer success is reinforced. Increasingly we believe that we can't be happy unless we have more. These are some common examples:

"I can't be happy until I have made a million dollars."

"I can't be happy until my bills are paid."

"I can't be happy unless my wife changes."

"I can't be happy unless my husband is more attentive."

"I can't be happy unless I have a better job."

"I can't be happy unless I lose weight."

"I can't be happy unless I win."

"I can't be happy unless I am respected or appreciated."

"I can't be happy with so much stress in my life."

"I can't be happy because there is too much to do."

"I can't be happy because there is not enough to do."

Initially getting what we want appears to work, but after a short period of happiness we are unhappy once again. As before, we mistakenly believe that having more will make us happy and take away our pain. Unfortunately each time we look to outer success for fulfillment, we feel more emptiness inside. Instead of feeling greater joy and peace in our lives, we feel more turmoil and dissatisfaction.

Without personal success, the more we get, the more unhappy we become. Why is it that the tabloids are full of unhappy stories about the rich and famous? For many celebrities, fame and money bring only misery, drug addiction, divorce, violence, betrayal, and depression.

---

**If we don't learn to create personal success,
getting more in life leaves us feeling more
dissatisfied and anxious.**

---

Their lives exemplify that external success can bring fulfillment only if we are already in touch with our internal positive feelings. Outer success can be a heaven or a hell, depending on the degree of personal success we have already achieved.

## Personal Success Comes from Within

Personal success comes from within and is achieved when you are able not only to be yourself, but also to love yourself. It is feeling confident, happy, and powerful in the process of doing what you want to do. Personal success involves not just achieving goals, but feeling grateful and satisfied with what you have after you get it. Without personal success, no matter who you are or how much you have, it will never be enough to make you happy.

---

**Personal success is achieved when you feel really good about yourself and your past, present, and future.**

---

To achieve personal success, we must first recognize the futility of making material success our highest priority. What good is it to achieve a goal and then feel it is not enough? What good is it to get what you have always wanted and then not want it anymore? What good is it to have millions of dollars and then look in the mirror and feel unlovable? What good is it to sing your song and have others love it, but hate it inside? To find true and lasting happiness, we must make a small but very significant shift in our thinking. We must make achieving personal success and not material success our number one priority.

## Experiencing Happiness

Lasting happiness comes from within. Getting what you want can only make you happy to the degree that you are already happy. Doing something well and learning something new can only make you more powerful to the degree that you are already feeling confident. Loving others can only be sustained to the degree that you already love yourself. Peace, harmony, and time to relax in your life can only be found to the degree that you are already relaxed and peaceful. The outer world can only bring us waves of love, joy, power, and peace when we are already feeling it inside.

---

**Material success can only make you happy if
you are already happy.**

---

When you are already happy, what you get in life allows you to feel it. It is like lying comfortably in a warm bath. If you lie really still, you won't notice the warmth after a while. If you move around a little and stir things up, you will begin to feel waves of warmth again. To feel the warmth two conditions must be met: you must be in the warm water and you must experience some movement.

In a similar manner, to experience waves of happiness in life, we must already be happy and then experience the waves generated by getting what we want. If we are already happy, it doesn't take enormous material success to generate delicious and delightful waves of joy.

If you are lying in a bath connected to your inner power and confidence, by just moving around you will experience waves of confidence. When you are lying in a bath of love and peace, your interactions will bring you waves of love and peace.

On the other hand, if you are feeling unhappy, unloving, insecure, or stressed, your daily interactions will bring you waves of unhappiness, disappointment, and distress. No matter how successful you are in getting what you want, it will bring only misery and stress.

## The Real Cause of Unhappiness

When outer success leaves us feeling unhappy, we conclude that the cause of our unhappiness is not having the next thing. It is easy to make this mistake. Most of the time, when we are unhappy, we are wanting something. We automatically conclude that we are unhappy because we don't have what we want. This conclusion is incorrect.

We mistakenly conclude that the cause of
unhappiness is not getting or having what
we want.

As you achieve more personal success, you discover that
wanting more and not getting it does not cause unhappiness.
Instead, wanting more creates positive and happy feelings like
passion, confidence, determination, courage, excitement, enthusiasm, faith, appreciation, gratitude, love—the list goes on. Wanting more is not the cause of unhappiness. When you are already
happy and confident inside, wanting more and engaging yourself
in the process of getting more creates waves of joy, love, confidence, and peace.

Desire or wanting more is the nature of the soul, mind,
heart, and senses. The soul is always willing to be more; the
mind is always seeking to do more and know more; the heart is
always longing to love more and have more; and the senses are
always wanting to enjoy more. If we are true to ourselves, we
will always want more.

Wanting more is the nature of our soul,
mind, heart, and senses.

It is natural to want more love in our relationships. It is good
to want more success in our work. It is normal to enjoy the pleasures of the senses and to want more. Wanting more is our natural state. There is nothing wrong with desire. Abundance, growth,
love, pleasure, and the movement toward more is the nature of
life.

Wanting more and having less is not the cause of our unhappiness. Unhappiness is simply the lack of inner joy and has nothing
to do with our external condition. The real cause of unhappiness is
the absence of joy. Unhappiness is similar to darkness. Darkness is

the absence of light. The way to remove darkness is simply to turn on the lights. Likewise, our unhappiness lessens as we learn to turn on the light within ourselves.

---

**Darkness cannot be directly removed, but it automatically disappears when you turn on the light.**

---

When we are connected to or are in touch with our true nature, we are automatically happy. Why? Because who we are is already happy. Our true nature is already loving, joyful, confident, and peaceful. To find happiness, we must begin an inner journey to recover and remember who we really are. By looking inside ourselves, we will discover that the joy, love, power, and peace we are looking for is already there. Those qualities are who we already are.

# CHAPTER 3

# *Selling Out to Outer Success*

I N LITERATURE and in the movies, there are often stories of people who achieve success by selling their souls to the devil or to the "dark force." Although these stories are fictional there is actually a lot of truth to the metaphor. It is much easier to achieve outer success if you give up who you are. Selling your soul or selling out simply means making outer success more important than your soul's desire to be loving, joyful, and peaceful.

Love, joy, trust, compassion, patience, wisdom, courage, humility, gratitude, generosity, confidence, and kindness, etc., are all human qualities inherent in every person. When you deny the natural process of developing and expressing these qualities, you are selling out. Outer success is then achieved, but it is not truly fulfilling.

When you devote all your attention to outer success, you get there faster but lose yourself in the process. You lose the ability to want what you have. You forfeit the ability to experience peace in your mind and love in your heart. Happiness is either fleeting or always just around the corner, out of reach.

---

**When you devote all your attention to outer success you get there faster, but you lose yourself.**

---

Many people have achieved great worldly success by not being loving. They deny their inner loving selves to become more powerful. It is easier to make decisions and do what achieves outer success when you do not care about anyone else. This is the dark side of material success. It does not apply to all, but it does explain why some very abusive people have so much power.

Without caring about the needs and feelings of others or about what is fair, they are free to be selfish. Unencumbered by the needs of others, they can ruthlessly move ahead. History abounds with powerful and corrupt people who achieved fame and fortune by abusing, neglecting, and stepping on others. All they cared about was power and not what happened to others. Outer success was more important than being true to themselves. Although their lives may have appeared prosperous and fulfilled on the outside, they were impoverished inside.

### Be Happy and Success Will Follow . . . but Not Always

On the other hand, some choose to be true to themselves, but often miss out on achieving outer success. They observe the popular idea of following their hearts, following their bliss, or simply going with the flow. "Don't worry, be happy," or "Let go and let God do it" are sometimes their mottoes. They believe that if they focus on being happy, success will happen. Though this sounds great, it is not always true. Being true to yourself can make you happy, but it does not ensure getting you what you want.

The world is full of people who are very happy without having much in external terms. While visiting villages in India, southeast Asia, parts of Africa, and other places around the world, I have observed many people who have tremendous joy and peace in their lives without outer material success. The world is filled with millions of people who are happy but poor. Even in wealthy countries, some of the nicest, most giving people still have difficulty paying their bills and making ends meet. These people have found degrees of joy and love, but they are not adept at getting what they want in the world.

---

**The world is filled with millions of people who are happy but poor.**

---

While some just don't care that much about material success, others reject outer success and condemn it as the root of evil or the cause of the world's problems, which is not necessarily true. They throw the baby out with the bathwater. They mistakenly reject their natural desires for more because others with material success have abused their power. Whether we consciously reject the material world or we just don't care much about it, a negative attitude about wealth is what keeps it away.

It is not enough just to be happy inside. If we are to live the life intended for us, we must also give ourselves permission to want more. If you are one who just does not care about money, it is good to reevaluate that feeling. You may unknowingly be blocking your inner desire for more. Although you are happy, you can be happier by embracing all the parts of who you are.

Sometimes when we don't get what we want, we deal with disappointment by denying our desires. Rather than feel our inner pain, we can avoid it by saying things to ourselves like: "It wasn't that important," or "I didn't really care anyway." This tendency can eventually numb our feelings and prevent us from feeling our natural desires.

## From Monk to Millionaire

In my twenties, I went through a phase of rejecting the outer measures of success. After living as a monk in Switzerland for nine years, I eventually "found God" and discovered a tremendous source of internal happiness. To a certain degree, I had renounced my need for outer success. Yet I still wanted to make a difference in the world, and I prayed, asking God to show me the way. My inner guidance directed me to California.

Living in Los Angeles, I rejected material success even more. I believed that rich capitalists were selfish and responsible for the problems of the world because they would get what they wanted by whatever means. Devoid of respect and compassion for others and the environment, they were just looking out for themselves and fulfilling their insatiable ambition for wealth and power. I rebelled, refused to get a job, and gave all my money to the poor. Within a few months I, too, was homeless.

One night, while sitting around the fire with other homeless people, I experienced a turning point. As I sat there teaching and sharing my ideas, one fellow passed me a beer and said, "John, we love to listen to you talk, but we have no idea what you are talking about." We all laughed.

Later that night, I kept remembering what he said. His one comment was the catalyst that brought me back. I realized that I needed to find my place in the world, a place where I was making a difference in a way that felt right to me. I also realized that I was missing the many comforts I had taken for granted before. Although my heart was full of love and joy, I was also miserable. This lifestyle was not right for me. I was cold, hungry, broke, scared, and lost. As I poured my heart out to God, I began to ask for help.

Although my nine years as a monk had taught me how to find inner happiness, that night I discovered that my soul was wanting much more. I learned it is not enough just to be happy with what we have; we must honor our material desires as well. As I began to ask God for more, it started to happen. Little miracles immediately occurred all around me.

---

**It is not enough just to be happy with what we have; we must honor our material desires as well.**

---

When I was hungry, someone would invite me to dinner. When I was tired of sleeping in my car, someone would invite me to visit for a while. I needed gas for my car, and my parents decided to send me a gas credit card. The joy and relief I felt in response to all these gifts helped me to begin releasing my negative beliefs and feelings about money and wealth. As this continued material success began to flow in, within a year, my life started to become comfortable again. I was still finding my direction, but my prayers were being answered.

I had always lived my life by the words of Jesus, when he said, "Seek ye first the kingdom of heaven within, and then all else will be given unto you." Well, from that night on, I began a new phase of my journey. I had found the kingdom of heaven within; it was now time for everything else to come my way. Throughout the next nine years, everything I had ever wanted was given to me and then more than I could ever imagine.

It had taken me nine years to go inside to find my true self and my connection to God. Coincidentally, it took another nine years to attract and create everything I had wanted in the outer world. Then, after another nine years, I was able to create success beyond my highest expectations and dreams and develop practical insights and tools for others to achieve their dreams much faster. Although it took me nine years of dedicated mediation, prayer, and devotion to God to find inner success, that time commitment is not necessary for others. As we enter this new millennium, it is no longer necessary to renounce the world and mediate ten to fifteen hours a day to find the kingdom of heaven within.

## Show Me the Money

As I look back at my own personal journey, I see many wrong turns and mistakes. Yet these mistakes were necessary for me to find my way. Fortunately I had enough love and support in my life to learn from those mistakes. After suffering deprivation, I gave myself permission to ask for more. I learned the hard way that if you don't ask, you don't get. Eventually, after asking God to show me the way, I learned that I could also ask God to show me the money.

---

**I gradually learned that I could
ask God to show me the money.**

---

Besides prayer, what helped me to move on was knowing I had the resources to make it in the world. I was not alone. God was helping me, and I had a family and friends who cared, who could and would help me to get started again.

I was able to bounce back so quickly because of the love and support available to me from God, my family, and my friends. For God's blessing to take hold in our lives, we must do everything within our power to get what we need. We cannot just expect God to do it all. It does not work that way. God only does the part that you can't do.

---

**When you pray, God only does
the part that you can't do.**

---

It is not enough just to find God to achieve outer success; you must also be able to get what you need to grow. The seed could be healthy, the ground could be fertile, but if you don't water the seed, it can't grow. To experience inner and outer success, fulfilling our emotional needs for love and support is essential. As we get what we need, we are able to look back at our difficulties and learn and grow from them. Without the support of love, we tend to look back with resentment and blame and miss the important lessons and growth.

For me, being poor and homeless helped me to open my heart even more to the material world. As I got back on my feet again, I really appreciated money. I clearly saw that money was a blessing from heaven or a ticket to hell. Money itself is neutral; we make it either positive or negative. The blessing from my homelessness was an enormous appreciation for the gifts money could offer me.

---

**Money can be a blessing from heaven
or a ticket to hell.**

---

I still remember the joy and appreciation I felt when a friend noticed that I needed money and gave me fifty dollars. I learned that a hungry man really appreciates the simple things of life. This appreciation for what I had plus the confidence that I could have more became a tremendous magnet to draw success into my life.

Even today, although I love the comforts and trappings of outer success, I travel around the world and sometimes live as a native in underdeveloped areas. Missing the simple comforts of our Western lifestyle keeps me from taking it for granted; primitive living protects me from losing my appreciation for what I have.

A tremendous amount of stress is taken from your life when your biggest worries and challenges are where to get bottled water, toilet paper, cooked food, a shower, and a bed. When the comforts of life are temporarily taken away, I experience once again that I can be happy without them. When the pleasure of the mind, heart, and senses are not available, the inner light of the soul has a chance to shine more brightly.

Yet this wouldn't be such a enlightening experience and positive challenge if I did not know that I also had the power to come back and to create material success as well. When I choose to give up the pleasure of civilization, it is not permanent. I still honor my desires from pleasure, comfort, abundance, money, family, friends, and health. After five or six days, I return to comfort. When I finally have a room in a nice hotel with hot water, I experience such physical pleasure and joy that I thank God for my outer success as well.

Let there be no doubt that the quest for money is hurting the world, but do not forget the reason why. Material abundance or the desire for it is not the problem. Outer success is only the cause of unhappiness when we make it our primary focus and neglect being true to ourselves. Once we have fulfilled our soul's desire to be whole, then money is one of God's blessings.

The desire for money and outer success is healthy and wholesome. Worldly success does not have to take us away from ourselves. You can have outer success and be true to yourself. You can get what you want and continue to love and take care of what you have. With an understanding of how to create personal success, you can experience both inner and outer success.

# CHAPTER 4

# *How to Get What You Need*

U P TO THIS POINT, we have explored the importance of being true to yourself and finding inner happiness before focusing on your outer desires. But how do you find inner happiness when you are not happy? How do you love yourself or others when that love is lacking? What can you do when you look in the mirror and you don't like what you see? You try to love your neighbor, but you are annoyed instead. You try to love your spouse, but you can't feel the love. You try to like your job, but you hate it or you are bored. You love your family, but you feel guilty because you want out. It's just work and chores. How do you find happiness when the world is bringing you down?

The answer to this question is "Identify your need and then get it." A car can be working fine, but if it doesn't have any gas, it can't go anywhere. In a similar way, when we are not getting what we need, we forget our true nature for a while. Happiness is our true nature. To experience and connect with it, we simply need to feel a particular kind of love and support. Until we open our hearts to receive what we need, we cannot find our way home.

---

**A car can be working fine, but if it doesn't have any gas, it can't go anywhere.**

---

Whenever you are not feeling inner success, it has nothing to do with not getting what you want in the outer world. We often think it does, but it doesn't. When life is too stressful to find peace, love, joy, and confidence, we need to remember who we are and reconnect with our inner nature. We cannot find our inner happiness unless we are first getting what we need.

When we are happy, we are getting exactly the kind of love we need. If we are unhappy, it is always because we are somehow deficient in a particular kind of love. Love is like a fuel, and when we stop getting the fuel we need, we automatically shut down. A lamp could be working fine, but if the power goes off there is no light. Receiving love gives us the power we need to connect with our true selves. Getting what we need is like switching on the power to turn on the light. The wiring is already in place; we need only to turn on the power.

## Love Vitamins

Just as the body needs water, air, food, vitamins, and minerals to stay healthy, the soul needs different kinds of love to grow and express itself fully through the mind, heart, and body. The mind assists the soul in fulfilling its purpose in the world by intention, setting goals, positive thinking, and believing. The heart assists the soul by drawing in what it needs to grow. The senses feed the soul by providing necessary information and pleasurable experiences in the outer world.

---

**The heart serves the soul by drawing in what
it needs to grow.**

---

Unless the soul gets what it needs, it is powerless to direct and bring fulfillment to our lives. Without a connection to the soul we are lost. We may think we know where we are going, but we will never truly be satisfied. To make a connection to our souls, we must be able to open our hearts and receive the kind of love we need. To be healthy and strong, the soul needs different love vitamins.

When our hearts are closed or our minds are looking in the wrong direction for happiness, we cannot achieve inner success. By learning to identify your love needs and then opening your heart to receive different love vitamins, you will always be able to reconnect with your inner self.

There are ten love needs, or love vitamins. To achieve personal success, you need each of the love vitamins. To know and experience your true self, you need to open your heart to receiving each of these vitamins. To immediately be free of struggle and begin to experience your power to create and attract success in your life, these different love vitamins are essential. They are:

## THE TEN LOVE VITAMINS

1. Vitamin G1—Love and support from God.
2. Vitamin P1—Love and support from our parents.
3. Vitamin F—Love and support from family, friends, and having fun.
4. Vitamin P2—Love and support from peers and others like us with similar goals.
5. Vitamin S—Love and support from ourselves.

6. Vitamin R—Love and support from intimate relationships, partnerships, and romance.
7. Vitamin D—Loving and supporting someone who is dependent on us.
8. Vitamin C—Giving back to our communities.
9. Vitamin W—Giving back to the world.
10. Vitamin G2—Serving God.

A rich and fully satisfying life will be fueled by each of these ten kinds of love and support. When you are dissatisfied in life (no inner success) or you are not getting what you want (no outer success), the basic reason is that you are not getting what you need. In many cases, your heart may be open, but you are looking in the wrong direction. At other times, you may be looking in the right direction, but your heart is closed, and you can't absorb the love your soul needs. By learning more about each of these love vitamins and how to get what you need, you will discover that you hold the power to make your dreams come true right now.

## Each Love Vitamin Is Essential

Each of these different kinds of love and support is essential if we are to be whole. Although each kind of love is just as important as another, it doesn't always seem that way. If your body is sick, it may be that you are deficient in just one vitamin. In this case, even though all the vitamins are important, the vitamin you are missing becomes more important for you. If you begin to take and assimilate that missing vitamin, your health will immediately improve.

In a similar way, if you are missing a particular love vitamin, no matter how many of the other love vitamins you are getting, you will not be happy. This is why there are so many approaches to finding happiness. Some people begin to thrive when they open up to God's love, while others thrive when they begin to love themselves and take responsibility to make their lives better. Some find happiness by being in a loving relationship, while others benefit most from spending time with their family or friends. People have different emotional deficiencies, and based on what is missing, they will have a greater need for that kind of love.

---

**Our needs for love vary according to our unique deficiencies.**

---

For example, when a person who is very deficient in perceiving God's love attends a spiritual event with his heart open, he will experience an incredible transformation. Yet others, who may be less deficient in divine love, will not have such a dramatic experience. They have a wonderful time, feel refreshed, but they are not overwhelmed. It is similar to eating. When a hungry person gets food, she is very, very happy, and the food tastes great. To someone who has just eaten a big meal, more food is not very satisfying, nor will it taste that good. Too much of anything good will eventually numb our ability to enjoy it. Instead of wanting more, we will be trying to get away.

Chris had been very devoted to his church. For years, he had been very fulfilled. He had a wife, a family, and a good job. He became depressed in his forties. In counseling, it came out that he even felt guilty because he was depressed.

He thought that because he had found God he should be happy. He had devoted his life to being good and serving God. He could not understand why he was so depressed. He felt guilty for not feeling the joy and connection that he used to feel when he first became spiritually involved.

After becoming aware of the love vitamins, Chris realized that he wasn't doing anything to have fun. He was deficient in vitamins F and S. He was so concerned with being good that he didn't do enough for himself. He was so serious in his dedication to God that he didn't take time to relax and enjoy himself.

To let go of his depression, he needed to shift his attention away from serving God and focus more on himself. He decided to take some time off. He bought a fun car and went on a road trip with his wife and kids. He let himself do things he would never have done before. He and his wife read some books on sex and romance and started having more fun in the bedroom.

As he shifted his attention to himself without guilt, he began to feel better. After being away from the active responsibilities of his spiritual community, he eventually came back and felt renewed appreciation and support. He needed first to understand that taking time for himself did not mean he did not love God.

## The Love You Need Is Always Available

Your soul has the power to attract the love it needs, but your mind must recognize what you need, and your heart must open up to receive it. The love you need is always available. When your heart wants what is not available to you, you are always looking in the wrong direction. Most of the time, when you are not getting what you need, it is because you are trying to get everything from one source. You are trying to stay balanced by attending to only one vitamin. The telling sign that you are looking to the wrong vitamin for help is the belief that you cannot get the love you want.

---

**When your heart's desire is not available to you, you are looking in the wrong direction.**

---

This happens a lot in marriage. When people get married, they often neglect their other love vitamins. They look to their partners for everything. Why? Because, in the beginning, everything is wonderful. They feel as if they are in heaven. And why not? They have found someone with whom to share love and to satisfy their need for vitamin R—love and support from intimate relationships, partnerships, and romance. Very quickly it begins to feel so good that they forget their other needs.

This heaven is temporary. While you are getting big doses of vitamin R, you are unaware of other unfulfilled needs or deficiencies. Although the soul needs all ten vitamins, the heart can assimilate only one at a time. Even if you were deficient in all ten vitamins, it feels as if you have everything you will ever need when one is being received.

---

**The soul needs all ten love vitamins, but the heart can only assimilate one at a time.**

---

If you were deficient in vitamin R but you also had other deficiencies, you would be blissfully unaware of the other unfulfilled love needs while you were getting vitamin R. However, once the need for vitamin R was fully satisfied, you would then begin to feel the emptiness of your other unfulfilled love needs.

Whenever one need has been satisfied, we will begin to feel dissatisfied to the degree we are deficient in our other love needs. At a certain point in intimate relationships, when we have received what we need from vitamin R, we will inevitably begin to feel the collective emptiness of any other unfulfilled needs we may have.

This finally explains the mystery of why so many couples fall in love and then fall right out. The beginning of a relationship is so blissful because we temporarily stop feeling the emptiness of our deficiencies. We connect with our true nature and feel great. As soon as our need for vitamin R is met, we begin to feel the same unhappy feelings we had before falling in love.

At this point, we stop feeling our love. No matter what we do or our partners do, it will never be enough. We become stuck.

Now things are even worse, because we mistakenly conclude that our partners are to blame. Instead of enjoying the presence of our partners, either we want them to change or we want to change partners. We lose touch with our heart's desire to love and get muddled by trying to make the relationship better or by finding a better relationship. Stuck in blame, we not only forfeit our power to get what we need, but we begin to hurt each other as well.

By learning to identify your different love vitamins, you will not be fooled by the illusion that there is not enough. When you experience obstacles to getting what you need, you will be able to change your focus, change your intention, and immediately begin getting the real support that you need. By knowing where to look and how to get there, you will understand that you can always get the love you need.

# CHAPTER 5

# *The Ten Love Tanks*

THE DYNAMICS of getting what you need can best be understood by using the visual aid of love tanks. Imagine that for every love need there is a love tank. Everyone has ten love tanks. If we are to stay connected with our true selves, our objective is to keep filling up our love tanks.

If we are disconnected from the qualities of our true selves, then one or more of our love tanks is getting low. By taking that particular love vitamin, you begin to fill up the tank. As a love tank is being filled, we are once again connecting back to our true selves.

The secret, then, to staying in touch with our true selves is to keep filling up our love tanks. As long as we are filling up, we not only will experience increasing joy, peace, and contentment, but will be able to stay in touch with our inner potential and power to create and attract more.

As soon as one tank is full, to stay connected, you must begin to fill another tank. If you don't shift your focus from time to time to make sure all your love needs are being satisfied, you become unhappy. For example, if you only look to your partner for love,

41

you will begin to resent that your partner is not giving you enough.

---

### As soon as one tank is full, to stay connected, you must begin to fill another tank.

---

The experience of being in love is actually the filling up of the R tank. If we continue to focus on getting more of that particular love vitamin after a tank is full, then we disconnect from our inner source of fulfillment.

Ironically, seeking the same love vitamin that was connecting us results in disconnection. When we disconnect from the true source of our fulfillment, nothing our partners do seems good enough. At such times, we mistakenly assume that working on the relationship will make things better. Instead, we need to focus on filling up another love tank.

When the vitamin R tank is full, we only make things worse when we focus all our energies and attention on solving the problems in a relationship. Without this insight, couples routinely hurt each in the process of trying to make things better. So much unnecessary struggle and pain can be avoided when couples learn to recognize the symptoms of a full tank and then begin focusing their attention on filling up another love tank.

George and Rose have been married about eight years. Although they were practicing many of the suggestions and ideas of good communication outlined in *Men Are from Mars, Women Are from Venus*, they were still stuck. It seemed that nothing George did was good enough. He tried to do the things he had learned, but it just wasn't enough for his wife, Rose. She felt he really wasn't connecting to her when she spoke, and that he wasn't giving her what she needed.

Rose was trying to be loving, but she felt that no matter how loving and giving she was, George would take her requests as criticism. She felt as if she were walking on eggshells. Although she wanted to be loving, her feelings of resentment kept building. It seemed that the more she tried to do the right things, the more resentful she felt that she was not getting what she needed in the relationship. George and Rose had lost the romance in their relationship.

After learning about the love tanks, George and Rose made a commitment not to expect anything more from each other for about six weeks. During that time, they were to sleep in different bedrooms and focus on getting their needs met elsewhere. They were to abstain from looking for intimate love, but were to take time for themselves and nurture their relationships with friends and family. They were to do whatever they wanted and not expect anything from each other.

After a few weeks of adjustment, they both began to feel happier and more fulfilled. When they stopped blaming each other for their unhappiness, they began to realize that they could have a good time. As they began to fill up their other love tanks, they began to feel better about themselves and were more content.

At the end of six weeks, they went on a special date to reconnect. They had a great time. For the first time in years, George felt real passion, desire, and interest in Rose. Rose really enjoyed his attention and was very appreciative. She was amazed that the things she wanted were there. He was attentive, connected, interested, and turned on to her. She was everything he wanted: appreciative, positive, happy to be with him, and responsive. To reconnect, George and Rose only had to take some time off from the relationship and then come back to it from a place of greater fulfillment.

## The Symptoms of a Full Tank

When a tank is filling up, we experience an increase of positive feeling. At those filling-up times, we may think it is our partners who make us happy, but it is actually the joy of connecting with our inner selves that makes us happy. Yet our partners' love and support allows us to get back to ourselves. When someone sees or treats us with love, we are then better able to connect to who we are. The different kinds of love help us to connect with the different facets of who we are.

When a love tank is completely full, the symptom is not continuous fulfillment. Instead, it is often boredom or restlessness and then dissatisfaction. Although we may think we are dissatisfied with our partners, we are actually feeling the collective emptiness of our other tanks.

---

**When a love tank is full, we then begin to feel bored or restless.**

---

Ironically, the inevitable symptom of fulfillment is the awareness that we are missing something. At such times, it is essential that we then know where to look, otherwise our minds make our partners responsible. If you are in a relationship and you are dissatisfied, instead of trying to make the relationship better, you will be more successful by stepping back and filling up another love tank.

When two people who were in love fall out of love, they are usually missing vitamin S (self-love). When we are low on self-love, we begin expecting too much from our partners. Since we don't love ourselves, we need more from our partners to feel loved. No matter what your partner says or does, it is not enough. When you are missing self-love, your partner's love cannot make you feel better—only you can do that.

---

**When you are not loving yourself, no one except you can make you feel better.**

---

If I believe that I am good enough, there is little you can do to make me feel inadequate. Likewise, if I believe that I am not good enough, there is little you can do to make me feel any better. If we are not loving ourselves, we cannot let in the love of others. We are the only ones who can fill up our self-love tank. In a relationship, when self-love is low, we begin to resent that our partners are not treating us the way they used to. We long for things to feel the way they used to and expect our partners to make us happy again. But that is not possible. With an attitude like this, things can only get worse.

We feel our partners are not responding the way they used to. We begin to compare what we are getting now with what we used to get. We start making lists of all the things our partners are not doing for us. "What have you done for me lately?" becomes our theme song. All these symptoms are clear signals that we need to shift our focus to filling up the vitamin S love tank. By focusing on loving and supporting ourselves and feeling more autonomous, we will gradually connect once again to our center. By taking some time for ourselves, time to do what we want, we begin to feel better again.

## Loving Ourselves First

I first discovered the love tanks when I was writing one of my earlier books. I was making great progress. I loved everything that I was writing. Then suddenly I didn't like anything that I was writing. For days I struggled, trying to make my work better. No matter what I wrote, it just wasn't good enough. Eventually I started rationalizing by saying things to myself like: "Every chapter can't be your best," or "It's not so bad; you are just being too critical." Eventually I completed the chapter and tried to be satisfied.

I invited my wife, Bonnie, to read the chapter. I acted as if it was fine and I was eager for her to like it as well. In retrospect, it is clear to me that I was hoping she would like it so that I could freely move on. I wanted her approval so that I could feel better about what I had done. When she read it, although she was polite about it, she thought it was a bit unclear and too complicated. Well, that is exactly what I felt, but I didn't want her to say it. I remember getting upset with her. I could not believe she could be so critical and negative.

I eventually realized in hindsight that she was not being too critical and she had not done anything wrong. Even her words were very polite. I had set her up to be the bad guy. Even if she had said she loved it, I would have felt she was not being honest.

I did not like it myself, but I was blaming her. Here was a clear example of how a relationship depends on self-love. If I had really liked my chapter and she didn't like it, the feedback would not have seemed so negative. Some part of me was looking to her love to make up for my not loving me.

Before I realized this, I was furious. I was annoyed about her response for the whole day. We even got into a big argument about something else, but this was the real reason. Most of the time, within five minutes of an argument, couples are arguing about the way they are arguing. They say things like: "You are not listening," or "You're blaming me." Then they bring up the old lists of past issues to defend their positions. That evening, although we argued about some financial issue, behind the disagreement was the real reason that I was not loving myself.

---

**Most of the time when couples argue, within five minutes, they are arguing about the way they are arguing.**

---

That night I went out with a buddy to an action movie. It had been quite a while since I had seen a movie, and I really like action movies. After the movie, I felt great. When I came home, I was easily able to apologize to Bonnie and felt very loving again. The next day, I reread the chapter, easily made some changes, and then liked it a lot. My writer's block was gone.

After this experience, I reviewed what had happened. First, I was blocked. I didn't like the chapter I was writing and couldn't make any successful improvements. I didn't like my wife for not liking it and then got into an argument. Then I went to a movie and felt better. That day, I realized that I had different emotional needs. I needed my wife's love, I needed to love myself, *and* I needed to have fun with my friends.

On that particular day, I could not feel, recognize, or appreciate Bonnie's love and support, because it was not the kind of love I was needing. In addition, I couldn't make any progress with my book because I wasn't feeling much self-love, either. I just didn't like anything I had written. When I was with my friend, going to a movie, I started feeling better and better.

To feel better about my writing and about my relationship, I needed to go back and fill some of my earlier tanks. I needed to spend some time with a friend and have some fun. On the way to the movie, I also shared a little of my frustration with another married guy, who knew exactly how I felt. This was some peer support. The result of filling up these two love tanks was that I felt better and could view the situation differently and with more love. By shifting my focus to getting other needs met, I could once again come back to my true loving self.

I started using this concept of different love needs with my clients, and it worked. Most of the time, when a couple was not getting along, instead of trying to get more from their partners, I pointed them in another direction to get love and support. When couples were not getting along, I would first recommend doing something to fill up their other love tanks. Then later we would successfully focus on improving their communication skills.

It's hard to focus on learning how to love your partner in the way he or she needs when you are already feeling empty and blaming your partner. I realized this insight applied to success in all areas of my life. By learning to keep the different love tanks full, I was able to sustain a powerful and positive attitude that not only made me happier, but allowed me to achieve all my business goals and beyond.

# CHAPTER 6

# Understanding the Ten Stages

THERE IS A natural order to the love tanks. As we develop from conception to maturity, there is a specific time period for the formation of each. These are stages when we need one kind of love more than another to develop all our talents and abilities. As we get the love we need at each stage, we are building a strong foundation for getting the next kind of love.

As we move on to the next stage, ideally we still need to keep previous love tanks full as well. If they are not full, as we succeed in filling one tank, we will need to go back and fill up our other tanks to stay connected to our true self.

As we move through a particular time period, to the extent that we are unable to get the love we need, the result will be that we can't know and develop some aspect of ourselves. We will never know that part unless we go back and get the particular kind of love that we did not receive.

For example, when children do not get the love, understanding, and attention they need, they don't realize or learn the full truth about themselves. They don't fully understand how special they are and as a result feel less lovable. As a result, when situations in life challenge their worthiness, they disconnect from their natural state of inner love, joy, peace, and confidence. In a variety of ways, they are held back in life until they learn to fill the empty or partly filled love tanks of the past.

These are the different time periods for getting certain love vitamins to develop who we are and to stay connected to our true selves:

## THE TEN TIME PERIODS

| Time Period | Love Vitamin | Love Need |
|---|---|---|
| 1. Conception to birth | Vitamin G1 | God's love |
| 2. Birth to seven | Vitamin P1 | Parents' love |
| 3. Seven to fourteen | Vitamin F | Family, friends, and fun |
| 4. Fourteen to twenty-one | Vitamin P2 | Peers and others with similar goals |
| 5. Twenty-one to twenty-eight | Vitamin S | Self-love |
| 6. Twenty-eight to thirty-five | Vitamin R | Relationships and romance |
| 7. Thirty-five to forty-two | Vitamin D | Loving a dependent |
| 8. Forty-two to forty-nine | Vitamin C | Giving back to community |

9. Forty-nine to fifty-six    Vitamin W    Giving back to the world

10. Fifty-six and beyond    Vitamin G2    Serving God

As we are growing through any of the above time periods toward full maturity at fifty-six, a particular love vitamin associated with that stage is most important for our growth. If we are not actively getting that particular need satisfied, then we will be wounded in some way. As we progress through the different time periods or stages of development, we will be missing something in varying degrees.

It is a little like trying to learn to read when no one has read to you first. Or trying to drive a car when you never learned to ride a bike. Or trying to run a business without basic math or reading skills. Although you can manage, there will always be extra struggle. In a similar way, each love vitamin becomes a foundation to develop the next. Getting each love need assists us in staying connected to all of who we can be.

As we grow more mature, most of the dissatisfaction we experience is not really about the needs of a particular time period. It is often because we are not getting what we need to fill up the other tanks.

When couples experience tension, the underlying cause is often that they are not loving themselves. This experience in my own marriage eventually led me to understand the different love tanks. Although once you read the ten kinds of love they are obvious, I had never heard it expressed in this simple manner.

This understanding of the love tanks and the different time stages is really just common sense. Any parent notices that as children start getting close to seven years old they become more independent and seek support and friendship from others, relying less on the parents. That is why there is a big difference between the preschool environment and first grade.

The next big change is, of course, puberty, and then another around twenty-one when we are considered adults. For many, this is the time they leave home to find themselves and experience greater autonomy. Each of these three stages is well known. What are not so well known are the later stages. People assume that our development is over at twenty-one, which is far from the truth. Following this same rhythm, about every seven years we go through a major shift in maturity that corresponds to the different love tanks.

Maturity increases up to fifty-six and even beyond. As you learn to keep all your love tanks full, you gain access to your complete potential at fifty-six. It is then that you know all of who you are and what you can do. For the rest of your life, you can serve God and everyone else by expressing that potential. Life is always a process of growth and development. When you stop growing, you begin dying.

---

**The maturing process does not stop at twenty-one, but clearly continues throughout our lives.**

---

As a counselor, I began to notice that at around twenty-eight clients and friends would go through big changes. It was as if they were all saying, "I can't live my life for anyone else. I need to lead my own life, I have to be me." The period of time around twenty-eight years old is when people finally have developed enough to form a clear picture of themselves, and they are ready to get serious about having intimate relationships. If they haven't taken the time to be themselves, then they are not ready to move on. They want to move back and feel free again.

When people get married in their early twenties, they often experience a big challenge around twenty-eight. Statistics show this time to have the greatest number of divorces. If they have given up themselves to nurture an intimate relationship, they suddenly begin to feel that they don't have what it takes to be married to their partners or vice versa.

As we move into the relationship stage between twenty-eight to thirty-five, naturally we begin to question if we are ready. If something is missing within ourselves because we did not take time to find ourselves in the twenty-one to twenty-eight period, we will not be able to connect with our inner guidance. It is hard to know what to do when we are disconnected. It becomes even more difficult to move on and have a healthy relationship or career if we have other earlier love tanks that are empty as well.

## Moving Back to Move Ahead

It is as if we have to move back before we can move ahead. There are many examples of this throughout life. Many people in their sixties, seventies, and beyond automatically begin to remember their childhood very clearly. Grandparents always love telling stories of the way things used to be. This is very healthy. To stay alive and healthy, they are automatically going back and remembering and reliving.

If they haven't healed the wounds of their earlier years and their tanks are low, they just can't move ahead until they heal their past. Their bodies become sick, because their love tanks are low. Some even lose their short-term memory and only remember their past. They literally can't move ahead and be fully present in the moment.

---

**When people are sick and not getting better,
they are not accessing the love they need.**

---

When a car is just not getting the gas it needs and the oil hasn't been changed, it stops. Likewise, when the tanks are empty, they can't assimilate the life force that streams in when we feel loved or loving. In many ways, the elderly regress to behaving like children or, because of a sickness, lose their autonomy and become dependent like children.

## Retirement Crisis: Age Fifty-six

At the transition points between stages, we particularly feel the emptiness of our other tanks. It is then that we feel the strongest urge to go back. If at the transitions we don't do something to remedy the situation, we continue to struggle by not realizing what we really need.

Let's first look at what commonly happens at the tenth love tank around fifty-six. Many men just can't wait to retire. They look forward to doing what they have always wanted to do. They want to relax and have fun. They want to move forward and do the things that they put off doing to be good providers. Instead of going forward, they go back. Instead of moving into the challenge of serving God, they feel the need to serve themselves. When their new lives eventually become boring, they die suddenly.

Insurance companies report that after a man retires he has a high probability of dying. If he keeps working, he will live much longer. The secret of getting older for a man is to continue working, but also to have lots of fun and to get lots of love. Men who continue to work often do it because they love their work. In this case, they have created a life where most of their love tanks have remained full. When you love your work, it is a sign that you are pretty connected to your inner self.

---

A man must continue to feel needed and responsible to others or he will lose his sense of purpose and vitality.

---

Women have less of a tendency to die around age fifty-six, but they may still regress. If they are not ready to move on, they tend to become rigid and opinionated. Instead of being free to share the precious wisdom of a lifetime and make a difference in the world, they may regress. They may defy what others think, much like an adolescent who says, "I will do what I want to do, and I don't care anymore what you think. I know everything I need to know." Too much autonomy can make a woman rigid and defensive. To stay healthy, a woman needs to feel that she is not alone and that she can depend on others.

---

**A woman needs to feel that she is not alone
and that she can depend on others;
too much autonomy is not healthy.**

---

When you reach fifty-six and your love tanks are full, then you are ready to move on to the next stage. You begin to feel the enormous exhilaration that now you are free to do what you are here to do. You are supported in this world, and you are needed. When you feel this way, there is no reason to get sick. You stay healthy and eventually die when you are ready, after many years of joyful and loving service to God and the world.

It is important that at each of the major transitions we listen to our hearts and work to fill the emptiness we may experience. If, at the transitions, we don't do something to remedy the situation, we continue to struggle, not realizing what we really need.

## *The Empty Nest Crisis:*
### *Ages Forty-nine to Fifty-six*

The next commonly discussed crisis is the empty nest. Around the age of forty-nine, many couples and single parents experience an emptiness in their lives. When the new challenge is to give back to the world, they suddenly feel the void inside themselves and their lives. They have little to give, and instead feel what they are missing. If married, they often blame their partners or the relationship for their unhappiness. To whatever extent they were not getting what they needed in their relationships as their children leave home or become more independent, they will begin to feel disappointed. The nest is empty. No one is home. Is this all there is?

For both married couples and singles, this can be the beginning of a greater freedom to enjoy their lives, or it can be a source of problems. By this age, either we have learned how to get what we need outside the relationship, or we are resenting our partners for not being enough for us. This is not the time to blame our partners or lack of partners. It is the time to continue growing to experience universal love and share it freely. This is the time to help make a difference in the world.

Either we have prepared for this time or we experience a depression about what is missing in our lives. It becomes harder and harder to move forward when we have not learned how to fill our different love tanks. While doctors search for ways to extend life, the answer is very simple. Keep your love tanks full, and you will stay young in spirit and healthy.

---

**The secret to staying young is keeping your earlier love tanks full.**

---

At this time, we begin to feel our mortality and want to stay young. This tendency is actually very healthy. We feel it most at this time if we have been neglecting our earlier love tanks. We may have disconnected completely from the energy we felt as children, teenagers, and young adults in our twenties.

Men look to younger women to keep them feeling young, while women look at their bodies trying to look younger. Around this time, if we have not found ways to stay young, that becomes our new quest. Again, focusing on ourselves, we may miss the challenge of this age period. By this time, we should be ready to get involved in helping the world. Ideally, this is when we have nurtured all our inner needs, and now we are ready to give back to the world.

If you are prepared, your greatest joy is meeting the challenge of being involved in making the world a better place or at least traveling the world and sharing your light and love in this stage. This is a time to meet people in other communities and cultures and to expand your influence beyond your community. It is wonderful to see people in their fifties and sixties taking time to see the world.

### The Mid-Life Crisis: Ages Forty-two to Forty-nine

Another much discussed transition point is the mid-life crisis. It generally occurs when a person is around forty-two. Before moving on to the next love tank, people begin to feel the emptiness of their past. If you were to skydive out of a plane, you would naturally want to check your parachute many times before making the plunge. Before people feel they can freely give back to their communities, they must be full within themselves. You cannot build a house if there is no foundation. You cannot begin writing checks to local charities when your bank account is low.

When it's time to move and you are not full, instead of moving forward you will begin looking back to all that you did not get. A man may suddenly want the freedom to sell his business and go mountain climbing. Or if he is married, he may feel the longing to be with other women. If he has been conservative in his life, he may want to buy and drive a fast car or have something he wanted in his teen years or twenties but never got. He will reevaluate his life and his priorities. Quite often he will want to throw off the responsibilities that make him feel old. The real reason he feels old is that he is not continuing to fill his earlier love tanks.

---

**When it's time to move forward, we long to move back if we are not ready.**

---

The areas in his past where he feels he sacrificed himself or he did not get what he needed will give rise to a growing dissatisfaction. To move on in his development, his challenge is to get what he needs without creating chaos in his life or hurting the people he loves. There are ways to fill his love tanks without disrupting his life.

---

**To move on, a man's challenge is to get what he needs without creating chaos in his life or hurting the people he loves.**

---

Around forty-two, a woman may also become dissatisfied in her life and often complains that she has not gotten what she wanted. She wakes up one day with a long list of the things she has given and the things she did not get back. She feels resentful and exhausted. If she does not have this understanding of love tanks, she will tend to blame her current life instead of going back and healing her past. She will pull away from love and often decide to dedicate herself to the community, but resent it quietly. To make matters even worse, she will feel guilty for resenting her life.

Certainly these feelings could be felt at any time, but the emptiness of the past tends to come up most at these transitions. If we do not honor our past and do something to heal it by filling up the other earlier love tanks, as we proceed in life, we will not benefit from being connected to our inner source of love and fulfillment. Without that inner connection, life will never measure up to our hopes, expectations, and wishes.

## The Secret Crisis: Ages Thirty-five to Forty-two

Around age thirty-five there is another crisis, but no one talks about it. The transition at thirty-five is the movement toward giving love unconditionally to a dependent. Children and later grandchildren are ideal dependents, but if we don't have children, then a pet will work as well. Around this time, the human spirit seeks to give unconditionally to someone who needs and depends on us.

Giving to our children or a dependent becomes our first experience of true unconditional love. The ideal relationship between parent and child is unconditional love. The child does not owe the parent anything. Some parents are unknowingly abusive to their children by giving the message that the children owe them. They say things like: "After all I did for you, you owe me." This is not correct. If, however, they are not prepared for this period, these feelings do come up.

---

**Some parents are unknowingly abusive to their children by giving the message that the children owe them.**

---

When the parent is full, the child gives the parent a great gift—the opportunity to give freely. It is such a joy to have the opportunity to love someone so much that giving to the child is like giving to ourselves. This situation gives the parent an opportunity to continue growing. The problem for many parents is that they had children before they knew how to give to themselves.

When people have children before they are ready, then

around age thirty-five they will begin to feel guilty for all the times they resented being mothers or fathers. They will regret not being able to give their children what their children deserved. Or they will resent that they gave so much, and their children have not given back more.

---

**When our tanks are not full, it is impossible
to give our love unconditionally.**

---

This is the silent crisis, because people don't want to talk about the resentment they feel about having kids. They love their children, and they love giving to their children, but they are also missing a life. To keep from resenting missing out on things while having children, parents need to learn how to fill up their earlier love tanks.

People in this stage who do not have a child or dependent they love and care for like a child will feel they are missing something. Rather than continuing to meet life's challenges, they will regress to doing just what they want to do rather than giving up a part of themselves for another. They will not know why nothing seems to satisfy.

If you are without children at this time, it is not enough to be spending time with nieces and nephews. It takes really being responsible. Every pet owner knows pets are a real responsibility. They have to be fed and walked regularly. They get sick, and you have to care for them. There are times of great sacrifice, just as in parenting, but it is all worth it. If owning a pet doesn't fit your lifestyle, then caring for a plant or garden can also be a way to express your nurturing instincts.

---

**If you are without children at this time,
it is not enough to be spending time with
nieces and nephews.**

---

Another aspect of the secret crisis is the frequency of sex in marriages. By this time, quite often the man is showing less interest and the woman is wanting more sex. This happens particularly if they got married in their twenties. After many years of wanting more sex than he got, a man just eventually turns off. Meanwhile, as a woman's body is better prepared for having babies, quite often her sexual desires increase.

> **Around age thirty-seven it is the women who complain about not enough sex and not the men.**

In my relationship seminars, I talk about how men gradually lose interest in sex with their partners if they feel rejected over and over. At the breaks and afterward, when I am signing books, there are always several women who approach me and share secretly, so as not to embarrass their husbands, that they have stopped having sex, but the women are the ones who feel rejected. She wants sex, and he does not seem as interested. When I ask their age, they are almost invariably thirty-seven.

As women move into this time of greater giving, they need romantic support, while their partners have in some ways given up on them and are finding their comfort playing golf. If a man hasn't gotten his romantic needs met, he will often regress to earlier needs and seek to satisfy them. Rather than try to initiate sex and be rejected, he would rather watch a ball game.

### Identity Crisis:
### Ages Twenty-eight to Thirty-five

"Who am I?" and "What do I really want to do?" are the ideal quests of the twenties. If we have not taken time to find ourselves and love ourselves, before we are ready to move to the next stage, at twenty-eight, we begin to feel we have to go back to find ourselves. We may seek to get out of a marriage or avoid getting into a relationship.

There are many single women in their thirties wondering what happened. For whatever reason, they did not find a partner. From the perspective of love tanks, the answer to this problem is that they did not find themselves in their twenties. They did not do what they really wanted to do. On one hand, they got into intimate relationships and lost themselves, or, in many cases, they sought to prove their equality with men in a manner that did not allow them to be true to their own wishes and wants.

The twenties is a time of exploration and experimentation. If they did not fully give themselves the opportunity to be themselves and explore their wishes and wants, they are not satisfied with what they got later on. When we are not connected to our true selves, when we are not loving ourselves, it is difficult for someone else to live up to our standards. When we don't feel good enough, just as we can be overdemanding of ourselves, we expect too much from others. No partner can ever measure up if we don't love ourselves. As a result, women may resist getting involved in relationships unless the guy is marriage material, and guys will tend to back off when it is time to make a commitment.

## Finding the Right Partner

When women become too picky about men, they stop appreciating what they can get and want what they can't get. If they are looking for a partner, they start shopping for a husband instead of a fun or interesting date. They won't go out with just anyone. They feel that if they go out with a guy, he should have a lot of potential. They don't want to waste time and get involved with the wrong guy.

In a sense, this is the right idea, but it is missing one important ingredient. The woman needs to be careful not to get seriously involved until it is the right guy. In the meanwhile, she needs to date lots of guys. If a man is interested and he seems interesting, she should just begin having a good time even though he definitely is not marriage material.

Women who don't have a strong sense of self have difficulty dating many men. It has to be just one, or they won't date at all. One method to avoid going too deep with just one man is to keep a steady stream of men in your life until the right one comes along. Always have one man on the way out, one that is a little regular, and one on the way in. Let them know that you see many men, and if that's a problem then . . . NEXT!

## Healing the Hurt of the Past

When people get to age twenty-eight, they tend to feel a lot of emotional turmoil, particularly if they have denied their feelings in the past. If twenty-one is a time of physical maturity, twenty-eight is a time of emotional maturity. If we have denied the unresolved feelings of our past, they begin to come back. As our souls are preparing to be vulnerable in an intimate relationship, we suddenly become more aware of what we feel inside.

Often, a surge of different emotions comes up. Whatever is left unresolved from our past surfaces. We begin to question everything we learned to be true from others. Now is the time to live our lives by our inner guidance. Certainly others can help us in our journey and give us direction, but now we must feel within our hearts what is true and workable for ourselves. What is good for one person may not be exactly right for you.

If in our relationships throughout our twenties (or further back) we have been hurt, then before we are ready to get involved, those hurts need to be healed. Before we can feel safe to open our hearts fully to another in an intimate relationship, we need to feel safe that we will not be hurt again. If we have pain in our hearts that has not been healed, we will continue to be afraid. This fear tends to make women overly picky and afraid of intimacy.

Although it does not hold a man back from getting involved, it will cause him to pull back from making a commitment. He will begin to get picky as soon as she is expecting a commitment.

As long as we have not healed the hurt of past relationships, it is hard to move on into our thirties to find one. We tend to get too busy in our careers and other work partnerships and relationships and avoid getting too intimate. The secret to coping with this is to start dating, but to avoid getting too intimate until you have healed your past. In later chapters, we will explore how to heal past hurts.

## Education Crisis:
### Ages Twenty-one to Twenty-eight

As our children leave home and go to college, there is a new crisis on many campuses. Some students don't know how to handle the freedom. They are not used to disciplining themselves. It used to be that when kids left home they had to get jobs and support themselves. This meant moving from one authority figure to another. If you wanted to survive, you did what you were told. Trying to earn a living, you did not have much time to think about who you were and what you really wanted to do.

In the past, we did not have the luxury of spending the years beyond eighteen to twenty-one being taken care of by our parents. We left home, were on our own, and had to get a job. Today many young adults leave home but don't have to get a job. Instead they arrive on campus and are suddenly free to control their lives. Since they haven't learned to discipline themselves, they go wild and lose control. They begin abusing their freedom with drugs, sex, and drinking, and many drop out.

Whether they continue their education or not, if people have not filled their earlier love tanks at this transition, they will feel insecure and go wild or sell out, seeking security. They may get married too early just so someone will take care of them, or they may forfeit their dreams because they don't believe in themselves. To prepare for their twenties young adults need lots of positive peer support in their teens. Association with mentors and friends who have positive goals and activities is immensely helpful. Even if their interests change, they will have experienced a sense of confidence that they can do things.

---

**Teens need group activities to give them a sense of confidence.**

---

If they get in with the wrong crowd, they can be greatly influenced and later feel unworthy of going for their dreams. They feel as if they don't have a place in the world. They need to know that the twenties is a time to find their place. They shouldn't give up hope. Many very successful people did not find their niche in life until after twenty-eight. If you find it before, it is by luck. Only a few do.

At a large parents' meeting for one of our daughters in college, the audience was asked how many had followed a career that directly related to the college degree they had received. Only about ten percent were working in fields directly related to their majors. Everyone was amazed. The point of the question was to reassure parents that it really did not matter what major their children picked. The point of education was for them to find their interest and learn about the world and themselves.

## The Hormone Crisis:
### Ages Fourteen to Twenty-one

At puberty, boys and girls get big doses of male and female hormones that create many new changes. Who they are as boys and girls is being greatly redefined. Quite suddenly their whole lives are shaken up. This transition is already dramatic enough if our earlier love tanks are full, but if we did not get what we needed, this is when it really shows up.

In the last few years, there has been much discussion about what we can do for our daughters and sons as they make the transition through puberty. Studies show that a dramatic shift occurs in a girl's self-esteem, and clearly many boys begin to display behavioral problems. Though this issue has been surrounded by silence in the past, experts are now working to correct the problem, and parents and educators are learning ways to help their children.

We must address this issue head on, but we must also recognize that our children are making the transition to the next love tank of peer support, and they are feeling the emptiness of the earlier stages. It is often not until puberty that we begin to feel what was missing previously. Only at this transition do young teenagers begin to feel and deal with the hurt of not getting what they needed at an earlier stage.

As our children reach twelve to fourteen, they make a radical shift. Our little children are teenagers, and every parent clearly notices this change. Teenagers are clearly more independent from their parents and family members and more vulnerable to peer pressure. Having fun is no longer a priority. They begin to do more schoolwork and focus on achieving projects and goals. If they did not have enough fun in the earlier years, they may resist their new responsibilities and want to have more fun.

Even though our teenagers have moved on to feeling their need for peer support, they still need the support of family and friends. Parental love and support is always the basis of our growth, but at this stage we depend on our peers and mentors to grow. Wise parents actively support their teenagers in getting involved in positive group activities. At this stage, one bad apple can definitely ruin all the apples in a basket. When kids become associated in a group, they are often swayed enormously by the leader of the group. This is particularly true when a teenager does not have strong and positive role models.

Teenagers need to look outside their close family to find out who they are and what they can do. It is as if they go out and learn from others and then come back to family and parents with something of their own. In my own life, my mother wisely encouraged and supported me in finding many mentors and group activities, from taking karate lessons to having a paper route.

There are a range of different interests possible. A teenager needs the time and opportunity to learn, find an interest, and excel. This is a period when confidence is building. It is important to discover what you are good at and experience a growing mastery of that skill. All different sports activities, singing, drama, and even after-school jobs are ideal.

It is important that parents not alienate their teenagers. As our children become more capable of independence, our roles as parents dramatically change. Though we were good managers before, we have to shift to becoming consultants. A manager controls, while a consultant is hired to give advice only when asked, and the clients then choose what they want to do.

Often this is a difficult period for mothers and daughters. Girls have a tendency to accommodate their mothers more at an earlier stage. When they reach their teens, to whatever extent they gave themselves up to please their mothers, they will tend to rebel and resist maternal authority. It is often hard for a daughter to pull away and find herself without pushing her mother away.

Mothers also have a harder time letting go of the task of managing their teenagers' lives. The nurturing instincts that worked so well in the earlier years can become too controlling or confining for a teenager. Parents need to realize that they now have less influence, and that is good. The teenager is supposed to begin finding greater support outside the family. As one teenager said,

"I don't need my mother as much anymore, but I am sure glad that she is there when I get home."

If you learn to give up telling your kids what to do, they will come and ask. Instead of telling them what to do this is the time to ask back, "What do *you* think?" They will continue to stay connected if you are able to listen more and ask questions, but are careful not to give too much advice or to tell them what to do.

In some activities, it is good for girls to share with girls and for guys to be with guys in a friendly activity. Having an outer focus is helpful in assisting them to get to know each other and to learn more about themselves and who they are becoming. In this stage, the growth happens by simply sharing with other peers who have similar interests, capacity, and goals.

## The Silent Crisis:
## Ages Seven to Fourteen

Leaving parents and starting first grade can be very traumatic for children, but often no one knows and no one remembers. It is a silent crisis, because when children leave home, the parents are not there to know what happens. Quite often, if children do not feel safe to express feelings, then not only do they not tell their parents, but they don't know themselves. Around this age, for children to know what is going on inside, they need someone to ask them interested questions to help them look inside to talk about their experiences, feelings, emotions, and wishes.

If children did not get enough nurturing in the first stage, then in the second stage at times they may resist having fun and continue to pull back into being a "baby." They may throw baby tantrums, wet their beds, suck their thumbs, or engage in other regressive behavior. Rather than shame children for such behavior, parents can recognize that these children are just trying to go back to fill their earlier love tank. Parents can help by creating special times and opportunities for children to get the nurturing they need.

When children are around seven years old, an active playfulness and need for fun and friendship emerge. It is as if we wake up from the dreamy state of our first seven years. From seven to fourteen is a time to develop social skills and learn to have fun. These ages are just general guidelines. Certainly some children wake up sooner, while others sleep a little later. If during our first fourteen years we do not feel safe to resist changes and work through a range of feelings, we do not form a clear sense of who we are or what we like.

The ability to delay gratification is learned in this playful stage. By taking turns and sharing, we grow in our ability to feel what we want and wait for it patiently. A big part of this process is to have many tantrums when we don't get our way. These emotional outbursts, when handled in a loving and nonsuppressive manner, are essential for our healthy emotional growth. Tantrums are the way we learn to manage strong passionate feelings without suppressing what we want. When a parent does not lose control in response to a child's tantrum, the child eventually learns how to have strong feelings while staying in control.

Even adults throw tantrums, but if healthy, they have learned how to nurture themselves without dumping their negative feelings on others. In most cases, when we blame others for our unhappiness, we need to fill this first love tank. Whenever you are pointing the finger of blame, three fingers point back to your earlier love tanks. To break free from blame, we must hear and understand our feelings in the way a parent would do for a child. In Chapter 10, we will explore how to keep those earlier tanks full without having to regress and behave like a two-year-old.

Keeping this early love tank full is the basis of feeling secure. If we have been neglected, we don't feel worthy of support. Even when have found outer security in life, we cannot truly feel secure, because we do not know what we deserve. On some level, we feel that it may all be taken away. We think we have to be good or right to deserve love. This is too much pressure for a little child. Children need pure unconditional love. When our early emotional needs for love are met, we are able to touch and taste the joy of being connected to our true selves. If we felt loved and nurtured in childhood, automatically we are able to love ourselves as adults. Without this foundation, we never tend to measure up to our standards for the rest of our lives.

By nature, we are already joyful, loving, peaceful, and confident. These are givens. Children automatically experience these inner feelings, but unless they continue to get the love they need, they gradually begin to disconnect from their true nature. Depending on the love we have experienced in early life, we are more or less connected to who we are. Just as love connects us to others, it connects us to ourselves.

As children, we have no ability to love ourselves. The only way we can consciously know ourselves is through the mirror of our parents' love and the way we are treated by our families and friends. When they treat us with respect, we learn that we are worthy of respect. When they treat us with caring, we see ourselves as special. When they help us and support us with time and energy, we feel worthy of that kind of support.

Throughout elementary school, or around ages seven to fourteen, children's greatest need is to feel safe. As they continue to grow and learn about the world and how they fit in, they need to have permission to make lots of mistakes and learn from those mistakes. A parent's job is to manage the child's life and protect the child from negative influences as learning occurs. This is a time of fun and free expression. Too much emphasis on perfection can interfere with a child's natural development.

As adults, we have a tendency to become too serious and work-oriented, because these expectations of us began at such an early age. Too much emphasis is put on doing family chores, working hard, and making sacrifices for the family. Ideally this is a time of joining with others who care about you, a time of innocence and unconditional forgiveness.

During this stage, as with earlier stages, the brain has not yet developed enough to understand the distinction: "I did something bad, but I am not bad." Instead, a child will conclude, "If what I did is bad, then I am bad." "If bad things happen to me, then I must be bad." Most adults have still not learned this distinction, because as children they did not have parents who knew the difference. When a child resists cooperating with your wishes, a better term than bad behavior is "out of control." There is then no negative association with who that child is.

Rather then punish children when they behave "badly," parents need to use time-outs, one minute for each year. If a child is eight years old, then eight minutes of time-out is appropriate.

When children misbehave, they are not cooperating with your wants and wishes, and they are out of control. By taking a few minutes of time-out, they will get what they need to come back into control.

A time-out is an opportunity for children to come back into control. Simply put the child in a room to be alone for a set period of time. This prevents children from acting out to disturb others, but also lets them feel and release their inner turbulent emotions. During that time, they may throw a tantrum. Children need to throw those tantrums in time-out to learn to control their emotions without suppressing them.

As adults begin to realize the importance of emotional fluency and recognize the value of emotional intelligence, they can easily recognize the value of giving children a chance to find control again with regular time-outs. God made our children little so that we could pick them up and move them to a time-out when they resist.

If they won't stay in their room or the bathroom, then it is best to hold the door closed rather than just lock them in. While children are upset about a time-out, it is good for them to know that they haven't been left and someone is right outside the door. Regular time-outs will free children to stay connected to their feelings and in particular the desire to make others happy.

This is why punishment does not work. Prisons are filled with people who were punished most by life and their parents. Ninety percent of the people in jail are men, while ninety percent of the people in counseling are women. When men are punished, they act out that mistreatment on others, while women act it out on themselves. This is one of the major reasons girls experience a big drop in self-esteem around puberty, and boys begin to act out. Boys tend to treat the world the way they were mistreated, and girls treat themselves the way they were mistreated.

Punishment gradually desensitizes us to our feelings, and we lose our natural desire to please our parents. People who are people-pleasers later in life become that way because they were never successful in pleasing their parents or family members. When parents make it easy for their children to be successful in pleasing them, children's self-esteem can be healthy and grow.

During this stage, parents may sometimes feel powerless to help their children. No matter how much you love your children, you cannot make them happy when their friends are not being nice to them. No matter how much you love them, you cannot make them love themselves. But you can help. By being understanding and listening, you help. Parents' unconditional caring will give children the support they must have to get what they need from family members and friends. Parents are also most helpful when they assist their children in having opportunities to be with other children and form friendships.

A big part of growing up through this stage is working through the social issues and challenges that inevitably come up. Although nothing is ever perfect, a parent's support is still very important, but too much support is not a good thing. When parents give too much, children will push parents away, because they must do certain things for themselves.

## Birth Crisis:
## Up to Age Seven

From birth to infancy, up to around age seven, we are in a kind of dreamy state of development. We have no ability to know who we are and what we deserve except by the way our parents treat us. As babies, we bond with our primary caretakers or parents, and then we grow through their loving support.

Our whole attitude about the world and our relationship to it begins at birth. Children are basically powerless to get what they need when they first emerge from the womb. If children are not taken care of, they will die. This being the physical reality, a child forms one of two basic attitudes: "I have needs and I have the power to get them met," or "I have needs and I am powerless to get them met." We move through life feeling either powerless or powerful.

---

**A child either feels powerful or powerless to get needs fulfilled.**

---

Our first impressions of life are always the deepest and most lasting. Although your brain wasn't developed at birth, you were able to feel and assess your situation. Either you felt that you could get what you needed, or you felt you couldn't. Because of the practice of separating the child from the mother that started about sixty years ago in hospitals, most of the baby boomers and later generations learned they could not get what they needed. Fortunately these practices are now being corrected. We have recognized the importance of bonding between the parents and the baby.

This attitude of powerlessness does not mean that we all grow up feeling powerless to get what we want. In many cases, a deficiency can make us more powerful. When we feel we can't get what we need, we automatically adjust in ways that may make us more powerful. We feel that no one is there for us, so if we want something we will have to get it. Depending on others is not a clear option.

If I feel that I can't get what I need, I conclude I have to grow up right away and do it myself. Suddenly, long before I am supposed to look to myself for everything, I am feeling too responsible and independent. I may experience a greater power to create outer success, but inside I will be missing inner success.

---

**When children grow up too quickly, they miss certain important stages of development.**

---

Another common reaction to feeling powerless to get what we need is an inability to know what we need or want. If we don't get what we need, it is hard to feel and define those needs. If we cannot clearly know our needs, it is hard to feel worthy or entitled to receive. On the other hand, the more we receive what we need, the more clearly we know we need it, and feel a greater sense of entitlement.

---

**Clear knowledge and experience of what we need creates a sense of entitlement.**

---

Without a clear sense of entitlement to receive what we need, we may try too hard to get it. To please our parents and get them to give us what we need, we mistakenly give up ourselves. Powerlessness can make us either overly dependent on others, or overly dependent on ourselves. If you feel an inner power to get what you need in this early stage, then eventually you will experience a healthy balance of dependence on others and on yourself.

When I assume that I can't get what I need, I shift to doing it myself and getting what I want. The distinction here is between needing and wanting. When we need, we are depending on others; when we want, we are depending on ourselves to get it. As children, we require many years of getting what we need before we develop our ability to get what we want. Until our twenties, we are much more dependent on what happens to us. At twenty-one, we have a much greater power to get what we need.

When we learn too soon to take care of ourselves, we think we have to do it all ourselves. We do not value the assistance of others, and we even push away valuable support. We do not feel comfortable feeling close or intimate. Go anywhere in the world where they don't separate children from their mothers at birth, and you will see how much closer the parents are to their children and how much more bonded the families are.

Although in developed countries we are suffering from the birth trauma of being separated from our mothers, it has had some good benefits. Sometimes we have to go in the wrong direction to find a new and better direction. Although the boomer generation has taken a big turn toward looking out for themselves and getting everything they want in the outer world, they are now coming back to the recognition that they need love. All kinds of therapies have developed to assist us in going back and healing the traumas of not getting what we needed at the early ages when we were most vulnerable and dependent.

## From Conception to Birth

Our first experience in this life is that of developing in the womb. During this time, we experience our relationship with God. It is not a conceptual relationship—the brain is not yet capable of that—but there is an experience. We generally forget this experience by the age of two when our language skills are rapidly developing.

For most people, the stay in the womb is a very heavenly experience. We are not responsible for anything. God or Mother nature does it all, and we don't have to do anything. People who are healthy, strong and growing are connected to this energy that created their bodies.

This energy that does everything for us is our first relationship with God. Unfortunately if, after we are born, others don't believe in or depend on that divine and positive energy, we gradually disconnect from it and forget that God is always there to take care of us and help us.

All healing comes from this divine energy. Doctors may give the remedies to assist the healing process, but God's energy does the healing. Sickness and healing are inevitable parts of life. When we are sick, that is a sign that we need to reconnect to the energy that made us.

Sometimes even in the womb we will begin to disconnect with the divine energy responsible for making our bodies. If our mother experiences negative feelings, that can affect us for the rest of our lives. If you want healthy and happy kids, the first step is to help the mother get everything she needs during the pregnancy.

Her relationship with God also makes a big difference. If she feels she has to do it all herself, then that nonspiritual message or attitude gets passed on to the child. A wise pregnant mother takes plenty of time to get what she needs and does not worry about her goals and ambitions in life. Most important, she focuses on letting go, getting out of her mind, and letting nature do her thing. Once she is finished raising little children, she has plenty of time left to focus fully on her ambitions again.

As people have shifted to depend solely on doctors and not God or nature, children don't get the reinforcement they need to know that the world is a friendly place that magically responds to all our needs. A mother needs to counter these tendencies to forget God by reading spiritual and uplifting books or spending lots of time in nature. If we are disconnected from the rhythms of nature, it is harder to feel good during the pregnancy.

In reading about these earlier stages, it is easy to become overwhelmed thinking we did not get what we needed and blame the past for our problems. If you are starting to feel powerless, you are awakening the feelings you felt as a child. Now you have the opportunity to give yourself a hug and say everything is going to be fine. The good news is that if you are reading this book you will soon have the power to fill those love tanks and start getting what you need.

# CHAPTER 7

# *Filling the Ten Love Tanks*

I F THE WALLS in your house began to crack, you would first look to the foundation to correct the problem. If your plants began to turn yellow and die, you wouldn't try painting them to make them look good. Instead, you would water them. In a similar way, most of our problems begin to go away on their own when we start filling up the ten love tanks. As we get what we need, we start connecting with who we truly are.

For most difficulties in life, the solution starts with making sure we are filling the first five love tanks. When we are stuck in life, it is enormously helpful to recognize that many of the feelings we experience are really how we felt as children. By taking some time out of our week to fill our past love tanks, we are able to move forward to create the life we want.

It is best always to be doing things each week that keep your tanks full. It is not enough to fill them up once. That love is needed to stay connected to who you are as you move ahead in whatever stage of life you are in. The basis to getting what you want and staying connected to your true self is keeping your love tanks full. If you have flowers in your garden, it is not enough to water them once. We have to attend to them all and keep nurturing them.

## Love Tank One:
## Vitamin G1

The first love tank is love and support from God. When we are missing vitamin G1, life tends to be a struggle. We eventually become tired and stressed, because we think we have to do it all ourselves. To fill this first tank, we need to have regular contact with God or a spiritual relationship in some way with the universe. We need to understand that we are not alone and that there is a higher power assisting us.

Although meditation is not religious, it is spiritual. Even if someone is an atheist or is not affiliated with a particular religion, they can satisfy this basic need with regular meditation. Often, after experiencing their spiritual connection, they will seek out and appreciate a religion to help understand their relationship with God and get the support of others with like minds and hearts. In Chapter 9 we will explore a wonderful meditation practice to fill up this love tank.

## Love Tank Two:
## Vitamin P1

The second love tank is love and support from parents. When we are missing vitamin P1, we tend to be held back in life by feelings of doubt, inadequacy, and unworthiness. We experience waves of emotional disturbance and distress in our lives. We may think it is the world or our jobs that create the distress, but it comes from within. The outer world just reflects our inner world.

Fortunately, as adults, now we don't have to depend on our parents or primary caretakers to get the unconditional love we need. Some parents will never be able to give us what we need, and some have died. As adults, we can pick and choose where to get this support, and we can learn to give it to ourselves.

When we are not managing our emotional experience of life in a loving, peaceful manner, this is the tank we need to fill. If we are not feeling confident or we are not happy, this is one of the first places to work on healing our past through filling up this love tank.

In a very practical sense, seeing counselors or therapists is like hiring parents. They listen to you, understand you, and give you unconditional love. As you get these needs met, you become capable of giving this support to yourself. As this tank begins to fill up, you discover either that your actual parents become more supportive of you, or that other people in your life give you this kind of unconditional love.

If meditating and connecting with God is like watering flowers, then healing our past is like changing the soil. A plant needs good soil to thrive. Many of the beliefs we formed in early childhood continue to hold us back. By changing the beliefs that were formed early in life, you make everything better right away. Regardless of what kind of support you got in childhood, you now have the power to be a parent to yourself and to give yourself everything you need.

I remember teaching a workshop at the San Quentin correctional institute. Never had I experienced working with people who were completely deficient in P1. Ninety prisoners began the workshop, and I had thirty-two volunteers to assist me. The volunteers, whose early love tanks were realtively full, did healing exercises with some of the prisoners.

When prisoners did excercies with each other, there was

much less impact, but with the volunteer assistants, there was great progress. At the end of the weekend, the thirty-two prisoners who stayed throughout each had worked with an assistant. It was clear that the exercises were effective when they were done with those who had experienced more love in their lives. The prisoners were so impoverished from their pasts that they could not do the exercises together.

In my own healing process, I found doing healing exercises with others—some trained professional and some lay partners in workshops—very helpful. Even to this day, I can remember many life-changing experiences. I will always be grateful for those healing moments. In Chapter 11, I will explain some of those healing exercises. They can be done alone or with a partner, at home, in therapy, or at a workshop.

### Love Tank Three:
### Vitamin F

The third love tank is love and support from family, friends, and fun. When your life is too serious and you are not having fun, you are deficient in vitamin F. If your primary relationship suffers from criticism, blame, or boredom, sometimes if you focus just on filling this tank, things will automatically get better. This third tank is filled by developing and enjoying friendships and having a good time.

To keep this tank full, we need to nurture our old friendships, and sometimes we need to create new friends as well. New friends help bring out new parts of who we are. Old friends help us to love and accept ourselves the way we are. Both are needed.

Sometimes people wonder why they don't have a lot of friends. The answer is that they never learned how to make friends. They assume that they are automatically going to like someone and want to be that person's friend. Or they expect others to like them right away. When you don't have friends, start doing things for others. By first giving to others and then receiving in return, you gradually begin to like each other more and become friends.

If it is difficult to make friends, sometimes the solution is to go to an earlier love tank and fill it up. This principle applies to each of the love tanks. Whenever we have difficulty getting what we need, we are looking in the wrong direction. By testing out the other tanks, you may find that one works better for a while than the others. Why? Because that is what your soul needs more than anything else at that particular time.

This concept explains why some people get so much out of therapy, while others may not. If they are feeling a big need for vitamin P1, then therapy really helps, but if they are needing vitamin F, then going to a football game with a friend will lift their spirits. Ultimately it is important to find ways to fill up each of the love tanks.

Friendship helps us to accept ourselves the way we are. To feel friendship, we need to feel safe being ourselves and expressing ourselves without fear of ridicule. Humor and play helps to fill this tank. When you are feeling down, it is very good to see a funny movie and get a big dose of F1. If you really don't want to, sometimes that is exactly what you need. We often resist the things we need, but once we get involved we start feeling better.

## Love Tank Four:
### Vitamin P2

The fourth love tank is peer support. To fill this tank, we need to be in a club or support group of some kind. Having a favorite sports team or activity is another way of finding this support. Although in a marriage you may share many interests, it is important that you have some interests separate from your partner. This needs to be your own thing that you share with others who are not necessarily the friends with whom you hang out or the person to whom you are married.

If you are into sports, one of the most powerful support groups is to attend a game of your favorite team. The stadium experience is more powerful than watching a game on TV, although TV does work. Feeling your connection with your team and with other fans gives big doses of vitamin F.

To fill this tank, go places where people group together. If you like movies, don't just get the video. Go to movie theaters where people with similar interests go as well. For even more support, go to a movie when it first comes out, when it is much more exciting. Those who really want to be there are there. That is the enthusiasm and focused energy with which you want to surround yourself.

If you are open to a particular religion, then participate in group activities. Sing together and pray together. Experiencing that regular support will provide not only vitamin G1 but also P2. You will receive an abundance of peer support.

If you like a particular singing artist, then go to concerts. Let your soul be nourished by the energy of P2. What a blast it is to go to a live Rolling Stones concert to bring you back to how you felt as a teenager. Not only is there a group of people who enjoy the music you like, but the music is what you listened to when you were young—that is, of course, if you are now over forty. The music you loved as a teenager will always be a powerful anchor to bring you back to feeling the energy of your teenage self.

Whenever you are filling up a particular love tank, you will be awakening that part of who you are and drawing in benefits from the particular energy of that stage. By awakening the teenager, you will have surges of enthusiasm, vitality, and energy to move ahead in life.

If you have any particular challenge that you need to overcome, attend meetings of others who have met similar challenges. Twelve-step programs for people who have given up addictions are an example of an excellent source of this vitamin.

## Love Tank Five:
## Vitamin S

Love tank five is self-love. To fill up this tank, you have to make sure that you come first. You must be in charge of your life. You must begin asking yourself what you want and then go for it.

If you ask yourself what you want and the answer is you want to make others happy, you are still missing the point. What you want means what *you* want. Look at what you are missing, what else do you want.

Certainly you want to make others happy, but that is not this love tank. What else besides making others happy makes you happy? What turns you on? What makes you happy? What is good for you to fill this tank? Go places where you feel comfortable asking for what you want and saying no to what you don't want.

---

**To love yourself, give yourself permission to experiment in life.**

---

Get away from people in your everyday life so that you are free to try on new outfits and behave differently. Give yourself the freedom to do things you would never have done. Go somewhere where you will never go again, so if you make a fool of yourself it doesn't matter, because no one knows you and you will not be back.

Much of the time, we hold ourselves back because we are concerned about what others will think of us. We want to do things, but we don't, because if we make mistakes we will be reminded of it forever. Also, being around new and different people always brings out some new part of who you are. Whenever you share with someone new and different, a new part of who you are has a chance to surface.

---

**Being around new and different people always brings out some new part of who you are.**

---

To find outer success and be happy, stay in touch with what you want and set your intentions each day. Imagine going into a restaurant and not ordering. The waiter asks what you would like, and you say, "Whatever you have." Unless you are just lucky, you will probably get leftovers.

To keep this tank full, take a few minutes every day to reflect on what you want, and then set your intention by putting in your order. We will explore this process in Chapter 10. By making sure you are planning your day, you don't end up with the world's leftovers.

## Love Tank Six:
## Vitamin R

The sixth love tank is relationships, partnerships, and romance. To fill up this love tank, you need to make sure that you are sharing yourself with someone. In some way, you depend on that person and that person depends on you.

In most cases, this need is satisfied by a loving, committed, sexual relationship. To share ourselves intimately most people need to grow together in love over time. It is hard for a woman to open up right away. She generally needs more time to feel that she is known before she can let this love in. A man can sometimes share himself right away, but before he can open up consistently he also needs to be in love.

> Vitamin R can come from any loving
> partnership where there is a loving
> give and take.

If you are not married or in an intimate partnership, it is important to date around to fill up this tank. Dating around does not mean that you have to sleep around. To find someone with whom you would want to be intimate or to share a partnership, take time to experiment. Just start dating and don't look for the perfect person. Particularly when people are looking to get married, they are held back by looking for the perfect person.

If you are not getting the right person, it is usually because you really need to be filling up some earlier tanks. Likewise, if you are in a relationship, after a while the love stops flowing until you take some time to fill other tanks that are low.

> If you are not getting the right person, you
> are looking in the wrong direction.

When the student is ready, the teacher always just appears. When you ask the question, the answer will come. When you are ready for a relationship and you are open to dating, the perfect person for you shows up. If you are desperate, the perfect person rarely shows up. Give up your neediness by having a life that supports your other needs, and you will draw the right partner for you.

It is important to remember that soul mates are never perfect, but they are perfect for you as partners. Since there is a deep connection, you are immediately connecting back to your true self by loving them. It is inaccurate to think that there could only be one soul mate for you. There are thousands of people with whom you could have a great partnership. A soul mate is one of those people you choose to share your life with.

> Soul mates are never perfect, but they are
> perfect for you as a partner.

In the past, people formed loving partnerships to survive. The relationship skills with which we were raised were based not on creating lasting romance, but on creating security. To get what you want in a relationship today, it is essential to learn new relationship skills.

The movies give us a taste of the romance our soul seeks, but they don't show us how to get there. To create love and lasting relationships, we need to learn new skills. It is important to remember that romance isn't automatic, even if we are filling our other love tanks. If we are not actively creating opportunities for romance to thrive, it won't. All the Mars and Venus books focus on learning those new skills for creating lasting passion.

Not only does romance fulfill our hearts' desire for greater intimacy, but it helps empower us to be more successful in the work world.

> When there is passion in the bedroom, that
> passion translates as power in the workplace.

All the techniques for creating more in the outer world require that we be in touch with our feelings and desires. If we are suppressing our sexual desires or are numb to them, we are cutting out a tremendous amount of power in our lives. Staying in touch with and acting to fulfill all your desires is essential to create and attract everything you want.

## *Love Tank Seven:*
## *Vitamin D*

Love tank seven is giving unconditional love to someone who is depending on you. Being responsible for the needs of others is an essential requirement of the soul. We cannot continue to develop after age thirty-five if we don't create opportunities to give unconditionally.

To fill up this seventh love tank, we need to take care of children and then later grandkids. If we don't have our own grandchildren, then we should offer our services to others. We must feel responsible to someone else whom we care for and love. With this special love, we can begin making sacrifices, giving up what we want for another.

This unconditional love and support is the appropriate relationship between parent and child. It is not the ideal relationship between intimate partners. It is misleading to encourage women to give unconditionally to their partners. When they resent not getting back what they need, they feel guilty for feeling that way.

People will experience resentment if they give more than they are getting back. If we don't have permission to feel this way, we don't feel the need to stop giving and start getting.

---

**People will experience resentment if they give more than they are getting back.**

---

Certainly a little unconditional love is fine, but it really is still conditional. You can give for a while without getting back as long as eventually you will have your turn and it will come back to you. This return should not be years later, otherwise you will wake up one morning completely empty, resentful, and closed. You will have nothing left to give.

Ideally we look to the first six tanks to fill up with love, and then we can overflow to our children. If we don't have children, then we mistakenly give unconditionally in our intimate relationship and then later get stuck in resentment. Without children we also may unknowingly sabotage a relationship or the possibility of a new relationship by overnurturing and treating a partner like a child.

We can give unconditionally only when our tanks are full, and we are overflowing. This is the ideal challenge in this time period of development. It is not enough to take care of the poor or a nephew or niece. Although this is helpful, if we are age thirty-five to forty-two we need to feel deeply responsible for someone or something alive. A good replacement is having a pet or garden to look after. Just like a pet, your plants are alive, and they need you. If we do have children, as they grow up we need to find a surrogate to give to. Grandchildren are certainly perfect for the job.

By feeling responsible and giving your love unconditionally, your soul will be strengthened.

## Love Tank Eight:
### Vitamin C

Love tank eight is giving back to your community, assisting in making your local world a better and more beautiful place. This is the ideal time to begin doing volunteer work to help others not directly related to you. Any kind of project to help the poor, the schools, the library, or the environment, to name a few, helps you as well.

In this stage of life, we need to be thinking about helping others. The gifts we have received in life are the gifts we have to share with our community. To fill this tank, start looking for ways to give back some of what you have received.

---

**The gifts we have received in life are the gifts we are here in this world to share.**

---

This is a period to give time and money to charities and worthy organizations that are trying to help your community. By extending yourself in this way, you begin to expand your spirit through your generosity. Be careful that you don't neglect your family in the process. This sort of giving can be so gratifying that we forget the other people we love. Ultimately it will lose its luster, if we are not making sure to nurture ourselves and to keep filling up our earlier love tanks.

## Love Tank Nine:
### Vitamin W

Love tank nine—giving back to the world—is an extension of love tank eight. In this stage, we need to broaden our horizons and extend ourselves beyond the boundaries of our community, race, and culture. This is a time to share with those of different backgrounds and traditions.

It is a time to become more interested in political ideals and ideas in your country and around the world. You might volunteer to help a candidate get elected or run for office yourself. To fill this love tank, you may get involved in some kind of world cause.

---

**Use your wisdom and power not only to help
yourself and your family, but to extend
yourself to help the world in some way.**

---

This is also an ideal time to travel and see the world and share your light. Take more vacations and broaden your experiences. If you do not expand your boundaries, you will not grow. Many people in this stage start feeling old and because they are not expanding. They don't know what they are missing. By getting out, they will soon get their old energy levels back.

Cruises and tours are great for this stage, not only because they make travel easy, but because they also offer the opportunity to fill the other tanks. By connecting and sharing yourself in other cultures, you will discover that, although people are different, we are all the same deep inside. Seeing the world will bring out new parts of who you are and will keep you young. This is a great time to travel around the country and create your own unique adventure with your partner, grandchildren, or friends.

---

**Seeing the world will bring out new parts of who you are and will keep you young.**

---

This is also a time when your business may thrive. When you are full within yourself and capable of giving back to the world, your own success dramatically increases. The more you have done for others, assuming that it is without strings attached, the more power you will have to attract what you want.

One study showed that men achieved their greatest levels of power between ages forty-four and fifty-six. At this time, a man is capable of thinking freely about the needs of others. As a result, not only do people trust and depend on him more, but he is in touch with intuition to make the right choices. Getting older can mean having more, not less.

## *Love Tank Ten: Vitamin G2*

Love tank ten is serving God. When we come into this world, God takes care of us. As we grow and fill up inside, we gradually can give it all back. At this point, we are free to serve God. As we fill up this love tank, we are automatically most in tune with God's will. This is when we can have the greatest impact in the world. Around the age of fifty-six is when we are fully ready to do what we are in this world to do.

This is when we reach our full glory. This is when we can be in touch with our greatest powers and gifts. When we have learned to fill all our love tanks, we can express each day to our full potential at this stage. Certainly, before this time, we can have glimpses of this stage, but until we have filled all the other tanks and fully developed ourselves, it is not possible. Many people immediately age and get sick at this time, because they cannot meet the challenge. Their other tanks are too empty to fulfill this new requirement to give selflessly in service.

---

**Many people immediately age
and get sick at this time, because they
cannot meet the challenge.**

---

When you reach fifty-six, the way to fill this tenth love tank is to surrender your will completely to the will of God. Although you may have done this at younger ages, you are able to do so at this age and continue to fill up all your other love tanks.

This is your time to bloom fully. Make sure that you are ready to enjoy it. If you are not ready, then at least now you know how to go back to fill up as you continue to ask for inner guidance. As you enjoy this state, you feel more and more that you are one with everything and everyone. Your greatest joy is in serving. The "I," "you," "he," "she," and "we" all melt into the one God energy. Life becomes a river of God's light and love gently rushing on toward more and more. You become a pure channel of God's grace to all you meet.

To lead a full and rich life is not only possible, but our duty. God wants you to have it all just as much as you do. By continuing to get what you need and fill your ten love tanks, you will always be guided to fulfill your divine purpose to make a difference in this world.

# CHAPTER 8

# *The Value
of Meditation*

To fill our first and most important love tank, we need to feel our connection to God. There are many ways to do that. Meditation is a very powerful way. Although it is not linked to a  particular religion, meditation supports all spiritual traditions. Anyone can benefit from meditation even without believing in God. As I talk about God, you may wish to interpret that to mean positive energy, love energy, higher power, greater potential, higher wisdom, glorious future, or whatever. Since my background involves a strong experience of and belief in God, I will use the word "God," but please feel free to insert your own meaning of that "something more."

Even if not religious, most people do believe in something more. That higher power can even be their own inner potential. At the very least, they believe in a better and brighter future. With any belief, meditation will help you to fill up your first love tank. Right away you will begin to experience greater peace and relaxation. Gradually you will feel joy, confidence, and love as well. By taking a few minutes every day to connect to God, you enrich your day.

I have taught meditation for more than twenty-eight years to people of all religions and walks of life. The value of meditation is recognized and accepted by all religions. Although viewed as a spiritual practice, it does not conflict with any religion. To enjoy the benefits of meditation, one does not have to be religious, yet, if one is religious, it strengthens one's religious interest as well. Regular experience of your connection to a higher power helps you to understand and honor the universal truths in every religion.

Regular meditation assists you in reconnecting to the aspect of your inner self that is connected to God. That connection is already there, but you have to become aware of it to experience it. Let's do a few awareness exercises:

Take a moment to become aware of your mother or someone who loves you. As you think about her, you will begin to feel your connection to her. This connection is always there. All you have to do is shift your attention, and you can find it.

Now shift your attention to your neck. Be aware of your throat. Notice how it feels. Be aware of the temperature. Suddenly you can't stop being aware of it. Soon your awareness will shift away, and once again you will forget your neck.

One part of your mind is always experiencing your neck as it connects the body to the head, but your conscious awareness only feels the neck or other parts of the body when you choose to direct your attention. In a similar manner, meditation involves shifting the attention to the part of yourself that is already connected to God. By learning to make this shift, you will begin to feel your connection with God, just as you can feel your neck attaching your body to the head, or feel your inner connection to your mother or someone who loves you.

---

**Meditation is shifting your attention to
the part of yourself that is already
connected to God.**

---

Without any interpretation, the experience of mediation is peaceful, calm, and relaxing. Gradually you begin to experience tingling energy or warmth in your fingers and hands. You feel a current of energy. And with the flow of energy you feel more confident, more loving, and more joyful for what appears to be no reason. These are the universal experiences of meditation, regardless of how you choose to interpret that energy.

I interpret that experience as feeling my connection to God. I feel God's love, grace, energy, and power flowing right into my body though my fingertips. It is literally like plugging myself into God's wall socket. Those who don't have a religious perspective will have a different interpretation of their experience, but the experience is usually the same.

## Meditation Works for Everyone

The experience of mediation is no longer for a select few. Everyone can do it and get immediate benefit. Times have dramatically changed since I began regular mediation twenty-eight years ago. I am amazed that students today experience this connection right away. One does not have to spend years out of society in the silence of the mountains to find God.

I lived as a monk in the mountains of Switzerland for nine years to experience my inner connection to God. Now, when I teach meditation, I see people progressing light-years faster than I did. Within a few weeks, they begin to experience the current of energy flowing in their fingertips. Ninety percent of the people who learn to meditate at my seminars have this experience in one or two days. To me, this is extremely exciting.

Throughout history this has never happened. To have such an immediate experience was unheard of. The great mystics and saints of our past had to spend years waiting to have a spiritual experience, and now practically anyone can experience the current of energy. Everyone experiences the peace and relaxation right away. When you meditate after work, the stress of the day automatically is washed away. Feeling this current of energy recharges you and helps you to feel immediately refreshed.

When you meditate at the beginning of the day, it prepares you to take on life's challenges with a positive attitude. Feeling your connection to God helps you to remember that you are not alone and that you have extra support. So much of our suffering and struggle occurs when we think we have to do it all ourselves. Fortunately we do not. Help is there, but we have to ask for it. The energy we feel moving through our fingers indicates that we are making the connection, and we are drawing into our lives the power, intuition, clarity, and creativity necessary to fulfill our wants.

---

### Suffering occurs when we forget our connection to God.

---

Mediation automatically begins to fill your first love tank. Certainly all the other love tanks are very important, but if this one is empty, it becomes the most important one. When we are low in vitamin G1, we feel the burden of life and its responsibilities. We feel we have to do it ourselves, and we don't know how we can do it all. When we are not aware of our connection to God, we automatically begin to look for it by expecting too much of ourselves and others. When we are not feeling a connection to something more, we expect others to be more and inevitably are disappointed. Instead of recognizing and rejoicing in God's little miracles each day, we focus too much on what we are not getting. We don't recognize that much of what we are wanting and needing is flowing into our lives. When this first love tank is low, whatever we get never seems good enough.

When you meditate on your connection to God, you feel more appreciative of what you have. This positive awareness coupled with strong desire increases your power to attract and create what you want. Naturally, when you radiate more positive energy, people want to be with you, work with you, give things to you, appreciate you, and trust you. In a very literal sense, you bring sunshine into their lives.

---

**When you radiate more positive energy, people want to be around you.**

---

## Meditation Is Simple

The most amazing thing about learning mediation at this time in history is how simple it is. In the past, the process was much more difficult. People did not immediately experience the pleasing current of energy. Meditation was tedious and boring and most students gave up. Teachers would often make you wait for a long time before teaching you. Meditation was only for the most committed and advanced students. Teachers would wait until they felt the student was receptive. Now, with an understanding of the importance of feelings and desire, this outdated practice of waiting is no longer necessary. In the past, when people were not as in touch with their inner feelings, having to wait strengthened their desire and passion, so that when they did begin, they could get a glimpse of spiritual experience to motivate them on their arduous path.

Teachers used to test students by having them travel long distances and perform many selfless acts before they would provide instruction. These traditions opened the students up to their inner feelings and longing to learn. At a certain point, the teachers would feel the flow of energy toward the students and teach. When you become open to receiving this energy, you, too, will be able to send it out to others.

This is the basis of spiritual healing. A laying-on-hands healer draws in the energy and passes it on to the person being healed. The same thing happened when the teacher taught higher practices of meditation. A teacher who could feel the energy flowing to the student knew the student had become porous enough to experience at least a glimpse of the flow.

Today, people I meet, within a few minutes of discussing the value of mediation, will begin to draw out that energy which indicates that they are ready. This is not the way it was twenty-five years ago or even five years ago. The world is quickly changing. We are so much more open to our feelings and aware of what we want and don't want. This ability to open our hearts and feel strong desires gives people the opportunity to draw in the energy if they just begin to feel their connection and ask. The process of meditation opens the channels for that to happen.

## Interactive Meditation

Interactive meditation supports you in learning to draw in energy through your fingertips. For me and the thousands of participants who have attended my success seminar, practicing interactive meditation along with making sure that the other love tanks are full is without a doubt a power tool for creating personal success right away in your life. Although I use and teach this technique, it is not the only way. There are other ways to meditate that are also very good and will assist a person in filling up love tank G1.

Until now, only the very adept or expert meditators knew how to draw in energy through their fingertips. Students were not taught, because they were not porous enough, and it just would not work. They could not feel the energy flow. But people today are ready. What someone can gain in a few weeks of practice took me more than fifteen years to experience.

Ideally it is good to learn meditation directly from an expert, but after teaching this technique on television to millions, I have received tremendously positive feedback that it works, even if you are not learning in a group at one of my personal success workshops. This great news encouraged me to share everything in a book. I would still advise learning in a group from an expert, but meditation can be learned at home as well. Particularly in the beginning, meditating in a group makes it easier to experience the flow of energy.

---

**This practice can even be learned from a book, although it is best studied in a group or with an instructor.**

---

Interactive mediation gives us the regular experience that we don't have to do it all. For me personally, this element has been very useful. Whenever people do something really creative, they wonder later, "How did I do that?" They then wonder if they can do it again. When we clearly experience that we are helped, that concern of "Can I do it again?" goes away.

If you just do your best, with higher help your intentions come true. Particularly in the Western materialistic countries, people need to remember that they are not alone, and there is extra support in making their big dreams come true.

When I write a book, sometimes people say, "You must have channeled that," implying that someone else wrote my books. This is not the kind of support that I am talking about. The support I get from interactive meditation is greater clarity to see my ideas, greater comprehension to put ideas together, greater confidence to sit down and work it out, greater energy to sustain a diligent and persistent schedule, greater ability to appreciate what works and change what doesn't, greater creativity to find a solution. This is the support I get. No one else does it for me. This help, however, does not come until I first sit down and do my best.

## Understanding Destiny

In the East, people have a greater sense that God's will is always being done. Although this can make you peaceful, it tends to negate your personal desires for more. Life is seen as a process of experiencing the results of your past actions rather than a blank canvas on which you paint whatever you want. From the perspective of personal success, life is a blank canvas as long as you choose to paint it. If instead you just go with the flow and see where you end up, then the momentum or "Karma" of your past controls your destiny.

Certainly we are always affected by our past; everything we experience today is the result of our thoughts and actions in the past. Yet this does not mean that we have to stay limited by that. At any time, we can choose how we want our future to be and begin making changes in that direction.

---

**A rocket in motion cannot immediately turn around, but it can gradually change direction.**

---

In a similar way, we are never limited to our destiny. Each day, we can begin anew and work on a new picture. Although we have the opportunity to paint a new picture, we are limited to the same colors to work with. To create our future we have to work first with what we have, but gradually by mixing colors, we can even create new colors.

If you tend just to let things happen rather than creating the life you want, you will benefit most by taking some time at the end of meditation to feel deeply your wishes and wants. Rather than passively accepting your destiny as God's will, take time to feel your will in tune with God's will to create a life of love, peace, confidence, and power, a life of abundance, pleasure, good health, and outer success as well.

You have the power to create the life you want. You are not limited by your past. By applying these principles of success you will create your destiny rather than act it out. Unless you are actively creating your future, your future is limited by your past. Interactive meditation sets the stage for you to act out your life the way you want it to be. You write the script, and you select the characters.

# CHAPTER 9

# *How to Meditate*

NTERACTIVE MEDITATION allows you to feel your inner connection to God or a higher power by inviting God into your heart. To practice interactive meditation, find a comfortable pose sitting or lying in an environment in which you will not be interrupted. It is best to turn off the phone and give yourself fifteen minutes to ignore all your responsibilities and turn inward. It's also fine to put on some soothing background music, although it is not necessary.

With eyes closed, reach your hands up in the air a little above shoulder height or wherever is comfortable and begin repeating this phrase: "Oh God, my heart is open to you, please come sit in my heart." Interactive meditation is primarily repeating this phrase quietly inside, over and over for fifteen minutes.

---

To meditate, quietly repeat the phrase:
"Oh God, my heart is open to you,
please come sit in my heart."

---

You begin by repeating the phrase out loud ten times, one time for each fingertip. As you repeat the phrase once for each fingertip, hold the faint intention to awaken and open the channels of energy in that fingertip.

Once you have said the phrase out loud ten times, continue repeating the phrase quietly inside for about fifteen minutes. Have a watch or clock nearby to check the time.

In the beginning, it is natural and normal for the mind to wander and have other thoughts. You may even forget the phrase. If you do, then simply open your eyes and look it up. It takes time before the process is completely automatic.

---

**During meditation, it is natural and normal
for the mind to wander and have
other thoughts.**

---

In the beginning, to remember and repeat the phrase you are using your short-term memory. As you continue to repeat it, long-term memory sets in and you actually begin to grow neuro-connectors in the brain to remember the phrase. With a little diligence and persistence the neural pathways gradually develop and the process becomes automatic.

Meanwhile, the channels to receive subtle energy will begin to open in your fingertips. To receive the blessings of God's energy, keep your fingertips up and not touching one another. If you do not feel the tingling right away, try saying the phrase aloud a few more rounds of ten.

---

**As you say the phrase out loud, once for
every fingertip, make a slight movement of
each finger as your awareness shifts to it.**

---

Sometimes in the beginning wiggling your fingers a little will relax them and help you feel the energy. Sometimes slowly moving the hands back and forth about a tenth of an inch will increase your awareness of the energy field around your fingers. In this way, as you direct your attention to your fingers while you open your heart to God, the energy begins to flow. The wiring is already there; you only have to turn it on. Just as your fingertips allow you to touch the world, they also allow you to touch God. This is wonderfully depicted in Michelangelo's painting of man reaching out and touching God with his fingertip in the Sistine Chapel.

---

**Just as our fingertips allow us to touch the world, they also allow us to touch God.**

---

Even in advanced states of meditation, it is normal for the mind to wander. In early stages, your mind will wander and think about things that may be bothering you or causing stress. In advanced stages, your mind wanders toward the blissful feelings and currents of increasing insight. Eventually, whenever you seek an answer to a problem or inner guidance, it may emerge as a delicate feeling while in a meditative state.

As you meditate, and you notice that your mind has wandered, simply come back to the phrase. It is natural to be thinking occasionally about shopping lists, duties, things people said, things you have to do, and so on. The benefits of meditation come even if you can say the phrase only a few times before your mind starts to wander again.

---

**As you meditate, and you notice that your mind has wandered, simply come back to the phrase.**

---

Every time you notice that you are thinking about other things, just come back to thinking the phrase and awareness of your fingertips. Just as it is effortless and easy to think about other things, it is also easy to think the phrase. The entire process is simple. It does not matter whether you think the phrase quickly or slowly, just think it, and that is enough.

---

Just as it is effortless and easy to think
about other things, it is also easy to
think the phrase.

---

Keeping your hands up in the air creates a greater awareness of the fingers. If in the beginning they get tired, it is fine to rest them on your lap, but keep your palms facing up and your fingers slightly apart. Make sure that your hands are not touching the bare skin of your legs. If you are wearing shorts, place a cloth over your legs. When your hands are directly lying on your skin, you tend to stop drawing energy in and feel your own energy instead. One of the benefits of interactive meditation is new energy to add to your own.

In a variety of ways, your experience in meditation will change. Sometimes the phrase will be clear and at other times faint; sometimes big, sometimes small; sometimes even and smooth, and sometimes like riding a wave up and down. Sometimes it feels very close, yet at other times very distant.

Your experience of the phrase will continue to change. Sometimes you will feel heavy and sometimes very light. Sometimes you will feel tired and other times alert. Sometimes the time goes really fast and sometimes it seems like each minute is ten minutes. Each of these variations is natural and indicates that the process is working.

---

In a variety of ways your
experience will change.

---

In the beginning, meditate two times a day so that the mind, heart, and body get in the habit of going within and opening up to

God's energy. Once the habit of going inside is established, regularity is not essential, but it is helpful. In the past, regularity used be more important, but now as soon as people put their fingers up, the divine energy begins to flow in. It feels so good that you will be looking for opportunities to do it more. It generally takes about six weeks of regular practice to fully open the channels in your fingertips.

Once you get in the habit of turning inward, you decide how much to meditate. Fifteen minutes twice a day is a good rhythm for most. If you are really busy one day, it is fine to skip, but then try to make it up later. Your body gets used to using the extra energy. When you meditate you get extra energy and clarity, which makes you more efficient. The best times for meditation are in the morning when you get up, after work around sunset, and before you go to bed.

---

**Fifteen minutes of meditation twice a day is
for most a good rhythm.**

---

Even if it seems that you have no time, it is a wise decision to take a few minutes to meditate. You will create more time by making the right decisions and pulling in more support. Usually, when we don't have time to meditate, it is because we are low in vitamin G1 and have to do everything ourselves. Remember, you are driving the car; you don't have to get out and push it.

Sometimes I spend many hours in meditation enjoying the flow of creative ideas that come when my mind wanders off the phrase. Or, before an important presentation later in the day, I will meditate longer to allow my energy to build up. More positive energy will always make others more attracted to you. More time in meditation, feeling the current of energy flowing, means more energy, creativity, love, joy, peace, and intelligence.

It does not work to use meditation to avoid responsibilities. You may think that if you just meditate things will get done. This is not the case. The engine of the car will take you where you want to go, but you still have to get in the car and drive. The car can have a full tank and be ready to go, but you have to start it.

---

### God will not do for you what you can do for yourself.

---

As you use the energy to get what you need and want, it flows more in your life. If you are not using it up in your life after meditation, it will stop flowing altogether. If you want more energy to flow, make sure that you are using it up. Some rechargeable batteries are this way. To fully charge them, you have to use them up completely. Then next time, they will charge up fully. In the case of meditation, if you put to use all the energy you get, you will get more and more. In this way, your capacity for more increases.

This current of energy is described in various cultures and religions. For example, in the Orient this energy is called *chi*; in India it is called *prana*; in the ancient Hawaiian culture it was called *mana*; and in the Christian tradition it is called the Holy Spirit. In many cultures, this experience is talked about, but never was it a common experience. People were lucky if they glimpsed it. Today, it is no longer a concept to describe how God works wonders in the world. For many, it has become a regular experience.

If you are an atheist and the word "God" doesn't work for you, then try, "Oh glorious future, my heart is open to you, come into my life." Everyone enjoys this phrase. It brings quite an exhilarating feeling.

You may also wish to experiment and put in any name you choose in the first part of the phrase. Depending on your faith you may wish to use any of the following phrases:

"Oh Jesus, my heart is open to you, please come sit in my heart."

"Oh divine Mother, my heart is open to you, please come sit in my heart."

"Oh heavenly Father, my heart is open to you, please come sit in my heart."

"Oh Allah, my heart is open to you, please come sit in my heart."

"Oh Great Spirit, my heart is open to you, please come sit in my heart."

"Oh Krishna, my heart is open to you, please come sit in my heart."

"Oh Buddha, my heart is open to you, please come sit in my heart."

If you already have a special spiritual connection open for you, then use this process to enrich it by placing at the beginning of the phrase the name of the energy or presence with which you wish to connect.

After about fifteen minutes, you will be flowing in the consciousness of your true self as it connects to God. This is the ideal time to ask for help from God by setting your intention and order your day. It does not take much time, because you are now connected. You are now ready to feel what you want and draw it into your life.

## Setting Your Intention

When your heart and mind are open and connected to the current of energy, this is the ideal time to ask for what you want and then begin to experience your power to create your day. If you don't order when you go into a restaurant, you don't get food. In a similar manner, to put this energy to work you need to feel your inner desires and intentions.

At the end of meditation, when you begin the process of setting your intentions, shift your phrase to "Oh glorious future, my heart is open to you, please come into my life."

Repeat this phrase quietly inside ten times with a little extra awareness of each finger, as you did in the beginning of meditation. Feel your openness for good to happen and then begin to reflect on how you want to feel that day. If by this time your hands are resting in your lap, raise them up again for this last part. Raising them all the way or partway is fine.

With your hands up and eyes still closed, reflect on how you want your day to unfold. Look at a best-case scenario. Imagine yourself moving through the day feeling happy, loving, peaceful, and confident. Take about a minute to explore each of these positive feelings. The more you are able to feel these positive emotions, the more power you will add to your day. As you imagine your day unfolding, ask yourself the following questions and then affirm the answers as if it is really happening.

How do you want your day to unfold?

What do you want to happen?

What else?
*Imagine it happening in great detail.*

What are you happy about?
*"I am happy that . . ."*

What do you love?
*"I love . . ."*

What are you confident about?
*"I am confident that . . ."*

What are you grateful for?
*"I am grateful for . . ."*

Feeling this gratitude, bring your awareness back into present time and slowly count to three with the intention to open your eyes feeling refreshed, peaceful, and focused. Then open your eyes and say, "Thank you, God."

## Practice Makes It Easy

In the beginning, setting your intentions may be a little awkward. You may have to keep opening your eyes to read the next question to focus on. With a little practice, this process of setting your intentions will become easy and automatic. Just as you can learn to throw a ball with practice, you can eventually learn to create positive feelings. These positive feelings will then attract into life what you want, and they will also assist you in staying connected to your true self.

The real challenge is remembering to set your intentions. In interactive meditation, it is just as important as repeating the phrase. To make a hard-boiled egg, you have first to boil the water, but you still have to put the egg in the water. It only takes a few minutes once the water is boiling. Meditation is like boiling water, while setting your intentions is like putting in the egg to be cooked.

We are so used to automatically starting our day that we forget to plan how we want to feel and what we want to happen in greater detail. Commonly, people go through their days passively accepting or resisting what happens. By setting your intentions, automatically things start coming to you. Right away, you get to see the creative power of thoughts. By setting your intentions, you are creating your day.

## Small Miracles

Let's look at a few examples of what happens when you set your intentions. I have thousands to pick from, so I will describe what happened today. Earlier in the day, I flew home to San Francisco from a talk I gave the night before in Illinois. While I was away for the night, I realized that my writing schedule had been so focused that for the last couple of weeks my wife, Bonnie, and I had not gone out on a date. I wanted to do something special and wondered what I could do. While setting my intentions, I asked for the information to come.

Later, when I was on the plane, the person next to me happened to be the assistant director for a play that Bonnie had wanted to see a few months earlier in New York. Now to my delight I learned that we could see it in San Francisco. I realized this was the answer to my request, and this nice man even offered to get us great seats.

This sort of small miracle happens daily when we start deliberately setting our intentions. We begin to see how life is always providing little miracles. In the example above, I had first imagined myself going out on a wonderful date with my wife. Then automatically that day my request was answered. I got the information to create a wonderful date.

By setting your intentions at the end of the meditation, you will see that you attract what you need to create what you want. As your confidence grows based on experience, the miracles just get bigger and bigger.

In the beginning, it is enough just to say, "I see myself at work feeling happy." Then, when you are happy at work, you notice, and you acknowledge with delight, "Okay, this is working. Thank you."

Yesterday, before making my trip to Illinois, I first imagined everything going smoothly and my feeling peaceful, confident, happy, and loving. Then on my trip everything was wonderful. I was met at the plane and driven by limousine to a nice hotel.

I was assured by my host that all my arrangements had been taken care of. When I checked in, the hotel couldn't find my reservation. I patiently pulled out my confirmation number, but they still could not find it. It seemed a comedy of errors. It took twenty minutes for them to find my reservation. Throughout the whole experience, I was amazed by how peaceful and unassuming I was.

Instead of getting upset or annoyed, I just relaxed and waited. I reassured my escort, who was terribly embarrassed, that everything was okay. I set him at ease by saying, "Thank goodness, I'm not in hurry. We still have just enough time to get to the talk." Although we had a setback, the trip was still smooth. As I reflected later on what had happened, I thought, "Thank you, God, for giving me grace and patience."

When you deliberately set your intention, things come to pass every day, and you have the wonderful opportunity to say thanks to God. This just strengthens your ability to cocreate your day with God and keeps your love tanks full. This added awareness of support and personal success keeps your heart open to attracting everything you want.

# CHAPTER 10

# *How to Decharge Stress*

A S THE CHANNELS in your fingers open more and you begin to draw consciously on the energy, you can learn to let go of stress most efficiently. Just as you can draw in positive energy, you can send out negative energy. When you have accumulated stress during the day, you can send that negative energy out of your body. This is called decharging. And it is just as important and easy as meditating and setting your intentions. By decharging stress, not only will you feel better, but you will be more free to create your day.

## *Understanding Negative Energy*

It is hard to explain negative energy in scientific terms, but everyone has certainly experienced it. When people are stuck in any of the blocks to personal success (blame, depression, anxiety, indifference, judgments, indecision, procrastination, perfectionism, resentment, self-pity, confusion, and guilt), they are producing some degree of negative energy. This does not mean they are bad or negative, but it does mean they are disconnected from their inner source of positive energy. In the absence of positive energy, they put out negative energy. If they are drawn to you, it is often because you make them feel better. They draw in your positive energy.

You have probably had the experience of going somewhere or being with some people who cause you to start to feel worse. Your neck might start to hurt or you might begin to feel tired. Although it may be hard to pinpoint any particular cause of discomfort, you still feel it.

In a similar way, you could be with others and automatically begin to feel better and better. Spontaneously little pains and aches start to go away. By being in their presence, you just feel good. Positive energy naturally makes others happier and more loving, peaceful, and confident.

These experiences are not random. They are the result of a definite exchanging of energy. When one person is low in energy, just being around someone with high energy will give that person a boost. Yet the person with high energy will have a little less. Energy flows from one person to another to find a balance or equilibrium.

Visualize two glass tanks that are connected at the bottom with a tube which is controlled by a valve. The valve allows fluids to pass from one container to the other. First close the valve and then fill up one tank with blue water. Now one tank is full and the other is empty. What happens when you turn the valve and open the channel between the two tanks? Automatically the empty tank fills up halfway and the full tank goes down halfway. In a similar way, when you have more energy it flows out to those with less.

Although this example explains the flow of energy, it does not explain the exchange of energy. It describes the flow of energy in quantity but not in quality. When positive energy flows out, it does not just become less, it will attract and absorb negative energy.

To understand this automatic exchange of energy, visualize

two tanks connected with a tube and a valve. First close the valve and fill up tank one with blue cold liquid and then fill tank two with red hot liquid. Now what happens when you open the valve? Automatically the temperature of the water begins to find balance and equilibrium. The red hot liquid flows to the blue cold liquid, and eventually both tanks are the same temperature and the color changes to violet.

In a similar fashion, if you are feeling good and you connect with someone who is feeling worse, after a while the other person will begin to feel better and you start to feel bad. You may not feel it right away, but within a few hours or days you will begin to notice that your good feelings are missing. Understanding this analogy helps to explain the exchange of positive and negative energy that occurs all the time.

When one person is stuck in negative energy, just being around a person with positive energy will make the person feel better. Gradually the person with positive energy will begin to feel a little less positive. A person who has a lot of positive energy will take a while before noticing that some negative energy has been absorbed. A person whose level of energy is low will notice and be influenced by the negative energy right away.

## Different Degrees of Sensitivity

The more sensitive you are, the more you will notice the different flows of energy and be influenced by them. If you are not sensitive, you will not be so influenced. Your valve, to different degrees, is closed. You are well protected, but you are also not able to draw in greater degrees of energy.

Some people are just less sensitive. They don't notice this flow of energy at all, and they are not influenced by it. They get their energy from food, exercise, air, sex, and that's it. They are more stable, they get things done, and they can be very successful.

They do what others before them have done and experience different degrees of success or failure largely depending on opportunities, effort, genes, childhood rearing, education, past actions, and the natural talent they were born with. Although these less sensitive people experience all degrees of success, great and small, they have not yet tapped their inner creative potential. They can repeat what they have learned, but they cannot create more. They give love according to the love they have received, but it is harder for them to forgive and love again after they have been hurt. They act out their destiny, which is sometimes good and sometimes not so good. To change their destiny, to discover their creative potential, to change their direction in life, they need to become more sensitive. By opening up to their feelings and practicing interactive meditation, they can find that power.

## Why We Don't Heal

On the other hand, many people suffer tremendously simply because they have not learned how to release the negative energy they absorb from others. They collect and carry around negative energy. Either they send it back out to others or they try to be really loving and good, and that negative energy stays stuck in their bodies and creates sickness and disease. This negative energy gradually weakens the body and blocks the natural healing energy that allows others to get better.

One cancer study investigated the psychological profiles of those patients who got better and those who didn't. The only common link the study found was that those who got better complained much more about the food, the accommodations, and the service.

Those who didn't go to great lengths to be polite and loving were actually the ones who got better. This does not mean that being polite and loving will make you sick. Being positive only makes you sick or unhappy when you are absorbing the negativity of others and not sending it out in some way. When sensitive people learn to decharge their negativity, they experience tremendous benefits right away.

Not only do their blocks go away, but they begin to experience their potential to create more. Even if they have been meditating for years and they have done everything in their power to get the love they need, unless they have learned how to discharge negativity, they will continue to suffer from the negativity of others.

## What Happens When We Absorb Negativity

To the degree that we absorb negativity and don't have a way to release it, we will continue to feel blocked. No matter how loving or good we are, we will stay stuck in negative feelings. These are four common symptoms of those who absorb negativity and don't know how to release it.

**1: Blocked love.** When we absorb negativity, we may want to be more loving, but we feel recurring waves of blame and resentment. Our love is restricted or restrained. We want to love more but can't.

This is very different from less sensitive people who may not be loving at all. They are disconnected from their soul's desire to be loving. As a result they don't feel an inner longing to love more or inner emptiness because love is absent in their lives.

**2: Blocked confidence.** When we absorb negativity, we may try to be confident and have faith, but we still feel rushes of anxiety and confusion when we take risks. Our confidence is blocked. We feel our soul's desire to be more and do more, but feel held back.

This is very different from less sensitive people who do not care about taking risks, but are quite content to live in their comfort zone of repeating what is familiar.

**3: Blocked joy.** When we absorb negativity, we may try to be happy, but we feel pulled down by depression and self-pity. Our joy is diluted and flat. We feel our soul's longing to be happy, but it is missing.

This is very different from less sensitive people who don't know what they are missing. They are somewhat happy, but it is nothing like the pure joy they felt as children. They have long forgotten what real joy is.

**4: Blocked peace.** When we absorb negativity, we may try to feel good about ourselves, but we still feel the occasional grip of guilt and unworthiness. We are unable to feel the purity of our innate goodness and innocence and the peace of mind that it affords. We feel tainted or stained by our past mistakes and are unable to forgive ourselves. As a result we experience being overly responsible for others. If as children we were punished for our mistakes, we will continue to punish ourselves.

This is very different from less sensitive people who may not even know that they made mistakes. When we are not sensitive to the feelings and needs of others, we are unable to recognize the mistakes we make. Even a really good person will be like a bull in a china shop without a certain degree of sensitivity.

Sensitive souls draw in the negativity of others because they are so open. The negativity they feel is a mixture of their own with others. Like a sponge, they draw in negativity wherever they go.

## What You Suppress Others Will Express

What allows others to be less sensitive is the ability to suppress feelings. If some people get upset, they don't need to process their feelings to feel better. They just need to ignore or reject their feelings, and eventually they go away. This technique works for those who are less sensitive, but it does not work for those who are more sensitive. When you are sensitive, you cannot ignore what you feel.

The most sensitive people are often considered the problem of the family or the "black sheep." Since they are more connected to their soul, they tend to be more sensitive. If they are much more sensitive than other family members, they will absorb the negativity of the whole family. What the parents suppress, the sensitive child will feel and express.

Every mother has experienced those very stressful days when she is doing her best to hold it together, but it is very difficult. At those times, she struggles to feel better by suppressing her fears, worries, anxieties, frustrations, and disappointments.

At those moments, her children become more needy, fussy, demanding, and unmanageable. Parents often wonder why their children have to pick the worst times to act out or lose control. The answer is clear. When a parent suppresses negative feelings, the sensitive child will feel what the parent is suppressing and lose control. The negative feeling the parent is suppressing will be absorbed by one or more of the kids.

Imagine two tanks connected by a tube and a valve. Let these two tanks represent parent and child. Fill the parent's tank with a blue liquid representing negative energy, and fill the child's tank with red liquid representing positive energy. Now open the valve. The liquids begin to mix very slowly.

Now put a lid on the parent's tank and press down. As you push down, what happens to the blue liquid? It very quickly gets pushed over to the child. This example illustrates what happens when parents suppress their feelings. What they suppress, their children will feel and express. A child becomes the black sheep of the family only when absorbing the negativity that everyone else is suppressing.

When people suppress their negativity, they not only send it out to others who are more sensitive, but they absorb less negativity from the world. It is as if they have a one-way valve connecting their tank to the feelings of others. They send out negativity, but do not draw it in.

In a similar way, some very loving and positive people get sick because they absorb negativity, but do not send it out. If you are sensitive, unless you find a way to discharge the negativity you absorb, you will continue to suffer unnecessarily.

## To Feel or Not to Feel

There are actually certain therapies that depend on helping others not to feel their feelings. They actually desensitize people from experiencing their emotions. By learning to turn off the emotions people find immediate relief. They stop absorbing negative energy, and all the symptoms go away.

If you learned how to suppress your emotions, many of your sicknesses and blocks might begin to go away, but your heart would slowly close. As you become less sensitive, you would stop absorbing negativity, but you would lose connection with your soul. Though your mind would become very clear, you would lose compassion and all the other benefits of connecting to your true self. As you learned to suppress your negative feelings, you would unconsciously be attracted to and create dramatic situations that would express what you were suppressing.

Some of these therapies rely on remembering painful events over and over with the intention of feeling nothing. If you were hurt by someone, you would remember the event, and describe it to another over and over until you felt nothing. Instead of remembering the past to feel the pain and heal it with love and greater insight, the goal is to deaden your negative feelings. Although you would learn not to feel, you would still experience some very impressive results.

Other therapies rely on analyzing your emotions and invalidating them. This process strengthens the mind at the expense of the emotions. Patients learn to invalidate their negative feelings and talk themselves out of feeling upset. Though self-talk is important to make sense of the world, one should not use the mind to suppress the feelings.

Fortunately there are other ways to send out negativity without becoming less sensitive. You don't have to give up your sensitivities to get better. With the skills for processing emotions that we will explore in later chapters and by regular decharging, you can learn to transform negative feelings without having to suppress them or become less sensitive in any way. Sensitivity is a precious gift to make all our dreams come true. Absorbing negative energy becomes a problem only because we have not learned to decharge it. By decharging, you will get the same immediate benefits without having to numb yourself. It is like curing a headache without having to take a pill.

If you are sensitive, a lifetime of negativity will begin to drain out of you as you practice decharging. By meditating and setting your intentions, you will be free to draw in tremendous positive energy to make your dreams come true.

The problem with becoming less sensitive is that you disconnect from your ability to feel your truly loving, joyful, confident, and peaceful self. When you suppress a negative emotion, you also suppress your ability to experience positive feelings. When you suppress negative emotions, you numb your ability to feel your true desires. If you can't feel sadness, then you can't feel how much you miss someone and want to be with that person. If you can't feel anger, then you can't feel what you don't want. If you can't feel your fears, then you can't feel your needs for love and support. If you can't feel your sorrow, then you have no compassion and life loses its meaning and purpose. All the negative emotions link us back to important aspects of our true selves.

---

**When you suppress negative emotions, you numb your ability to feel your true desires.**

---

If you suppress your emotions, you can still be somewhat loving, happy, confident, and peaceful, but you do not continue to grow. These positive feelings lose their richness. Instead of living in full color, you live in a black and white world, and often you don't even know what you are missing. In the short term, by suppressing your feelings, you find immediate relief, but in the long term, you stop growing.

When you don't feel fear anymore, you feel tremendously confident in the short term, especially if you have been stuck in fear and it was holding you back. Suddenly you are free to do what you have been wanting to do. You feel propelled into life, like an arrow that has been pulled back and then released. But like that arrow, which drops, you lose momentum after a short while.

In life you lose momentum because you have suppressed your ability to feel new desires. The passion you feel briefly when you release a fear comes from the old desire that was being held back. To feel the next new desire and passion, you must be in touch with your feelings and not suppress them.

When you don't feel anger, you feel very loving and grateful for what you have in the short term, especially if you have been stuck in blame and resentment. Suddenly you are free to love again, but after the immediate rush, down the road you feel less intimate or connected to others. You don't experience conflict, but you are missing passion in your life and relationships.

In a similar manner, suppression makes you more fulfilled in the short term, but in the long run, it disconnects you from your inner feelings, which is how we connect to our inner source of happiness. We become increasingly dependent on the outer world, and our lives become devoid of passion, creativity, and growth.

## The Exchange of Energy

The more sensitive people are, the more negative energy they draw in. People who are overweight are very sensitive. They cannot lose their weight because it protects them from feeling the negative energy surrounding them. Unless they desensitize themselves in some way, they are affected too much and either become sick or feel negative themselves. Overeating is one way to desensitize ourselves or numb our feelings.

---

**All addictive behaviors are attempts to suppress and avoid feeling what we feel.**

---

When people are stuck in any of the twelve blocks to personal success, they are often chronically disconnected from the positive energy of who they truly are and send out negative energy instead. A sensitive person automatically takes on this negative energy. This is why some people never get better in therapy. They work on feeling better, and as soon as they go back out into the world, they just pick up more negative energy and get stuck.

Some people exude negative energy because of their lifestyle, friends, and thinking habits. They could be sending it out all the time or just part of the time. To the degree that you are sensitive and porous, being around these people will actually make you sick.

---

**Being around negative people can make you sick.**

---

Other people who are more in touch with their true nature automatically send out positive energy. They could be sending it out all the time or just sometimes when they are doing something they are really good at or love to do. To be around these people will actually make you feel better. This is why we are drawn to successful people.

There are numerous examples of great presenters in all fields—acting, singing, dancing, teaching, entertaining—who shine when they are onstage, but are the opposite when they are offstage. It is not that these people are not what they appear to be onstage. The opposite is actually true. Who they become offstage is not who they are. As these presenters open up and shine onstage they are sending out positive energy. As they send out positive energy, they begin drawing in all the negative energy in the audience. People begin to feel better and better because the presenters are taking in their negativity.

---

**A positive presenter attracts
negative energy like a magnet.**

---

Part of the reason that the audience loves these presenters so much is that their blocks to loving have been temporally removed. They are filled with positive energy, and it begins to flow more freely. They express that relief and joy by giving a standing ovation. Although the presenters get to enjoy and receive all that love, they will also absorb negativity as well, as will any person who is sensitive or in touch with feelings.

---

**When you have a lot of positive energy,
you don't notice that you
are absorbing negative energy.**

---

The solution to absorbing negative energy is not becoming less sensitive. That would only lesson the ability to draw in and recharge with more energy. By learning to decharge, you can freely share your energy with the world. Just take time to recharge through meditation, and then discharge any negativity you have inevitably absorbed.

## *How to Decharge*

The first step in learning to decharge is interactive meditation. Just as you have the ability to draw in energy through your fingertips in meditation, you have the ability to send it out. Once you have learned to meditate, it is incredibly easy to decharge.

The second step is sending out the negative energy where it will do no harm. Negative energy is automatically absorbed and transformed by nature. This is why if you are stressed you automatically become more relaxed by going for a walk in a forest or garden. This is why some people enjoy the beach or lying in the sun. The elements of nature absorb our negativity and send out positive energy. By directing or decharging our negative energy into nature it is automatically transformed into positive energy once again.

A good example of this on the physical and more tangible level is photosynthesis. Green plants use energy from light to combine carbon dioxide and water to make food and oxygen. All oxygen on our planet comes from this energy-converting activity of green plants. Humans and animals then inhale oxygen and exhale carbon dioxide. Plants absorb the carbon dioxide exhaled and then again give off oxygen. This cycle of conversion maintains earth's natural balance of carbon dioxide and oxygen. In a similar manner, nature absorbs our negative energy and puts out positive energy.

After meditating for ten or fifteen minutes with your hands up, open your eyes, lower your hands, and point them in the direction of a live plant, fire, or body of water. Continue to repeat the meditation phrase over and over with a simple intention to send your negativity out and into whatever you are pointing at. After some practice, you don't even have to meditate first. You can just begin the decharging process and do it with eyes open or closed.

These are some basic discharging phrases:

"Oh God, my heart is open to you, please come sit in my heart, take this stress, take this stress."

"Oh God, my heart is open to you, please come sit in my heart, take this negativity, take this negativity."

"Oh God, my heart is open to you, please come sit in my heart, take this sickness, take this sickness."

Discharging is an incredible experience. You will feel a flow of energy out of your fingers. For many, it feels as if you were standing in a shower and the water is running down over your fingers and fingertips. You may feel tingling energy throughout your hands as the negative energy leaves your body and goes into nature.

As it leaves, the energy does not in any way feel negative. It just feels good to be moving the energy. It is as if you are being entertained by a great performer. As the performer absorbs your negative energy it does not in any way feel like you are sending out negativity. It just feels good. The same thing happens when you send your negative energy to an object of nature, it just absorbs all your negativity and you feel better.

By taking time to recharge and then discharge any negative energy, you will most effectively continue to increase your personal power. Your soul has a chance to grow and thrive when you breathe in positive energy and exhale negative energy.

When people first hear about discharging into an object of nature, they sometimes think it does not seem right to direct negative energy to nature. But it is not hurtful at all. Nature absorbs and recycles the energy you discharge. Nature thrives when we offer up our negativity.

## *Where to Decharge*

Plants, flowers, bushes, and trees are usually the best objects in which to decharge. For most people flowers are the most powerful. Now we can begin to understand why there are flowers in every performer's dressing room, why we throw flowers when we give a standing ovation, why a man brings flowers when he wants to make up.

Performers may not know why, but they like to receive flowers. Women may not know why receiving flowers works, but it does. Now you know. When a man brings flowers to his partner, those flowers automatically help her to decharge and let go of her negative feelings. Women particularly appreciate flowers, because women tend to be more sensitive than men.

---

**When a man brings flowers to his partner,
those flowers automatically
help her to decharge.**

---

Think about funeral traditions. We send flowers to comfort the bereaved. Certainly the loving thought counts as well, but we don't send gizmos or gadgets to comfort them. Nature absorbs our negativity. When we have opened the channels in our fingers and we begin to direct the energy out, the process is much more efficient and effective.

Just as we reach up to heaven to receive our blessing, we need to reach down to mother earth to take our negativity. As we are able to feel the tingling in our fingertips, our ability to decharge dramatically increases.

---

**We reach up to recharge and down to earth
to decharge.**

---

Another place to decharge is into a sink filled with water, a bathtub, hot tub, pool, pond, river, lake, or ocean. The bigger the body of water, the more powerful the decharge. Water will absorb negativity. This is another reason it is important to drink more water. To keep the energy flowing and to get the benefits of regular meditation, it is important to drink eight to ten glasses of water a day. If you are a bigger person, you will need more.

---

## Water absorbs negativity.

---

Fire is another powerful aspect of nature we can use to decharge. Think back to the wonderful times you may have spent telling scary stories around a campfire. The stories would bring up the fear, but then the fire would absorb that negative energy right out of us. Memories of sitting around a fire are so strong because we were decharging.

Walking barefoot on the earth, the grass, or the beach is also a powerful way to decharge. As you walk, continue to say your meditation phrase and direct your fingers down to the earth. This can also be done while walking in a forest. It is fun to aim your fingers toward the trees and send out your negative energy like little ray guns and receive nature's blessing. Working in the garden and putting your fingers in the dirt is also a great activity that allows you to decharge automatically.

Think about the tradition of Christmas trees. In the cold of winter, people could collect around and decorate a tree. As they sent their love and affection to the tree, it would absorb some of their negative energy. Naturally they felt better. Evergreen trees or simply live branches with leaves were needed because people were not spending as much time outside in nature. It was too cold to go out so they brought nature inside. With this insight there are countless examples of ancient traditions and rituals in all cultures that begin to make sense.

---

### Every culture is rich in traditions for decharging.

---

Once you have experienced the energy flowing freely from your fingers, you can try holding leaves or a flower so that your fingertips touch and then practice decharging with your eyes closed. It is just like meditating, but you are holding a few fresh leaves or flowers in your hands.

Just as you feel the energy by holding your fingers up, you will feel the energy flow out of your fingers as well. I suggest learning with your eyes open and hands pointing down, because many people experience the flow of energy better that way. Once you feel the flow, you can hold or touch a natural object and continue to feel the energy. The most efficient and powerful way to decharge is to do it with your eyes closed and holding a fresh leaf or flower. The other ways work and should be enjoyed, but holding leaves and flowers works in the shortest amount of time.

## *When to Decharge*

You can decharge any time you feel negative energy. It will always help you to feel better. As a practice, it is good to do at least a few times a week for five or ten minutes. In the beginning, you may wish to do it much longer. For sensitive people, a whole lifetime of negativity begins to drain out. The best rule of thumb is to decharge as much as is enjoyable. You cannot overdo it. Nothing bad can happen.

---

### The best rule of thumb is to decharge as much as is enjoyable.

---

If you work in a stressful or negative environment, it is a good idea to decharge every day. A few minutes of decharging can be done while you are in the shower. To lessen stress at work and home, it is important to be surrounded by live plants and water.

Even though decharging can create unbelievable benefits right away, learning to meditate is the first step. Through regular meditation, you open the channels to receiving positive energy, and with this positive energy flowing in, you can most effectively send out the negativity.

Decharging will also assist you in removing all the twelve blocks. In some cases they will automatically disappear. Women by nature are more vulnerable to taking on negativity and experience an incredible lift and relief through decharging.

Though decharging frees you from absorbing negative energy, you still have to look within yourself to let go of your own blocks. By learning to decharge, you are free to create your future instead being held back by the blocks of others. At least when you are blocked, you know it is your block and not the world's.

## Giving Up Any Fears of Negative Energy

These remarkable insights about energy can easily be misunderstood. A person may become anxious about being around negative people or get caught up in blaming others for problems. Taking in negative energy is an inevitable part of life if you have more positive energy. You cannot escape it. Rather than seek to avoid negativity, we just need to be responsible for decharging it as well.

This natural exchange of energy is very similar to weather patterns in nature. A low pressure system will always attract a high pressure system. Heat always rises in a cool room. If your house is warm and cozy, but you don't have double pane glass, then there will be drafts in the cold of winter. The warmth draws in the cold from outside. If you put your hand by the window, you can feel the draft.

Nature always seeks a balance. Likewise, when you have a lot of positive energy, you will attract negative energy. The secret of personal success is to continue to recharge and then decharge the negativity you absorb.

Trying to avoid negativity is only important if you are tired and sick, but if you are recharging every day through meditation, then sharing your love and light with the world is what brings the greatest fulfillment and strength. As you develop your ability to draw in positive energy and decharge negative energy, confronting the challenges of negativity will make you stronger.

# CHAPTER 11

# Letting Go of Negative Emotions

T HERE ARE BASICALLY two ways to fill our love tanks. Giving and receiving love with God, and giving and receiving love with our parents, family, friends, peers, self, partnerships, children, community, and then world. By practicing meditation, setting your intentions, and discharging negativity and stress, you will always be strengthening your foundation. To make your dreams come true, you have to keep your love tanks full to stay in touch with your true self.

The number one obstacle to receiving love in each of the love tanks is the inability to feel and to release negative emotions. After years of helping people move through their negative emotions in a very short time, I discovered twelve basic negative emotions. The whole area of emotions is greatly misunderstood. In the name of letting go of negative emotions, people unknowingly suppress them. All it takes is to feel guilty or judgmental about our emotions and it keeps them from coming up to be released. There is a big difference between letting go of negative emotions and not feeling them. To let go of them, we have to feel them. They are essential for us to come back to our true self. When we are not regularly feeling negative emotions and letting them go, our love tanks can't fill up.

One of the major reasons people are able to make such fast progress in meditation today is that they are able to feel more fully. Through feeling and releasing negative emotions we are able to fully discharge negative energy. The reason for extraordinary material progress, creativity, and power in the world is more awareness of what we are feeling and what we want. Emotion is always connected in some way to our desires. Feeling emotion, whether positive or negative, is pure energy that connects us to God and the world. It is the fuel that fills our love tanks.

When emotions are blocked or not felt, either we cannot get the energy and love we need, or we are unable to get the power to attract and manifest what we want. Just feeling emotions is not enough. They must be managed carefully and skillfully and then be released. In releasing negative emotions, we will become more empowered by knowing what we want and motivated to get it.

Some people block their potential by suppressing, numbing, or repressing emotions; others feel their emotions, but are unable to release them or let go. They become stuck feeling negative emotions and attract situations in their lives to mirror their negativity. This is one of the reasons people are so afraid of negative emotions. When you are stuck in them, what you attract in your life is more situations to make you feel that way.

There is one other category: people who selectively feel their emotions. Some may let themselves feel angry feelings, but not more vulnerable feelings like sadness or fear. Some are quick to feel shame and sorrow, but resist their feelings of anger. There can be any number of combinations and permutations. Regardless of the particular situation, the result is the same. To the extent that you dwell on negative emotions you will attract that in your life.

To the extent that you deny your emotions you will disconnect with your power to create what you want.

## Process Your Feelings

Processing your feelings means identifying your negative emotions and releasing them by getting in touch with your underlying desires and positive feelings. Processing negative emotions is using them to come back to the true self.

One way to imagine the usefulness of negative emotions is to think of life as a process of riding a bike. To keep balance, we are constantly making adjustments from left to right. To get where we want to go, we need to move the handlebar. Getting in touch with your true wants is like moving the handlebar to guide you. Feeling and releasing negative emotions is what keeps you from falling over. Regular meditation and asking for God's help gives you the power to move ahead. Meditation is moving the pedals up and down, around and around.

Unless we process our negative feelings, we will still be falling over all the time. Balance is achieved by regularly going off center and then coming back. Wiggling from side to side is the process of sustaining balance. In the beginning, this wiggling is very dramatic, and quite often we fall over and have to start again. As we get the hang of it, we learn gracefully to make small adjustments to keep our balance.

Going off balance is exactly similar to a negative emotion. You are still connected to the self, but you are moving away. A pure emotion is always connected to the true self, but it is a symptom that we are disconnecting. It is more that just a warning signal that we need to come back to balance; it is the experience of moving away from center.

The only way we can keep balance on a bike is to notice when we are moving off center to the left or right. When we move to the left, we need to move back to the right to find balance and then back to the left and then back to the right. In this process of back and forth, we find our balance again. Likewise in the process of living. For the soul to interact in the world, there is a balancing process. When we move off center to the left, a negative emotion comes up. As we let go of that movement and return to center, we move the other way, and another negative emotion emerges. Once again, by feeling the next negative emotion, we realize we are moving too far to the right, and we adjust that movement to come back to center.

Imagine how difficult it would be to ride a bike if you could move only to the right. It would be impossible to find balance. When people suppress certain feelings and only allow others, they cannot find balance. It is the back and forth movement that allows us to find center.

After we get back to center, we can stay there for a while. Then the whole process starts over. With a bike, we don't expect always to be in perfect balance. It is enough just to stay upright and experience a smooth graceful ride. We don't expect always to be in the center, and we know how to find center. When it comes to negative emotions, we mistakenly assume that to stay balanced in our center or true self we should never feel pain or negative emotions. We resist the process, because we don't know how to deal with our negative emotions to find balance again.

As you get better at riding, keeping your balance is practically automatic. In a similar way, as you learn to process your negative emotions, it will become an effortless part of your life. To experience the richness and fullness of life you have to have to stay in touch with your emotions—all your emotions. Through staying in touch with your feelings you can fully enjoy the richness of life's simple pleasures. You enjoy the wind on your face, the warmth of the sun, the freshness of spring, the coolness of autumn, the joy of dressing up a child at Halloween, the love shared between friends, the pleasure and excitement of romance, the exhilaration of learning something new, the thrill and pride of accomplishment, and the ecstasy of drawing in and expressing God's gift in the world through service.

## *Four Ways to Process*

As you begin to process your negative emotions, for some it is difficult to identify them, while for others it is difficult to release them. When you learn to use the four ways to process feelings, these challenges become easier. One method is not better than another. To use these different methods, just move through them until one of them works. The methods for processing emotion are:

1. Change the emotion.
2. Change the content.
3. Change the clock backward or forward.
4. Change the subject altogether; shift from feeling your pain to feeling the pain of another.

The first way to process is to feel whatever negative feeling you can, and then change the emotion. If you are angry about something, write out those feelings for a few minutes, then change your feeling to another negative emotion. This is similar to riding a bike and finding balance by moving in the opposite direction, which will then put you off balance in the other direction. Moving back and forth between negative emotions releases any blocks and greatly assists you in finding balance.

Though others try to minimize their feelings, the best approach is to temporarily expand or increase the negative feelings you experience. Most of the time, when people are stuck in any particular emotion, it is because they are blocking another emotion. No one emotion is always the culprit. Any negative emotion that is not being felt will block the flow of energy and keep you from letting go. When one emotion is blocked, a person will tend to stay stuck in another emotion.

The second way to process feelings is to change the content. When you experience a feeling, but it doesn't fully seem to relate to what you are upset about, simply change the content. If you are angry with your boss and don't seem to be able to let go, make a list of all the possible things you could be angry about. Feel your anger and ask yourself what else you are angry about. Whenever you stay upset about something that can't be changed, it is generally a clue that you are really more upset about something else.

The third way to process feelings is to change the clock. If you are upset by something and can't seem to feel and release your feelings by using step one or two, then recall a time in your past when you may have experienced similar feelings. Sometimes the feelings we experience today are intensified by the wounds of the past.

For example, if you felt abandoned as a young child, those feelings can still be affecting you. As soon as someone rejects you a little, it can seem much more painful because of your past. When this is the case, the best way to process is to link what you feel now to something you felt then. While pretending you are in the past, process your feelings by giving yourself the ability to feel, identify, and express your feelings.

The past is always easier to process. If we are afraid now, we don't know what the outcome will be. When we look back to the past, we can always reassure ourselves that things have and will work out. Even if we couldn't get the support we needed in the past, we can imagine ourselves getting that support. In this way, we can heal the wound of the past.

The fourth means of processing is to shift the subject away from your pain to someone else's. Sometimes we just can't get enough perspective from our pain to feel it and let go. We feel we are the pain and nothing else. To get perspective, we need to find someone outside ourselves and experience that person's pain. This is probably the easiest of all the methods, the oldest form of therapy known to mankind. It can be found in literature, comedy, theater, singing, movies, CDs, and TV.

Telling stories and sharing with friends or sharing in a support group of like-minded people are important ways to step out of our pain, but not away from it. As we hear the pain of others and cry with them, laugh with them, and feel with them, our own feelings are being felt and released. For people who can't find their pain to process, the fourth way is often the most direct in assisting them to begin to look inside to feel and heal. Always in my workshops as I work in front of the room helping one person to feel and release negative emotions, the whole room automatically goes through the process. People become aware of and release feelings they had long forgotten. By caring about another who is processing inner wounds, they are healed as well.

## *Method One:*
## *Change Your Emotion*

When upset, many people try to change their negative emotion right back to a positive emotion. This is one of the major reasons people get stuck. They try to release their negative emotion too quickly.

When you are stuck in a negative emotion and you don't have a lot of practice finding balance, it is very difficult to find another emotion that you feel. With greater insight into each of the twelve negative emotions, whenever you are stuck you will know where to go. Understanding these twelve emotions was like learning to ride with training wheels. It makes it much easier to experience finding balance.

The twelve negative emotional states we naturally feel to find balance are as follows:

1. "I am angry."
2. "I am sad."
3. "I am afraid."
4. "I am sorry."
5. "I am frustrated."
6. "I am disappointed."
7. "I am worried."
8. "I am embarrassed."
9. "I am jealous."
10. "I am hurt."
11. "I am scared."
12. "I am ashamed."

When you feel stuck in anger, take some time to feel and express what you are angry about, and then ask yourself what you feel sad about. Anger is generally a reaction to what happened; sadness is a reaction to what didn't happen. Right away, you will begin to experience a release of your angry feelings. As you shift to another feeling you will begin to go deeper. The negative emotions will move you back to balance. As you begin to move back to center, you will start to feel better.

If you are stuck feeling sad, then shift to feeling afraid. Whenever we are focusing on what didn't happen, it is because at a deeper level we are afraid about something that might happen. Fear is generally our reaction to what could happen that we don't want to happen. In each case, as you go down the list, you will experience a dramatic shift and release by looking a little deeper. When you get to number twelve, begin again at the top of the list. If you are stuck feeling ashamed (number twelve), then after feeling ashamed shift to feeling angry (number one) about an aspect of the situation.

Sometimes before you get a complete release, you may need to move down two to three levels. I make it a basic practice to shift down three times unless I feel a release sooner. If I am angry after writing feelings of anger, I make the first shift to sadness. Then I make the second shift to fear, and then I make the third shift to sorrow. Between each of these shifts, it is particularly useful to write out what you want, like, wish, or need. At the end of the process, it is important to write out the positive feelings that naturally emerge after we release negative emotions. Write out feelings of love, understanding, trust, appreciation, or gratitude. This exercise is called the feeling letter, and I have written about in all my other books. For additional information and support in processing feelings, refer to my book *Mars and Venus Starting Over, or What You Feel You Can Heal.*

Sometimes it is hard to find where to start on the list. In this case, don't try to be so accurate. View the list in another way, like this:

**Level One:** "I am angry, frustrated, or jealous."

**Level Two:** "I am sad, disappointed, or hurt."

**Level Three:** "I am afraid, worried, or scared."

**Level Four:** "I am sorry, embarrassed, or ashamed."

As you look at any one category, see what fits. If lots of feelings fit, then start anywhere. If you can't clearly pick one, just start at level three with "I am afraid that I will pick the wrong level." Write a few minutes about any one level, then shift to the next level down. If you start out at level four, after exploring any feelings of sorrow, embarrassment, or shame, shift to level one. In this way, by shifting levels of negative emotions you will eventually find the release, and you will begin to feel more positive and loving. Remember to write out those positive feelings and what you want, particularly how you want to be, how you want "things" to be, and what you want to do and have.

Sometimes to complete the process of writing out what you feel, it is necessary for you to write a response letter. After writing out your feelings, imagine what someone listening could say or do to make you feel better. If you were upset with someone, imagine that person writing you a letter saying he or she has heard you, he apologizes, and then goes on to say great things about you and gives you what you want.

By taking time to write this letter, you get the opportunity to experience how you would have felt and you are back to center again. Even if the person would never say those positive things, by imagining how you would feel getting that support, you will experience letting go of your negative emotions and coming back to your true loving self. You cannot even begin to imagine how effective this approach is until you try it. Later, in Chapter 17, we explore a variety of emotional exercises to experience this amazing immediate transformation.

## Method Two: ## Change the Content

Most of the time, when we are stuck, not only are we disconnected from our negative feelings, but we are focused in the wrong direction. We may think we are upset with someone when really we are upset with ourselves or afraid about something at work. In most cases, when we cannot seem to release an emotion, it is because we need to redirect our emotion at something else that may be bothering us.

If I am stuck being angry with a business associate, I would ask myself who else or what else I am upset about. Suddenly I may begin to feel that I am upset that I am behind schedule on another completely different project.

Once I change the content of my upset, I feel I am on the right track, but the anger is still not releasing. Then I would simply use method one and change the emotion by asking myself what I am sad or disappointed about. As I begin to feel my sadness or disappointment, my anger automatically lessens and I start to become more understanding. With greater understanding, my thinking becomes more open and forgiving. Since I am now coming back to center, the negativity is mostly gone. My attitude shifts as I feel greater trust that I can find a solution. Automatically I begin to appreciate once again what is working and release my focus on what is not working.

As you practice this release technique, you will discover that much of the time what you think you are upset about is just the tip of the iceberg. By getting inside yourself and exploring other things that may be bothering you, you will find that you can give up resisting what you cannot change and that what you are really upset about can be changed either by a little shift in your attitude or by a change in your behavior.

## Method Three:
## Change the Clock

When any of the previous methods don't seem to be working, we need to change the clock either backward or forward. Let's first explore looking back. By linking what we are feeling now to events in the past, we can very effectively find a release.

If you can make the link to your past, it is always much easier to feel and release your emotions. When we are angry in present time, it is harder to surrender and let go because we think we have to be angry to get things done. When we are sad in present time and feeling a loss, we are not yet experiencing that the future will always bring more. When we are afraid in present time, we don't know what the future holds, but when we look back and reexperience the fear we felt in the past, we have the added benefit of knowing that things were not as bad as we thought they were and that things did get better. With the advantage of hindsight, it is much easier to release negativity.

Think for a moment about all the times you got really upset about something and later realized that it was not such a big deal. Think about the times when you were afraid of the worst happening and it didn't. Even when the worst has happened to us, things eventually change and get better. This is a benefit we can give to ourselves by going back and linking what we feel today with what we have felt in the past.

After we have made the link, we need to pretend that we are back in time with the adult ability to process our feelings. Once we have written a few levels of feelings, we can write out a response letter. We give ourselves the loving response we would have wanted. If we had received that loving response, we would have felt more centered and aware of who we really were, instead of being left feeling powerless or unlovable at difficult times. Reliving and then enriching the experience by writing a response letter will help you to release your negative emotions.

When unresolved feelings from our past come up, they don't introduce themselves by saying, "Hi, I am your fear of abandonment which started when you were sent off to the relatives to live." When our past is coming up, we often can't make any sense of those feelings. We may be afraid, but we don't know of what; we may be sad, but things are not that bad; we may be afraid, but there is really no great danger; or we may feel jealous, when we already have so much. Quite often, our feelings seem too much. We can't share them with others, because they seem too negative, so we begin to suppress them. Instead, we can link them to a time in the past when those feelings would have been appropriate reactions, considering what we thought was happening and our particular stage of development in life.

From the mind's perspective, which has to make sense of

everything we feel, it is not appropriate to be a happy, fulfilled, and successful adult and to feel sad or depressed for long when we suffer a business disappointment. Yet, when I was starting out and I didn't know that I would eventually achieve success, I was naturally more upset when I experienced a particular setback. By linking my current feelings to a past setback, my mind automatically gives my heart permission to feel the emotions more profoundly. If a lot of feeling still does not flow up and out, I could go further back in the past to feel more deeply.

The further back we go, the more permission we have to feel negative emotions. The younger we are, the less capable we are of making sense of the world. Naturally the emotions will be strong and more negative at times.

---

**The further back we go, the more permission we have to feel negative emotions.**

---

When a parent drops off a child at the baby-sitter and that child screams as if he is going to die, we can be sympathetic because we know the child's mind is not yet developed enough to realize or remember that Mommy or Daddy will come back. That is one of the most important lessons we need to learn in growing up. When our source of love goes, we are still safe, and that person comes back. Until we learn this lesson and many others in childhood, we have very strong emotional reactions.

By linking strong feelings in the present to the past, we give them a context in which to surface. Sometimes, when we are blocked from our feelings in present time and feel nothing, it is because there are no rational reasons to feel the strong emotions inside. By learning how to link feeling to the past, whatever was not fully healed or resolved gets a chance to be felt and released.

So if linking feeling to the recent past doesn't juice up my ability to feel the flow of negative emotions, I could link my feelings even further back, back to a time, at six years old, when I was taken away from my family for a week.

On a summer vacation to California, my parents asked who wanted to visit the relatives. Someone told me they lived across the street from Disneyland, so I volunteered. I thought we were going to Disneyland, everyone else would come, and after a fun day, we would return back that night. When I got to my aunt's I discovered no one else had come, and we didn't even go to Disneyland. I spent a week there. I didn't know if I would ever get back and was very sad and afraid.

Using this memory, I can link any feelings I have in present time with the sadness and fear I felt then. By linking my current feelings in this way, I can create an appropriate context for my strong negative emotions.

Whenever you are upset and you don't know why, clearly what you feel has nothing to do with right now. In this case, to feel and release the emotions, you have to create a context that can nurture and release the feeling. Changing the clock is a very important skill to learn, because if you can't find a reason for your feelings, your mind starts to create one.

If we can't create a safe context in which to feel and release emotions, we are automatically drawn to or attract situations to validate these unresolved feelings. What keeps us from moving ahead to creating the life we want is the tendency to repeat the past, because we are not willing or able to experience the feelings that come up. If you are not willing to look at your past and to continue filling the earlier love tanks, your past will come to you by repeating patterns. If we are not willing to look at what is needed to be released, we are drawn again and again to situations that will validate our pain.

I first became aware of this tendency years ago. I was pacing back and forth waiting for someone. A part of me was really starting to get angry, but I was too nice ever to let myself feel such negative feelings. Then something amazing happened. I felt an urge to walk over to the kitchen sink and wash my hands. I moved the handle to the left. As the hot water continued to get hotter and hotter, I was peacefully enjoying the view, not even noticing the steam coming up. Without even realizing what I was doing, I put my hands in the scalding water to wash them. Instantly I screamed in pain.

Although my hands hurt, another part of me was relieved. I had unconsciously created an opportunity to feel my suppressed emotional pain. The burning hot water made me feel my pain, and as a result, although physically I was burned, emotionally I felt better.

From that moment on, I began to be more aware that we are always either attracting or being attracted to a variety of experiences. When we attract negative situations that are not even close to what our mind is wanting, the soul is drawing in situations to help us get in touch with and to release our negativity. The soul knows that sometimes there is no other way to reconnect with our true self unless a context is created to feel the pain we are suppressing.

## The Personal Empowerment Process

Sometimes, rather than looking back to process our feelings, we can look ahead. If we are upset and we can't seem to release our feelings, one shift can make a huge difference. For a few minutes, imagine that whatever is happening continues to get worse. See everything that you are angry about continuing on. See your biggest fears actually coming to pass. Imagine yourself in the future having that experience, and then process your feelings. By making this simple shift, using your imagination, you can create an appropriate context to allow your feelings to surface. Once they are up, take a few minutes to link them to your past, and then use method one to process and release the negative emotions. This is called the personal empowerment process.

Jack was feeling really nervous about giving a presentation

at work. For days before a big event, he would lose sleep and feel anxious and uncomfortable. In the personal success workshop, he practiced looking ahead to release his fear.

He wrote down all the worst things that could happen. He imagined everything that could go wrong. Once he started writing, it was easy but painful. He imagined that he didn't make any sense; no one laughed at his jokes; no one was impressed; his ideas were not up to standard; and he wouldn't get another opportunity, since he would be fired.

By looking directly at his fears, he felt sad, hurt, and discouraged. Then he linked his sad and hurt feelings to a time in his distant past when he gave a talk for someone else, was unprepared, and *was* rejected by the audience. He linked his feelings back to that time and began processing his past using method one. As a result, his nervousness went away. Occasionally it would come back, but he knew just how to let it go.

## *Method Four:*
## *Change the Subject*

The fourth way to get unstuck and process your negative emotions is to change the subject. Instead of focusing on your pain, take some time to focus on the pain of others. By shifting the attention from ourselves to others, we are then free to stand back from our pain and eventually to let it go. When something happens in a movie and tears well up in your eyes, you may not even know why you have such a strong reaction, but clearly it's because of something in your past. A nerve has been touched. Something occurred in the story that made you feel something your heart needed to feel.

Although home videos can be just as good, there is an added benefit to being in a movie theater with other people sharing what you feel. Reading books has the same healing influence. By living through another person's pain and joy, we can more fully stay in touch with our own. The reason for drama is that the characters act out the problems we experience in life. Since their circumstances are more tragic or more humorous, it is easier for us to feel with them.

In our own lives, we often suppress our feelings, because our minds invalidate them. Movies, great stories, books, and theater help to dramatize our pain. We accept the pain and sorrow of characters in the story. As we share in their pain and eventual resolution, we experience the release.

Music and singing also heal the heart. Classical music continues to have meaning because the composers often captured the dramatic movements of the soul with such extreme emotions as elation, salvation, hope, devastation, rage, betrayal, and despair. The same range of feelings can be expressed by poetry and song lyrics.

In my workshops, I always use different kinds of music to assist participants to feel what needs to come out. A big part of making a successful movie that can carry us through our different feelings is the musical score. Certain music signals something tragic is about to happen, other music warns of danger, or music gives us relief and lets us know that everything is going to be okay.

Another way we can change the subject and help ourselves is through support groups. When we heal the pain of others as we give them compassion, our own inner pain has a chance to come up and is sometimes automatically released. If you have difficulty connecting with your past feelings, I recommend being in a support group or attending a workshop. My own ability to connect with my feelings has been enormously enriched by being around others who were more in touch.

With an awareness of each of these four methods, you now have powerful tools to process your feelings. You have the power to get in touch with and release any negative emotions. As you practice these skills, you could be up and riding your new bike to wherever you want to go within a few months.

# CHAPTER 12

# *How to Get What You Want*

THE SECRET OF personal success is to be true to yourself and to continue to want more. To achieve personal success, it is not enough to be happy. You must also grow in your desire for more. Passion is power. When you really want more, you will get it. People who don't have more don't give themselves permission to want it. In some cases, they might like the idea of having more, but they don't go all the way and really want it.

To have outer success, we must want it so much that it hurts when we don't get it. At the same time, we must learn how to release and heal that hurt so that we can experience inner happiness as well. We must be consistently able to find inner joy, love, confidence, and peace, while dealing with the inevitable waves of frustration, disappointment, worry, and other negative emotions that come with the desire for external success.

This insight explains why many people who have found great degrees of personal success had humble beginnings. As children, they may have been poor, deprived, or even orphans. They learned the hard way how to be happy with less, but continued to want more.

> By wanting more but appreciating
> everything they had,
> many have unlimited success in life.

There are endless stories of how becoming successful or getting what they wanted eventually weakened some people, making them "too soft," and their lives and careers took a dive. After achieving outer success, "the good life," they stopped producing, creating, or attracting success, because they lost touch with their desire for more. They either slowly descend or they take a dive, but not all stay down.

After bottoming out and losing it all, quite often people make a comeback. They rise again by fully feeling their longing for more and all the feelings that come with that desire. By releasing their pain and then relearning how to be happy with less, they once again create the fertile ground to plant the seeds of desire.

By feeling the pain of losing it all, they strengthen their desire enough to attract and create outer success. Once they lose it all, they accept and appreciate what they have. With acceptance and desire, their wave of success rises again. Fortunately, with insight and wisdom into the secrets of personal success, you don't have to go to such extremes to accept your life and strengthen your desires. By learning to get in touch with and to transform negative emotions, you don't have to lose it all to feel your inner passion for more.

## The Secret of Outer Success Is Desire

The secret of all outer success is desire. You must know what you want, feel it deeply, and believe. Passion, belief, and desire are power. When you continue to feel and act on what you want, the universe responds to your will.

When you exercise your will with actions to satisfy your desires, your desire becomes stronger. The more you persist, the more you believe, and the more you feel. When you can fully feel your desire, contained in that feeling is the intuitive knowledge of what to do, and the belief that you will succeed. By taking action to get what you want, you strengthen your belief. The world will not believe in you until you believe.

---

**The secret of all outer success is desire, feeling, and belief.**

---

Almost every great success story is filled with examples of rejection, failure, frustration, worry, and disappointment. There are always setbacks, betrayals, and delays. Those who think big or desire big draw in even bigger obstacles to overcome. With patience and persistence, if they continue to exercise their will to fulfill their desire, they succeed. Rome was not built in a day. It takes time to create and attract what we want, but most important, it takes passion.

This, then, explains another of the great mysteries of creating what you want. It is not what you do that counts, but what you want, feel, and believe. Certainly some action is required, but it doesn't have to be a struggle, and it doesn't have to wear us down. Yet action does serve an important purpose. It strengthens our belief, which is what attracts success.

---

**The world will believe in you and respond to your wishes when you first believe in yourself.**

---

When you take the risk, when you make the commitment and follow through, when you make the jump into the abyss of the unknown, you are reinforcing your belief in yourself and the possibility of getting what you want. Pushing yourself to extremes is not necessary when you know how to tap into intuition. Once you have learned to access your inner intuition and confidence, you will not have to push so hard or take big risks to attract success.

Doing too much is sometimes the result of not believing in your power to attract and create success. Many people are exhausted because they are not getting what they want. Their overgiving and overworking prevent them from achieving success. By relying fully on "doing" to achieve, they disconnect with the belief that they can get what they want.

---

**By relying fully on "doing" to achieve, many people disconnect with the belief that they can get what they want.**

---

On the other hand, some people do achieve success after becoming completely exhausted. They try everything, do everything, and give it everything they've got. They push themselves until there is nothing left. They crash. They give up. They beg God. But then, by feeling their intense longing and letting go to accept what they have, they create the secret alchemy of success.

Thomas Edison described his genius to create thousands of inventions as ninety-nine percent perspiration and one percent inspiration. He would try everything, and when his mind gave up, he would let go and finally experience the inspiration of a genius idea. After trying everything to figure out a solution, after trying everything he knew, his mind would give up and the solution would come. By trying everything, he demonstrated his belief in the possibility of success. By persisting and not giving up, he allowed the fire of his passion to be ignited, and he could attract great and brilliant ideas.

> The fire of passion, once ignited,
> attracts great and brilliant ideas.

By applying the secrets of personal success, you will learn how to feel the passion in your heart without having to go to such extremes. You will learn how to demonstrate that you believe in yourself without having to gamble everything again and again. You will learn how to sustain your success without having to bottom out and rise once again from deep despair. You will learn how to tap into your natural ability to get what you want.

## The Power of Surrender

Whenever we push ourselves to our limit, we feel our limit by experiencing negative emotions. The limit means we can't feel positive about this anymore. When we push to our limit and then let go, we are turning it over to God, spirit, or that mysterious source of brilliant ideas. How you label a higher authority is up to you. If you are religious or spiritual, you may experience that power as God. If you are an atheist or an agnostic, maybe your higher, intuitive intelligence will suffice.

Regardless of your particular orientation, when you let go after doing everything you can, you will receive what you want. Just feeling a little desire and then surrendering is usually not enough. We really have to want something and to feel confident. When we believe that we are just lucky or that God's angels help us, being successful is much easier. When I learned how to ask for help and get it from the higher source, my life shifted to much higher levels of productivity with much less stress. I know that I get lots of help in everything I ask for.

When we remember that we don't have to do it ourselves,

we can relax a lot more. This is another reason that regular meditation is so valuable. Just taking fifteen minutes to remind ourselves that we do not have to do it all helps to set the right intention for the day. Instead of feeling as if it is all up to us, we remember that we have help.

---

**Just fifteen minutes of meditation to experience that we have help sets the right intention for the day.**

---

Without taking the time to meditate each day, it is too easy for me to think I have to do it all. Regular mediation helps me to practice letting go of all that responsibility. To get a sense of this right now, pause and do this little experiment. Move one of your fingers back and forth very quickly for half a minute. Do it again, but this time be aware of the fact that you really are not doing it. You are just driving the car, so to speak. You are just telling your finger what to do, and your body does it. And you have no idea how it does it.

It is very important to realize that you are the commander. You call the shots. You drive the car, but you don't have to make the engine work. As the driver, you don't have to get out and push. The car does all that for you. You just have to turn the key and steer the way.

---

**When you drive the car, you don't get out and push.**

---

When we experience our connection to spirit, it becomes easier to remember that we are not alone and that we are helped. By simply asking that certain things happen, you become aware of all the things that happen for you. We get so caught up resisting life that we forget that so much is done for us. By setting your intentions at the beginning of each day and then experiencing that the world responds to your desires, not only are you more successful, but you don't have to do so much. Instead of taking three years to achieve something, it might take three months. And then instead of three months, three weeks.

Confidence that we can do something is trusting that our intended outcome will occur. Pianists don't sit down and think about moving their fingers, it just happens. Once you have learned how to type on a keyboard, you don't even have to think about it. Your fingers automatically move and type out what you want to say.

Whatever we do, we are really just telling the mind, body, or heart what to do. It either happens or it doesn't. What makes it happen is a connection to the true self and a clear awareness of what we want. Practice helps only because it give us confidence. Confidence and intention result in success.

## Letting Go of Struggle

Without this insight into how we can choose to surrender to a higher power, we would always have to struggle and push hard to our limits to experience the vast creativity accessible to us. Many of the great writers, poets, inventors, scientists, healers, and leaders of the world led extremely troubled lives that forced them to humble themselves, to let go, and to surrender. With these valuable insights of personal success, you can do the same without so much misery and struggle.

With the understanding of filling the love tanks to connect with your true self to achieve great success, you need only stay in touch with what you want, do your best, and events will move as if by magic to fulfill your desires. When we achieve outer success the old-fashioned way, we push to our limit until we can do no more, and then turn it over to God.

If you can just turn it over to God each day but continue to direct, you do not have to push that hard at all. Turning it over to God means remembering that you don't have to do it all, just as you don't have to get out and push the car. All you have to do is know how to drive. We still have to do our best, but it is much easier when we know and trust that extra power is already there.

---

**If you turn it over to God each day, then your whole journey becomes so much easier.**

---

There are some who do turn it over to God, but don't get what they want in the outer world. They put it all in God's hands. This doesn't work, either. To have success, we need to do both. We need to feel responsible *and* ask for help. If we depend too much on God, we stop feeling our own inner wants and wishes. When things don't happen, instead of feeling disappointed, sad, or afraid, we just trust God and have faith.

To attract and create what we want, we must be able to feel and release the negative emotions that naturally arise when we really want something and don't get it. This process of feeling negativity and releasing it is essential for staying in touch with what we want. When all our love tanks are full, what we want is also what God wants. To know God's will for us, we must open our hearts, and then simply ask ourselves what it is that we want. When we act on the true desires that emerge, we have the power to create what we want without much actual doing.

---

**When all our love tanks are full, what we want is also what God wants.**

---

God helps those who help themselves and then ask for help. You have to do it, and then God sends his angel or divine energy to help. As you continue to practice meditation on a regular basis, you will begin to feel the tingling energy coming into your fingertips. Gradually you will feel it throughout your body.

God helps those who help themselves
and then ask for help.

Whenever you need a boost, you can just hold up your
hands and draw in more support. This divine energy will give
you vitality, clarity, and the power to connect with your inner
creativity. If you put everything in God's hands, you stop feeling your part and the energy can't continue to flow into you.
The energy is always there, but you have to draw it in.

## Why Positive Thinking Does Not Always Work

Positive thinking does not work when people use it to deny their
true feelings and wants. When they are always trying to be positive, they tend to suppress their negative emotions. They don't
want to bring others down, nor do they want to feel negative.
Instead of feeling the pain of not having what they really want
or the disappointment of not getting what they want, they
choose to focus on the positive.

They believe in positive thinking, positive feelings, faith,
goodness, loving kindness, generosity, enlightenment, angels,
Karma, destiny, God's will, or God's grace. Though positive
thinking may make people happier, they are unable to experience
their full power to create, attract, and get what they want in life.

In their attempt to be positive, they unknowingly weaken
their inner ability to guide their lives. Unable to feel passionately
what they want, they focus on being positive and loving what life
brings them. They live primarily by such positive beliefs as go
with the flow, accept and forgive, surrender and let God's will be
done, give up your desires, be of service, give up your ego, rise
above negative emotions, fear is just illusion, sickness is an illusion, expect a miracle—ad infinitum. They focus more on accept-

ing, loving, and wanting what they have, and don't focus enough on wanting more.

---

### Focusing too much on inner fulfillment can block outer success.

---

When and if they have negative feelings, they feel guilty or ashamed. Although these spiritual concepts are undeniably important, we must also recognize the significance of negative feelings as a doorway into our feelings and desires.

To achieve personal success, we need both inner spirituality and outer success. We need to make sure that our positive thinking doesn't prevent us from feeling our negative emotions and having strong desires. In this sense, we not only need to practice positive thinking, but also need to have a more positive attitude about negative emotions and desires.

# CHAPTER 13

# *Find Your Magic Star*

I REMEMBER WHEN my daughter Lauren first learned about the magic of asking for what you want and having faith. When she was about five years old, we were on vacation in Hawaii. She found a box of "magic stars" in a little bookstore. She picked one up and asked me what it was. I took one and read the instructions, which said something like this: "Hold this magic star close to your heart, close your eyes, and then make a wish. You can have anything you want."

When she heard this she lit up with such excitement. It was as if she had made the discovery of a lifetime. She said, "Can I ask for anything?" I said yes. She asked if I would get her one. As we were walking along the beach, she was beaming with a huge smile. She was so happy. She was holding her magic star next to her heart and making wishes. This was just the coolest thing she could imagine.

Then after a few hours, she asked, "Daddy, how come my wishes aren't coming true?" I thought, "Oh God, how can I answer this?" Well, I didn't have to. My wife, Bonnie, responded by saying, "As long as you keep your heart open and continue to make your wishes, then they will come true. But they don't always come true right away. It takes time, and you have to have patience." Lauren was satisfied with this answer, and she continued to beam.

In that one statement, Bonnie had summarized the secret of outer success, which is probably why she has so much in her life: Keep your heart open and continue to want what you want. This secret explains why so many people lose their creative power. When they don't get what they want, they give up and stop believing. The secret of creating is sustaining a strong, willful intention. It feels like this: "I will have that, I really want it, and I trust that it will come." In this way, desire and trust turn into a strong, willful intention.

## Knowing What You Really Want

By getting in touch and staying in touch with your deepest desires, you can find your own magic star. By continuing to focus and feel what you really want, you will increase your power to create your life. First in your mind and heart and then through your actions, you will be increasingly successful in creating what you really want.

Knowing what you really want is not as easy as it sounds. There are many ways we get distracted from our true desires. Sometimes it is just too painful to feel what we really want, and we believe that we will never have it. Fear is one of the major reasons we don't give ourselves permission to feel what we want. If we want something that is not as important to us and we don't get, it is not so painful. If we let ourselves really feel what is most important to us, it may be too painful to fail.

When I began giving public talks twenty-eight years ago, I felt tremendous anxiety and fear. I felt most nervous about speaking because that was one of my gifts in life, what I came here to do. If

I failed at speaking, I would be devastated. If I failed as a computer programmer, it would not be so crushing because my gift was not programming. That was not my purpose in life. Whenever you risk doing that which is closer to who you are, the thought of rejection or failure is greater. It is one thing to be rejected by others for the clothes you wear; it is an entirely different story to be rejected for your beliefs.

When you are true to who you are, you are exposed. If you are rejected or criticized, then it cuts much closer and it hurts more. It pushes your buttons and brings up unresolved issues and feelings from the past. My anxiety was just playing out unresolved feelings from my past. By eventually learning to process my past feelings of abandonment, failure, and powerlessness, I was free of anxiety in my life within a few months.

From this experience, I learned that fear is greater when we risk being true to ourselves. Often, we can't even feel our soul's desire because we are blocked. It is risky to believe we can have what we want so we automatically deny our true wants. To uncover our power to create what we want and experience greater confidence, we need to become very conscious of the ways we may be pushing down or denying our true desires.

## Trust, Caring, and Desire

When we have a desire that is not fulfilled, quite commonly we give it up in some way. We stop caring as much, we stop wanting, we stop trusting. When a man stops believing, he will stop caring. When a woman stops believing, she will tend to stop trusting. In both cases, they will give up hope. Hope is vitally important to stay in touch with our ability to feel our desires fully.

Trust, caring, and strong desire are the ingredients of power. We need all three. To cultivate these attitudes, you must be in touch with how you feel and what you want. When you don't get what you want, it's important to let yourself feel deeply disappointed and sad. Why is that some famous and rich people are always taking drugs and getting into fights? They lead intense lives, because they have strong wants and feelings. At the Academy Awards, there is a lot of love and goodwill, but just under the surface is an ocean of fear, anxiety, and jealousy. After the awards, there is great joy for some, but much more disappointment, sadness, fear, anxiety, and jealousy. Sometimes you have to pay a big price to get to the top, and then even more to stay there.

Yet all this intense feeling doesn't have to rip our lives apart. When we know how to manage our feelings and release negative emotions, intense feeling can be mostly positive. To continue caring, when others get what you want, you naturally feel hurt, disappointed, and sad. When others prevent you from getting what you want, you feel jealous, frustrated, and even angry. When it seems that you may not get what you want, you naturally feel afraid, worried, and scared. When you fail or don't live up to your expectations, you feel embarrassed, sorry, or ashamed. Risking these feelings and many more are all natural when you really want something.

## Feeling Emotions and Letting Go

Getting in touch with feelings helps us to care more, while letting go of these emotions builds trust. As we learn to let go and move on, we can stay open to the next possibilities of getting what we want. Women often can feel many of their emotions, but they have a hard time trusting and letting go. Men, on the other hand, have had a little easier time letting go and knowing what they want, but it is much harder for them to feel their emotions fully. By focusing a lot of his energy on what he wants, a man sets the stage for getting in touch with his feelings. By setting goals and really going for it, if things don't always work out, he can feel his loss more deeply. As a result, the power of his desire and belief will increase. Taking reasonable risks and pushing to his limits helps him to feel his emotions. Taking time to share his feelings with others is not as important for a man.

---

**Taking reasonable risks and pushing to his limits helps a man to feel his emotions.**

---

Women can build trust and learn to release their negative emotions by focusing more on acknowledging the different wants and needs behind their painful emotions. As a woman connects more with her wants, the inherent knowledge and wisdom of how to get them emerges and provides her with greater trust. Taking risks and pushing to her limits is not as important for her, but sharing her emotions in a supportive context assists her greatly in feeling her wants.

---

**Sharing her feelings in a supportive context assists a woman in feeling her wants.**

---

A big aspect of a woman's ability to grow in trust is to experience her own inner worthiness. As she feels her emotions and desires more deeply, she begins to believe, "I deserve to have more, I deserve to be successful, I deserve greater abundance in my life right now." By taking time to listen to and nurture her inner feelings, she is then able to find trust and let go of negative emotions.

As a man is able to connect more with his feeling and wants, he is able to increase his caring. As he is able to "feel" his desires, the intuitive knowledge that he can get what he wants emerges. His confidence increases, and he feels up to the job at hand. By taking time to review his goals and acknowledge his feelings as they come up, he is able to keep his edge. He can continue to stay hungry for more and motivated to get it.

---

**Increased caring and trust enhance your power to create what you want.**

---

When your desires are strong, the intuitive knowledge of what is possible comes into focus. It just becomes evident to you. Increasing trust and caring create passion and enhance your power to create what you want. Then, if you just focus your attention on what you want, that desire will begin to manifest in your life. Not only will your thinking be more creative, but things will just go your way.

The secret to increasing your power to get what you want is to feel your negative emotions when you don't get what you want and then release them. As you learn to release negative feelings, you are left feeling your true desires. By connecting with your true nature, you once again have the power to create what you want and want what you have.

## The Process of Denial

When we don't know how to release our negative emotions, the easiest way to leave them behind is to stop wanting. The process of denial is simple to understand. If not getting something I want bothers me, I simply stop wanting it or lessen my desire. If I adjust my desire always to accept what I get, I can be free of negative emotions. Some people are very happy doing this, but then wonder why they may be bored or why they are not getting more of what they want.

Denial is perfectly described in the fable of the fox and the grapes. The fox really wanted to taste the grapes, but when he realized that he couldn't have the grapes, his reaction was to deny his desire. After discovering that he couldn't get what he wanted, he said to himself, "Well, I didn't want those grapes anyway."

In this way, we deny our deepest dreams when we don't realize our inner power to make our dreams come true. We all have a magic wishing star. We just have to keep feeling our wants and wishes as we increase our confidence in the art of getting what we want.

If you could wave a magic wand and take away all the denial, you would not only be happier in life, but you would get more of what you want immediately. When we believe in our future, we open the door for more to come in now. We must believe and we must ask. If you don't ask, you don't get. With belief based on the experience of getting what you want, the awareness of what you want, and the ability to feel fully, you have the three most important ingredients for outer success.

## What's Wrong with Being Nice

Most people who deny their wants are the positive ones. We tend to believe that if we do good, then good happens back. As you sow so shall you reap. This is only partly true. How did Scrooge get so much money? How did Hitler get so much power? Why do some of the nicest people finish last?

The answer to this question is denial. Nice people deny their wants and needs for the good of all. The Scrooges and Hitlers of the world don't really care how others feel. They do what they want to do, and they passionately want what they want. There is nothing wrong with nice people, except that to be nice they often deny themselves. But you can be nice and get what you want.

To get what you want, you don't even have to believe in or experience God. There are plenty of people who have made millions, even billions of dollars who don't believe in God. In some ways their lack of belief in God has helped them to desire even more. If you don't believe in God, then you know you have to do it yourself. If you trust God, sometimes you trust too much and give up doing your share by feeling your wants and asking for more.

If you have strong desire, you get what you want. The universe responds to all desires. What you desire is what you get. That is what is meant by the blessing of free will. We have the power to will ourselves into hell or heaven, not after we die, but right now.

Contained within strong desire is the knowledge of how to get what we want. It doesn't matter whether you believe in God or not. If you believe that you can get what you want, then you will. With that strong belief, you will feel trust, which builds determination, persistence, and strong passion.

When you suffer setbacks and disappointments, that trust will help you to let go of your negative feelings, get back up, and keep going. Blind ambition will always succeed in the outer world. But as we have discussed, though you may have outer success, you will not be connected to your inner self.

When you sell out to achieve outer success, no matter what you get, it will never be enough. If you shift your priorities and begin to get the different kinds of love in your life, you can find balance. It is never too late to find personal success. Whether you have outer success or inner success, or you are missing both, you can achieve personal success. If you have worldly success, you don't have to give it up to find inner success. All you have to do is take steps one and two for personal success. Recognize the importance of inner success and then get what you need. Start filling up your love tanks, and you will begin to enjoy your abundance.

Asking for God's help in achieving outer success just makes the whole process more fulfilling and less stressful. The process is still an adventure. It is still challenging. Too much dependence on God will only weaken you. Like a wise, loving parent,

God can only do for you what you can't do for yourself. When children are young parents do more, and as they get older, parents let them do more so that they can gain confidence and independence. God helps most when you do all that you can do.

God always gives us the opportunity to do all that we can do. That is how we grow in confidence, but it is also how we grow in faith. Miracles happen most when we clearly have done all that we can do. You realize that what you ask for, you get.

## Chance Meetings

Let's look at a recent example. When the *Men Are from Mars* board game was released, I went to New York to do some publicity to promote the launch. For months, I had been wanting to meet the top officers of Mattel to talk about ideas I had for promoting the game. Nothing had worked out because of mutually busy schedules.

During my trip to New York, one of the interviews was postponed. With a little extra time, I decided to stop by the Toy Fair to see the display. While I was there for a brief twenty minutes, the president of Mattel came by and we met, then the CEO and vice president. When the main buyers for Toys "Я" Us came by, I was able to tell all of them personally about some marketing ideas. There is no way anyone could have arranged all these meetings at that time. It just happened by good fortune. I had set the intention and it just happened.

My wife, Bonnie, calls it the God Corrective. Whenever some disappointment or setback happens, she knows that things are constantly adjusted so that events can happen when they are supposed to. If my publicity interview had not been postponed, then the Mattel meeting would not have happened. The meeting turned out to be much more important than the canceled interview.

A few weeks earlier, for several days after meditation I had visualized having a great meeting with all the executives at Mattel. That week, I was disappointed that it didn't work out because of schedule conflicts. Without any more planning on my part, it just happened to happen.

The day of these chance meetings, I had also set my intentions. I wanted all my publicity to be a great success and motivate the buyers at the Toy Fair to order plenty of the new game for Christmas. I imagined getting feedback from everyone that I had done a great job.

That day, just by chance, my past intentions and the intentions of the day were realized beyond my expectations. This is what commonly happens when you regularly set your intentions. After a while, you recognize that there are few chance meetings. Instead, what might seem like chance is the direct result of setting your intention and letting your intuition guide you to getting exactly what you want.

By setting your intentions, your confidence begins to grow when things happen. The secret is to start small. Just set your intentions for things you want to happen that you think can and will happen. Always throw in a few extra things just to open the door for more to come in. Then when things happen, you realize your power to create the day the way you want.

Belief, faith, and trust all grow when you experience that your intentions are fulfilled. Through setting your intentions each morning you clearly recognize that life is really a series of little miracles, and occasionally some real big ones start happening. Things get organized that you could never orchestrate yourself. People change overnight in the way they deal with you.

From another point of view, all miracles are really the same magnitude. After all, it is all God's grace. Just the act of moving your finger up and down is a miracle. It's just that it happens all the time and we take it for granted. When you start setting your intentions and things start to happen, you start to be excited by your newfound power.

## Green Lights and Red Lights

As your experience increases, your whole attitude changes. You begin to feel incredible confidence. Instead of noticing red lights and stop signs, you begin to appreciate all the green lights. Instead of thinking about the people who resist you, you think about the people who love you. Instead of focusing on what is missing, you start noticing what you are getting. Instead of dwelling on your mistakes, you think about where you are headed. Rather than feel stuck, you appreciate the movement and freedom you have in life. Rather than toss and turn at night, you sleep more soundly. When there is an abundance of green lights in your life, you don't mind the occasional red light.

I remember riding in the car with my daughter Juliet, who was a teenager at the time. When we were stopped at a traffic light, she asked me why the lights in our town were always red. I said, "Let's do an experiment to see if indeed all the lights are red."

As we began driving around our town, we discovered that there were many more green lights than red lights. We just didn't notice the greens, because we were quickly driving through. It takes only a few seconds to drive through a green light, but it takes much longer to wait at a red light. Naturally we noticed the red lights more, because while we were waiting, we really wanted to be moving.

---

**It is easy to miss the green lights
and focus on the red lights.**

---

This example clearly explains the way most people look at life. They wonder why there are too many red lights. Either life doesn't seem fair, or they don't expect much. With this experience, they stop trusting that they will get what they really want.

By taking time to appreciate the green lights and giving thanks for what you attract every day, you are more inclined to trust that you can attract what you need and create what you want. An attitude of gratitude increases your trust and faith.

Even more powerful than a general attitude of gratitude is gratitude that the specific thing you asked for has been delivered. To take the struggle out of your life when you want more, just ask God. People who believe in themselves do have the power, but they also experience enormous pressure to sustain it. If you ask for help each day, the wear and tear of life diminishes. When you ask, God is happy to help, but you must ask. That is a matter of free will again. The angels in heaven wait for your requests to become active. Otherwise, they are just waiting for a big tragedy or emergency, when you say, "Okay, God, if there is a God, would you help?"

---

**The angels in heaven wait for your requests.**

---

Many people don't ask for help, because they don't want to bother God. If you believe in God or divine energy that has infinite power, then realize there is no limit. God's power is unlimited, and there is no end to it.

You cannot ask for too much, and you are never bothering God. God wants you to ask. All loving parents want to help their children. The difference between God and our parents is that God is all-powerful and unlimited. You can't wear God out or be offensive by asking for too much.

---

**All God needs from us is the invitation and the request.**

---

You prevent God's assistance and your own inner power when you suppress your inner will and desire. As you grow in self-awareness and in your connection to God, the distinction between God's will and your will becomes very fine. Your power increases when your heart is open and love is flowing. At such special times, God's will becomes your will, and your will becomes one with God's will. The more your will is aligned with God's, the more a tremendous power is literally at your fingertips.

## Becoming Aware of Your Denial

When we feel abandoned or unsupported, quite often our automatic reaction is to suppress our true needs or feelings and deny our wants. When children are not touched, they begin to turn inward after a while and stop crying out for what they want. They become very peaceful and content and hum to themselves. It becomes too painful to feel the pain of not getting what they need, so they stop feeling altogether and become peaceful.

As children, we don't know what we want. All we know is that we are in pain, because we are not getting what we want. So we cry out. If we have loving parents who know what we need and give it to us, we are able to identify our true needs and wants. When we don't get what we need, we never really get a clear sense of what we need.

---

**Unless we first get what we need, we cannot know what we need.**

---

One day when my daughter Lauren was about six, she was pulling on me and making a big fuss for attention. Her older sister Shannon said, "Lauren, stop giving your dad a hard time." Lauren's response was: "I'm having a hard day, I just need someone to hold me and read me a story." We were all amazed by how articulate she was. I told her that I would do that soon. She was then able to wait patiently because she trusted that I understood her request. Quite often children get upset because if you are not giving them what they want, they assume that you don't understand what they need. They become even more upset when they don't know what they need. This insight can only come from repeatedly getting what they need.

Depending on the support we have received growing up, we are able to feel and articulate our true needs and desires. Without support, we will feel our frustration and eventually suppress or deny our needs. This is another reason that feeling negative emotions is so important. If we give ourselves permission to be upset about things, we look a little deeper and begin to find out what it is that we really want and need.

As we begin learning to fill our love tanks by getting the love we need, our true desires begin to come into focus. Our tendency to deny what we want diminishes, and we become aware when we are beginning the process of denial. Just noticing that we are starting to deny a feeling or desire is enough to bring up that feeling or desire to be processed.

# CHAPTER 14

# *Giving Up Resistance*

W HY IS IT that when we don't want something, it tends to follow us through life? Quite often what we resist persists. Yet, unless we resist negativity, how can we change it? This one belief is what holds us back much of the time from getting what we want. We think that by resisting what we don't want it will go away. Well, it won't. In many cases, it is only by giving up our resistance that we are free to create what we want.

When we resist what we don't want, it is putting gasoline on a fire. We just add power to someone or a situation when we actively resist it. When we resist what we don't want, we are giving it our full attention, and we are acting from the belief that we can't get what we want because of this situation or circumstance outside ourselves.

Let's look at a few examples. At work, the people we resist the most are somehow the ones we are forced to deal with on a regular basis. When we resist our children's feelings, they just seem to get stronger. When we resist the desire for dessert, we just want it even more. When we resist paying bills, they seem to overwhelm us. When we resist the traffic, we continue to pick the slowest lane. In some mysterious way, much of the time what we resist just gets stronger.

Through resistance, we deny our inner power to create and attract what we want. Actively focusing on what we don't want weakens our power to get what we want. It is difficult to feel confident that we can make our dreams come true when we are focusing on what we are not getting. It is difficult to experience our state of inner happiness, love, and peace when we are focusing outward to find it.

It is not that you should ignore the things that you don't want. But, instead of resisting them, use them and the negative emotions they evoke to support you in feeling and focusing on what you do want. Our power to create our future is all in our attitude and approach. Instead of resisting, feel and release your negative emotions and then focus on what you do want.

Resisting reinforces the belief that we cannot get what we want. Automatically we begin collecting evidence that we are powerless and we disconnect with our creative potential. What we believe is what we create. Our thinking is far more powerful than most people understand. Ninety percent of what gets done in life is caused by thinking, while ten percent is action.

If you believe you can have more and you don't get more, by looking deeper into your feelings, you will see that there are still parts of you that don't yet believe. By continuing to feel your wants at times of hopelessness, you will strengthen your belief and passion. When you believe, challenges make you stronger and increase your belief.

---

### What we believe is what we create.

---

When hopelessness begins to win out over our inner confidence, we begin to resist the world unnecessarily. Instead of being open to what we have and working to get what we want, we use up all our power resisting what we have. When we resist a person or situation, we misdirect our desire.

Instead of wanting peace and cooperation, we start wanting someone to leave. Instead of wanting to complete a project, we waste tremendous energy not wanting to do the project. Instead of wanting to make up in a relationship, we waste energy wishing our partners would stop a particular behavior. We focus on what we don't want and bring our thoughts to all the times we didn't get what we wanted. Instead, we need to focus more on what we do want and remember all the times we got it.

We resist our partners' behavior by feeling they never love us. Instead of focusing our energy on wanting them to be happy and to show some interest in us, we wait for them to mistreat or disappoint us again. In a variety of ways, when we are resisting a situation, rather than getting what we really want, we unknowingly waste our energy and continue getting what we resist. What you resist will persist. What you focus on is what you get. What you put your attention on in life just increases. When you attend to someone with strong negative emotions, you will attract what you resist.

---

**What you put your attention on in life just increases.**

---

When you resist something, you continue to create it, because you are believing that it won't go away. The place you come from when you resist is hopelessness. Hopelessness emerges when you are believing that you can't get what you want.

---

**When you resist, you are reinforcing the belief that you can't get what you want.**

---

Imagine that you knew you were going to get a check in the mail for a million dollars. If you then got a lot of bills in the mail, you wouldn't resist paying them. You wouldn't dread having to write those checks. You wouldn't want them to go away. Instead you could accept them peacefully and go about paying them or patiently postpone paying. You do not resist because you are feeling confident that you have enough.

Imagine that your partner was sick but you knew for sure she would get well soon. In this case you don't mind picking up the slack and taking care of your partner. You don't take it personally that you are being ignored. You don't resist the sickness, nor do you feel burdened. Your resistance goes away, because you are assured of getting what you need and want later. Your confident belief in what is to come frees you from getting caught in the bind of resistance. With this insight about resistance it becomes clear that to achieve success we need to give up resistance.

Achieving outer success is like a snowball rolling down a hill. As it rolls, it gets bigger and bigger. Likewise, as you experience some success, you believe more and you get more. As you get more, you believe more and your success grows. Your confidence then increases and you become more excited and enthusiastic; you begin to glow with positive energy and belief.

Once people get on a roll they often keep going for a while. Nothing builds success like success. By understanding this, you can appreciate why it is so important to set your intentions each day. When you put in your request and things happen, you get excited as you comprehend your inner power to attract results in your life. If, however, you are not open to appreciating the little miracles, you will never draw the really big ones. Instead, you will get caught up resisting the things that you don't want to happen.

---

### Nothing builds success like success.

---

To experience personal success, we must feel and act on our true desires. Yet most of our desires throughout the day come from resistance or "not wanting." These are not our true desires; in a sense they are false desires. Instead of attracting what you really want, a false desire wastes energy and reinforces the belief that we are powerless to get what we really want.

---

**Focusing on what you don't want just reinforces the belief that you can't get what you want.**

---

Let's say you are in traffic jam. If you are in a hurry, you may want the cars to move, but you are really not wanting to be stuck in traffic. By resisting the traffic, you are focusing your attention on what you don't want, and that just attracts more opportunities to resist. As a result, you will intuitively pick the slowest lane to drive in, instead of picking the quickest. If you don't actually pick the worst, at least you will think you picked the worst.

Why is that in the grocery store every time you are late or in a rush and feeling anxious, you pick the slowest checkout line? This is not just chance. It is too predictable. When you are off center and in a hurry, you pick the slowest line.

---

**When anxious at a grocery store, we tend to pick the slowest line.**

---

When driving in traffic, if you are off center, you will unconsciously or "intuitively" pick the lane that is slowest or the route with the accident. It is inevitable that when we are resisting we will attract more opportunities to resist. When we focus our attention on not wanting to wait then more waiting is what we get.

## Why the Past Repeats

This is another reason that it is important to heal the wounds of our past. When we have been hurt in a business deal or a relationship, we approach life from the perspective that we do not want to be hurt again. Our resistance to being hurt actually attracts opportunities to be hurt again. On the other hand, when we have not been hurt, we don't think much about it. Instead, we naturally focus on what we do want and that is then what we attract in our life.

---

**When we don't want to be hurt,
then opportunities to be hurt again
are what we attract.**

---

Once we have something bad happen to us, it is very difficult not to resist it. Once it has happened, we clearly want to avoid it. Yet by focusing on what happened and by actively not wanting it to happen again, we begin to attract it back into our lives to some degree. The more we have healed our past, the less we are affected by the ghosts of our past. Unless we can let go of the pain associated with a past event, we tend to get stuck in a negative pattern of repeating certain aspects of it.

For example, if we passionately don't want to be alone, that is what we get. If we really don't want to be rejected or ignored, that is what we get. If we hate the possibility of failing or losing at something, that is what we get. If we dread going to an unhappy job, then it continues to be a source of pain. If we just can't stand working with someone, then we get stuck with that person.

---

**The more passionately we don't want
something, the more we will attract it.**

---

By learning to heal the pain of the past, we can let it go so that we are not always secretly hoping it will not happen again. When the pain is healed, then the fear and belief that it will happen again goes away. At this point, we are more free to focus on what we want. Our positive desires increase in power as we are able to let go of past hurts.

If you resist looking at your past, then it just keeps visiting you again and again. If you resist looking at your feelings, then you are automatically attracted to situations that will call up those feelings. Besides interfering with attracting what you really want, resistance drains your energy. It is like punching a hole in your love tanks so that they never fill up. Your power is always leaking out rather than being used constructively and consciously.

As an experiment, notice all the negative thoughts and beliefs that you actually put in words in a day. It is amazing how undisciplined we are when it comes to how much resistance we feel in a day. And how we express our resistance is only the tip of the iceberg.

Our negative comments reflect a world of resistance within. Although our real challenge is to heal those inner feelings and beliefs, start by being aware of what you say and being careful with your words. As you gain more confidence in creating your life, you will begin to experience that what you say *is* what happens. The power of your words is enormous, particularly when you express a true desire.

## The Resistance Game

The resistance game can be fun. My twelve-year-old daughter Lauren and I sometimes play. One day, we went shopping together and simply noticed all the negative expressions that came out of our mouths. Then we tried to express the thoughts differently. We made it a playful game so that we weren't seriously resisting our resistance. Here is an example of just a few of our comments:

I said, "There are probably no good parking spots so let's park over there." I could have said, "Let's see if there are any good parking spots." We then went to where we really wanted to park and found a spot.

She said, "I hope we don't have to wait long; I have so much homework." Then she reworded it as: "I hope everything runs smoothly, and we get in and out. I want to have plenty of time to do my homework."

When it was about time to leave a store, I said, "Your mother won't like it if we are late." We reworded that to: "If we get home soon, your mom will be really happy."

In the car at home I said, "Don't forget to bring the shopping bag," which we reworded to: "Let's make sure we have everything we need."

## Give Up Resisting Your Partner

These same principles hold true in relationships. Instead of focusing on what you don't want your partner to do or how you don't want your partner to feel, begin putting your attention on the behaviors and responses you do want. Instead of resisting your partner's negative mood, focus on wanting your partner to notice what a great person you are. Remember a time when your partner was appreciative of you. Feel inside, "I want my partner to love me and think I am wonderful." Instead of thinking, "My partner never helps me anymore," remember times when your partner helped out, remember how that made you feel, then set your intention to feeling that way and then think, "I want my partner to offer to help out." In this way, by shifting your attitude, ninety percent of the problem is solved. By setting your positive intention, you are awakening your inner belief that getting what you want is possible. As you believe it more, it begins to happen.

---

**Asking for what you want in a positive way makes it happen.**

---

On the level of communication, practice making positive statements and requests rather than complaining, criticizing, or demanding. Try to avoid expressions like: "don't," "you didn't," "you should have," "you never," "you always," "why didn't you," "why don't you." Have some fun trying to reword your expressions in a more positive way or as a direct request.

Instead of saying, "We never go out anymore," say, "Let's do something special this weekend."

Instead of saying, "You forgot to empty the trash again," say, "Would you get the trash next time? It got really full so I emptied it."

The secret to asking for more is do it without conveying a message of blame, shame, or guilt. It works best if you use an easy tone, as if you are asking your partner simply to pass the butter. There is no need to demand or doubt that your partner will hear you.

---

**If you are communicating with the idea that your partner won't hear, then your partner won't hear.**

---

If you resist certain behaviors or attitudes, at a moment of positive feeling briefly ask for what you want in friendly terms and then patiently persist. Continue to ask again occasionally, but each time ask again as if it was the first time. After a few requests, your partner will become aware that they are not giving you what you want and then really appreciate you for not giving them a hard time. This appreciation will free your partner from resistance and motivate your partner to do more for you. This same approach applies to every relationship in the office, at school, or at home.

## The Power of Memory

Just as negative experiences increase resistance in our lives, remembering the positive will increase our confidence. When I really want something to happen, I remember other successful times. As I set out to write this book and meet my deadline, I took some time to remember all the occasions when I did make my deadline. I remembered the satisfaction of doing my job and doing it well. I remembered everyone's positive comments and appreciation. This then empowered my belief that I could do it once again. And I did!

If you do not actively remember the positive, your fears and doubts begin to come up. Even though this is my tenth book, when I begin a new project I experience fear. I begin to resist the process of writing. Some part of me is afraid that my best years are gone. I am afraid that this project will not be as good as the others. I am afraid that it will not happen this time. These fears are very real and could hold me back if I didn't know how to process them.

Every writer has to face them, successful or not, beginning or seasoned. At that moment of creation, you have to have a blank mind, not knowing if you can do it or how you do it. And then it begins to happen. Each time, I am amazed. Clearly it is a gift, but it has also been forged by years of practice, persistence, frustration, disappointment, worry, and anxiety. After each success, the confidence grows and the gift or power to create increases. Clearly I could not do it by myself. I do my best and then God does the rest.

---

### When you do your best, God does the rest.

---

Taking time to remember your positive experience is essential for building confidence and belief. It is similar to noticing the green lights and not just the red lights. If you notice only the red lights, you resist the flow of your life. If you remember the thousands of green lights in your life, you will build confidence.

If you don't have a lot of green lights, you can create green lights by healing your past. By linking present negative feelings to past situations, you can relive your past and enrich it with your more mature and loving perspective. When you were a child, you were dependent on your parents to know the truth. As an adult, you can go back to experience the feelings you had as a child and make corrections.

When you felt abandoned as a child, you did not know that one day you would have the power to get the love you need. Without this insight as a child, you formed such beliefs as: "I will never be loved," "I can't get the love that I need," "Something must be wrong with me," and so on.

As children, we did not have fully developed brains capable of reasonable thought. At that fragile age, we formed beliefs that were incorrect, yet they continue to shape and mold our lives. Although we can't change the past, we can change the beliefs we formed. We can reevaluate what happened and how we felt. Our limited and incorrect beliefs can be corrected by going back and revisiting the past and using the processing techniques described in Chapter 11.

## Learning to Love Yourself

When we feel emotional pain, we are in some way experiencing a negative and untrue belief. Pain is always caused by believing what is not true. When we feel pain, the mind believes something, and the soul is saying it is not true. To change the belief, we have to get back to feeling the pain. If the source of our pain is the belief that we will never be loved, then as the mature mind reconnects it begins to self-correct. As children, we did not know that one day we would have the power to get the love we needed.

---

**When we feel pain, the mind believes something, and the soul is saying it is not true.**

If we felt unloved at times and began to believe we were unlovable, when we go back and feel the pain, it automatically begins to lift. As children, we did not know how beautiful and precious we were. When we were ignored, neglected, or mistreated in any way, we don't get to find out how special we truly are. We miss a chance to connect with our true selves. Even today in my own life, sometimes I forget what a wonderful person I am. Fortunately, when the feelings of doubt or unworthiness come up, I know how to process them. In a few minutes, they are gone.

I simply link what I am feeling with something that happened when I was seven years old. I give myself permission to feel like a little seven-year-old who thought that he would never find his way home and that his family had forgotten him. For a few minutes, I imagine I am there, feeling the fears I had at that time. Then I give myself a hug and remind that little seven-year-old that he is loved and that he is not forgotten and that nothing is wrong with him.

I reassure myself that soon I will be loved. After just a few minutes of connecting to the little part of me that was wounded growing up, I am back to feeling as if I deserve to be loved by everyone and if people don't love me, then it is clearly their loss. By finding a few sore spots from your past, you can always go back to those times to fill your first four love tanks. To keep attracting more in our lives, we must continue to experience new levels of self-love and confidence. There is no end to the process of creating more and more.

# CHAPTER 15

# *Honoring All Your Desires*

RECOGNIZING AND HONORING all your desires is the basis of finding your true self. Although your soul's desire is the basis of personal success, you must also honor all your true desires. You have many kinds of desires: your soul's desire, your mind's desire, your heart's desire, and your body's desire.

When you are not experiencing inner success, you are not in touch with your soul's desire. When you are not experiencing outer success, you are not connecting with your mind's desire. When you are not attracting what you need, you are not fulfilling your heart's desire. When you are not healthy or vibrant in your body, you are not fulfilling your body's desires.

Staying in touch with and honoring all your desires gives you a clear direction in life and ensures personal success. Honoring a desire does not mean you have to act on it. When you listen to and honor all desires, they begin to become more harmonious. When a desire felt at any one level is in harmony with the other levels, it is then a true desire.

---

### When a desire at any level is in harmony
### with the other levels, it is a true desire.

---

There are many ways we unknowingly disconnect from feeling our true desires. Since we have different kinds of desires, sometimes they conflict as well. The mind wants things to make us powerful, while the soul wants to be loving and happy. When we cannot see the whole picture, the mind may want money right away and not care about being happy or loving in the process. This tendency to suppress our soul's desire to be happy and loving creates an inner conflict.

In this example, the mind won the battle between the mind and the soul. Generally speaking, in Western materialistic circles, the mind dominates the soul and wins this battle. The mind says, "I do not care about being happy or loving today. I would rather have money and then I will be happy."

In the Eastern traditions, the soul tends to win the battle. The mind wants to be happy and yields to the wisdom of the soul and then believes that happiness can only come from within. The mind honors the soul's desire, but suppresses its own passionate desires for outer success. The soul's desire to be happy and loving is fulfilled, but the mind does not achieve what it wants in the outer world.

The good news is that there does not have to be a battle any more. As we have already explored, we are now more capable of the abstract thinking necessary to make the leap to know when something is not necessarily better or worse, even though it is different. In a similar way, one kind of desire is not better than another. The soul's desires are not better than those of the mind, heart, or body. All are different, but can coexist and work together.

We can win the battle by honoring each of the four levels of desire: body, heart, mind, and soul. When we are in touch with all our desires, we have the opportunity to feel our true desire.

There are twelve ways we interfere with the process of listening to all our desires in order to feel a true desire. By being aware of these tendencies, we can begin to recognize the difference between what we may know, think, feel, or sense we want, and what we really want.

---

**A true desire is always in harmony
with each of the four levels:
body, heart, mind, and soul.**

---

There are generally twelve ways we disconnect from feeling our true wants. They are revenge, attachment, doubt, rationalization, defiance, submission, avoidance, justification, rejection, withholding, reaction, and sacrifice. Let's explore each in greater detail.

## *1. Get Mad but Do Not Get Even*

If you are angry and you do not know how to let go of anger, one of the ways you tend to push your anger away is by getting even. When we want to hurt someone or make that person suffer, we are not in harmony with our soul's desire to be loving. When one part of us wants to be loving and another part wants to hurt someone else, our power is neutralized.

The old saying, "Don't get mad, get even," is sure to take you away from your soul's desire. Since you have strong feelings and a lot of passion, you may be successful, but you will not be happy with the result. You will have just wasted time and energy, which could have been focused on what you really want.

Your time, energy, and attention are limited. If what you really want in life is to be loving and happy, it is a complete waste of time and energy to get even. Even hoping that something bad happens to someone who hurt, disturbed, or betrayed you in some way will leak away your power. Whenever you are caught up in the grip of blaming others, you get sidetracked from believing you can have what you want.

Instead of believing in yourself and God, you forfeit your inner power. You begin to believe, "I can't be happy, because of what that person did. I can't get what I want, because of what that person did. I can't be loving until that person changes, goes away, or suffers the way I did." Even when you do manage to get even, the satisfaction is short-lived. Revenge provides relief, but it does not heal anything. You may feel satisfaction, but you will always have to justify your revenge by believing that because of that person you can't get what you want. When you seek to get even, you are not only denying your soul's desire to be loving but also your power to create what you want.

By learning to release blame with forgiveness, you will be free of this tendency to waste your energy and power trying to get even. As long as you are holding on to the desire to punish, get even, or teach someone a lesson, you will just be giving them space in your brain free of charge. The energy you have to make your dreams come true gets wasted on them. When you let go of revenge, you take back your power to be happy and fulfilled within yourself without depending on the outside.

## 2. Give Up Attachments and Keep Desiring

Quite often when we lose someone or something, we feel a range of such negative emotions as sadness, fear, sorrow, and frustration. Feeling these emotions is healing and a necessary part of letting go. If you do not know how to process and let go of negative feelings by healing the heart, you will continue to want what you can't have anymore.

When our hearts are not healed, we hold on to what is no longer available. When we cling to our past, we unknowingly push away our glorious future. Ultimately there is nothing wrong with attachment. The tendency to hold on is beautiful. It can be a pure expression of love. When we love someone, we want to hold on. The secret of continuing to love is to let go when it is time to change. When it is time to change, we must be able to let go.

Holding on becomes a sickness when we refuse to let go of what is no longer available to us. When we learn to let go, accept, and trust change, we clearly experience that every change, no matter how tragic, always opens the door to more.

---

**Every change, no matter how tragic, always opens the door to more.**

---

When we suffer a loss or setback in life, the cause of our suffering is attachment. To let go of the attachment, we need to find love in our hearts again. We mistakenly believe we need someone specific or some particular thing, when really what we need is what that person or thing provided us. A special person is special but what that person provided us with is love, and that can always be found elsewhere. By letting go, we open the way for something new in our lives. Change is only painful when we can't let go.

---

**The only real lasting tragedy of a loss or setback occurs when we do not open our hearts to find love again.**

---

To let go, it is helpful to understand why you become attached in the first place. When we are used to getting love and support from someone, when we lose access to that support, we disconnect from our inner selves. To feel loving, we think we need that person and do not yet realize that we really need the love and support that person provided us. The support to reconnect with ourselves can be found elsewhere. No one could ever replace that person, but there are always other ways to fill up our love tanks.

Until we are able once again to fill up our love tanks, we will temporarily suffer from our emptiness.

We can also become attached to our desire for more as well. When we are attached to wanting more, we "have to have" something to be happy. Believing that we "have to have" something negates the truth that we are already happy within ourselves. We think more money or a new big-screen TV will make us happy. Since we think that having the TV will make us happy, we become attached to having it. We believe temporarily that we must have it to be happy. This kind of clinging attachment arises when we have not yet learned how to connect with our true selves by getting the love we need.

When you mentally try to give up attachment, you run a great risk of denying your inner passion and desire. You cannot achieve the power to make your dreams come true if you stop dreaming. You must feel your inner passion. To give up attachment, some people make the mistake of giving up their desires. They say, "I shouldn't be so attached" and release their attachment by suppressing or negating the importance of their true desires. In giving up attachment we must be careful to not minimize or suppress our desires.

As you learn to fill your first love tank through prayer and meditation, you will experience a lift in your spirit. When you can directly taste the happiness you thought only the new TV would bring, you are no longer so attached. You still want the TV, but not because you have to have it to be happy. You want it, but you are not attached. This kind of unattached desire is also passionate and holds a lot of power.

## 3. Doubt Your Doubts

To access your creative power to solve problems and create what you want, you have to start from uncertainty. To draw in more knowledge and insight, you need first to feel a certain degree of not knowing or uncertainty. There is a big difference between doubt, which is not believing, and simply not knowing. From a place of not knowing, you can still believe that something is possible.

When afraid, you can say, "I really do not know. Maybe it could happen or maybe not. But definitely it could happen." By shifting doubt into uncertainty, you are free to believe again in the positive possibilities that exist. When you are stuck not believing when really you are just uncertain, then doubt your doubts and look at what could be possible.

---

**By shifting doubt into uncertainty, you are free to begin believing again in the possibilities that exist.**

---

By experiencing uncertainty without doubt, you open yourself to your most creative self. If you already know something, you are not open for more. But when there is a question, the answer will come. When the need exists, the solution is always nearby. The challenge with uncertainty is to keep asking for answers. One of my favorite prayers is: "Show me the way." Whenever I do not know what to do next, I ask, and eventually the insight comes and I get what I want.

Whenever I feel anxiety, I can release it by reminding myself that I have started to doubt instead of accepting that I just do not know. I have learned to recognize that uncertainty always precedes getting a new answer, a clearer insight, or something wonderful.

To let go of anxiety, I do this little process. I ask myself what I am afraid of. Then I ask myself, "Do I know for sure that those things will happen?" This frees me to see that when I am uncertain, I also have no certainty that anything bad will happen. Most anxiety is believing our fear instead of remembering that we really do not know. By opening your mind to all possibilities, you can begin to tap into your inner guidance and to feel trust again.

---

**When you are uncertain, then you have no certainty that bad things will happen.**

---

When we doubt that something we want is possible, we automatically stop wanting. Doubt kills passion and stops the flow of feeling. An easy way to release doubt is to acknowledge that we are just not sure but open to all possibilities.

Sometimes when I do laying-on-hands healing, I do not feel a strong current of energy flowing into a person. The natural healing energy becomes blocked because some part of them is missing faith and they are doubting. When I ask them to express out loud what they want, the energy immediately begins to flow. When people say and feel what they want, they are automatically connecting with the part of them that knows or believes that they can have what they want. Letting go of doubt allows you to focus on what you want rather than waste your power resisting what you do not want.

## 4. Recognize Your Rationalizations

Another way we block feeling our true desires is by rationalizing away our true desire. Even when our heart says we do not want to do something, the mind dominates by explaining why it must be done. We may say, "This is my job," or "These were my orders." When the Nazi war criminals were asked how they could treat their prisoners so inhumanly, their response was: "I was just following orders." Although common people are not ruthless killers, people mindlessly do things that are against what they feel by rationalizing their feelings.

Another example of rationalization occurs when we do not

believe that we can do something or we think it is not possible for us. Rather than continuing to want what we want, we rationalize our desire. If I am disappointed that I did not reach a goal, I might begin talking myself out of the feeling. I might say things to myself like: "Do not be upset," "You can't win them all," "It's just not your thing," "Your goals were unrealistic," "It's not yet possible," or "It's not the right time."

Self-talk is actually very helpful as long as we first get a chance to feel and then release our emotions. We mistakenly conclude that to let go of negative emotions, we have to talk ourselves out of them. In the long run, this does not work. It will either increase them or suppress them, along with our ability to feel what we want. Many people, after years of suppressing feelings, do not know what they want. In a very real way, they are impotent to fulfill their needs and desires.

In many cases, just the time spent becoming aware of and then feeling negative emotions is enough to release them. Little children all have this ability. Children will return automatically to positive feelings if able to feel freely and share their negative emotions with a loving and understanding listener.

As adults, we are not so dependent on others to help us release our negative emotions. After about age twenty-one, we can begin to exercise our potential to listen to ourselves with love and understanding. That is good, since other adults generally do not want to hear negative emotions. As adults, if we just take the time to write down our thoughts, feelings, and desires, we can listen to what is going on inside. If we learn to listen without judgment or resistance, the negative emotions will lead us right back to our true positive self.

As soon as we rationalize or try to talk away our negativity, we will cause suppression and disconnection from our true nature. Rationalization may work temporarily to create relief, but in a variety of ways it is counterproductive. Besides disconnecting us from our true selves, it drains us of life force and results in sickness, boredom, and lifelessness. Suppressing emotions takes away energy.

Even more important, rationalizing can cover up our feelings of remorse that allow us to self-correct. We may do something that hurts others, but by rationalizing we deny our soul's desire to be compassionate. We say to ourselves, "There was no other way to get what I needed," or "I shouldn't feel bad, I wasn't responsible."

With this denial, we disconnect from our compassionate selves. Even when we are not responsible for a loss or tragedy, it is natural to feel sorrow and wish that it could have been different. These kinds of cold rationalizations harden the heart and prevent us from connecting to the world.

---

**Rationalizing can cover up our feelings of remorse, which allow us to self-correct.**

---

Quite often we will do things though our hearts will say no. Our minds come in and create reasons that we should not follow our hearts. When I was sixteen, I first experienced this conflict. I was driving my car while delivering newspapers. I suddenly heard a big thud. I stopped my car, got out, and saw a hurt dog. I first felt very sorry and thought, "What can I do?" I was afraid that someone would blame me for hurting the dog and I would get in trouble. I moved the dog to the side of the road, got back in my car, and continued on.

In hindsight, I recognized that I made a mistake. I listened to my mind rather than my heart, which wanted to help the dog. My mistake was not doing something more to help the dog. At least I could have knocked on a few doors to let others know about the accident and help in any way that I could. But I did not.

Later in life, I realized why I had done that. At the time, I saw what had happened and thought, "I wasn't speeding, I did not see the dog, I certainly did not mean to hurt the dog." After I focused on these rationalizations, I stopped feeling sorry. I felt as if it wasn't my fault, got back in my car, and drove on. I have since forgiven myself, but I have not forgotten the lesson. I am careful not to rationalize away my natural feelings of sorrow, which are the doorway to conscience. One of the greatest sources of energy and motivation is feeling compassionate for others. It awakens your true desire to be of service and make a difference.

## 5. Defy Your Defiance

Sometimes, when someone really annoys us, we will want to defy that person or rebel against what that person wants us to do. Often it is some authority figure who is trying to control us, and we seek the feeling of freedom by defying and rebelling against doing whatever that person asks. We refuse to do something, not because we do not want to, but because a certain person wants us to do it. We act not because we really want to, but because we want to defy. This is not a true desire.

If we are annoyed by someone and that person does not want us to do something, we will do it in defiance. We may get great satisfaction from doing the opposite of what the person wants, but we will have leaked our power. We think we are "showing them," but all we are showing is that the person is still controlling us. We are the ones who lose when we do not do what we want.

All power comes from doing what you want. When we change ourselves because of someone else's bad manners, we are the ones who lose. We think we are proving that we are free, but we are still being controlled by someone else, bound to doing the opposite of what that person wants.

---

**When we defy, we think we are proving that we are free, but we are still being controlled.**

---

I remember one man who hated his father. His father said he would never amount to anything, so the son set out to defy him and prove him wrong. He succeeded in becoming a millionaire, because he had strong desire and passion. His passionate defiance gave him the power to create and attract success, but unfortunately his heart was closed, so he could not enjoy his money.

Sometimes we want to do things just to defy someone or prove them wrong. What a waste of time and energy to allow someone we do not even love to affect our behavior that much. This tendency is actually rampant in our society. There is so much energy wasted in lawsuits. Although sometimes a suit is valid, so many are frivolous. Rather than waste money, time, energy, and focus on a lawsuit, move on and create what you want. Lawsuits are another way we affirm that we can't have what we want until someone out there gives us the power.

When I get the urge to defy someone and do something that I did not really want to do until that person came along and annoyed me, I resist the urge to defy. I defy my defiance. I say to myself, "Is this really what I want to be doing with my time? How would I be feeling if this person approached me in a nice manner? How would I respond then?"

## 6. Surrender Your Submission

When we are disappointed, instead of surrendering to accept what has happened, we sometimes give in and submit. We stop believing in ourselves and God and give up our desire. There is a subtle distinction between surrender and submission. When we surrender, we are giving up our resistance to what is. We embrace what we have and accept what we cannot change. It does not mean that we stop wanting what we want.

---

### Surrender is
### giving up our resistance to what is.

---

When we surrender, we are just making an adjustment in our expectations of how soon we will get what we want. Surrender frees us from demanding what we need in a particular wrapping. Surrender nurtures patience but does not preclude persistence and strength.

In the process of healing our past, we may have to surrender the expectation that our parents will ever love us the way we want, but we do not have to stop wanting to receive pure, unconditional love. Surrender frees us and opens us up to receive what we want in a variety of different ways. Ultimately, who cares who gives us what we need, as long as we get it? Then we can get back to our true selves and feel our true desires.

Through surrender, as we receive feedback from the world, we sometimes find out that our immediate requirements are unrealistic and we have to adjust. Adjustment does not mean we stop wanting. Instead, we accept what we have and keep thinking of what we really want and how we can get it.

Another prayer that aptly describes the difference is the serenity prayer: "God, grant me the serenity to accept the things I cannot change, the courage to change the things I can, and the wisdom to know the difference."

## 7. Avoid Avoidance

Once we recognize the futility of avoidance, we are motivated to stop doing things that are really attempts to avoid doing what we really want. Many times, what we think we want is the opposite of what we really want. When our desires oppose one another, they cancel out, and we lose the power to create and attract.

Often, when we feel helpless to get what we need and want, we will replace our wants with secondary wants. For example, sometimes when I am working on a book, a part of me is not wanting to write that day. At those times, it is amazing how I will find so many other things to do. Suddenly I really want to clean out my closet, read my faxes, balance the checkbook, go shopping, or do anything that will keep me from writing. Although I "1`want" to do those things, they are not what I really want. They are replacement desires.

Much of the time, when we think or feel we really want to do something, we are actually seeking to avoid doing what we really want to do. Often we are afraid of failure so we put things off. Unless we have clarity about what we really want, we cannot harness our inner powers. We could spend much of our lives going in the wrong direction when we just need to make a few adjustments and take a few steps in the right direction, and everything will start to work out. The right direction is the direction you are truly wanting to go toward.

---

**When you make a few adjustments to
honoring your true desires,
everything works out.**

---

Quite often, when we are looking for a partner, we are really seeking to avoid our feelings of loneliness. When we hunger for success, we are sometimes running away from feelings of failure and inadequacy that still need to be healed. When we are tired or want to take a nap, sometimes we are running away from feeling responsible for something. In myriad ways, our desires for more may be an attempt to avoid our inner feelings. When this is the case, we have less power to create what we want.

Whenever our desires are seeking to avoid, they are not pure, strong, and positive. People may feel stressed at work and dream of another job. What they really want is to be happy at work, to have a job that they enjoy and feel challenged by, to be doing something purposeful each day. Without that clarity, they loose power. When we run away from our problems, they will be waiting wherever we go. By dwelling on a replacement desire, you weaken your true desires, which have much greater power.

---

**When we run away from our problems, they will be waiting wherever we go.**

---

Soul power comes forward most strongly when our conscious desires are aligned with what we really want. When we seek to avoid situations rather than focus on attracting what we really want, we lose the opportunity to fulfill our soul's desire.

So much energy is wasted when we procrastinate. One technique to overcome procrastination is to keep visualizing doing what you are procrastinating. Imagine how you will feel when you finally get around to it. See yourself doing it easily and effortlessly. See yourself begin the task and complete it, feeling good and happy at both ends. By continuing to do this and asking God to help, you will find yourself starting to do those things. As soon as you shift from feeling what you do not want to what you do want, you realize a tremendous creative power.

## 8. Defend Against Your Defenses

Some people lose touch with what they truly want by overdefending or justifying their position. Rather than make up after an argument by looking at how they contributed to the problem, they refuse to acknowledge their contribution until the other person apologizes first. By making their feelings of regret and responsibility depend on whether they get an apology, they disconnect with their inner desire to learn from everything and grow. They justify what they did rather than feel true compassion or remorse.

When I make a mistake, it is always possible to explain why I did it. There are always good reasons, and certainly I did not mean to do it. These are all givens when we make a mistake, but a mistake is still a mistake. If we do not acknowledge our mistakes, we cannot fully connect to our inner feelings of regret, sorrow, and remorse. Without these feelings, it is almost impossible to self-correct our attitudes and behaviors. We lose touch with our natural desire to learn and grow. By becoming aware of your tendencies to defend and how they hurt you, you can appropriately defend yourself from your defenses.

Let's say on Monday I affectionately patted you on the arm. It was a friendly gesture. Then I see you again on Friday. I am unaware that you have hurt your arm because your wound is covered. I say hello and affectionately give you a pat on the arm, exactly where I touched you last time. This time it hurts, and you scream in pain.

The big question now is: "Did I make a mistake?" It amazes me that very defensive people will say no. They justify their behavior and deny that they made a mistake with statements like these:

"I am sorry if I did anything wrong."

"I am sorry if I hurt you."

"I did not know that you hurt your arm."

"How was I supposed to know?"

"You should have let me know that you were hurt."

"It's not my fault, anyone would have done it."

"I was just trying to be friendly."

"Hey, there's nothing wrong with giving a friend a pat on the arm."

"Well, I do regret that you were hurt, but how was I supposed to know?"

Each of these statements limits our ability to self-correct. They are examples of how the mind will deny your inner feelings of sorrow and block you from feeling your soul's desire to correct your actions and to learn from every mistake. These defensive tendencies emerge because we are afraid of being punished for our mistakes. All success hinges on our ability to self-correct and not to continue repeating behaviors or attitudes that do not work.

Let's explore in depth a few of these justifications and defenses. Someone who says, "I am sorry if I did anything wrong" appears to be taking responsibility for the mistake, but really is not. Taking responsibility would sound more like: "I am sorry I made a mistake" and not "I am sorry *if* I made a mistake." Likewise the statement, "I am sorry *if* I hurt you," completely ignores the reality that you just hurt someone and that you want to do something to make it up.

When we acknowledge that we made a mistake, our heart's desire is always to find an appropriate way to make it up. We want to comfort the person or compensate in some way. Wanting to make it up is an important link to our inner feelings of conscience, which motivate us to do what is good and wholesome.

When we feel, "Well, I did not know that was a wound" and make the other excuses, we not only deny our natural remorse and regret, but we suppress our desire to be more attentive and caring. There is always a lesson to learn when we recognize we made a mistake. When we excuse ourselves by saying we did not know better, we are telling ourselves that we did not make a mistake when we did. Rather than excuse ourselves, we need to forgive ourselves and trust that others will forgive us as well.

## 9. Reject Rejection

When children are deprived of touch, often the result is that later in life they do not feel comfortable being touched. If we are deprived of an important need while growing up, rather than feel the enormous pain of deprivation, we stop feeling our need. Then later in life, if someone tries to give us what we need, we will reject it. When we have denied our inner needs, and our soul keeps drawing into our life the love and support we need, with our minds we keep rejecting it. People offer their support to us, but we are not interested.

To break this tendency to reject what we really want and need, we must ask someone we trust to give us what we know we need but feel uncomfortable receiving. As the person gently persists, we give ourselves permission to resist and explore and process all the feelings that come up. When you are able to experience and release the negative feelings linked to your rejection, you will begin to appreciate receiving what you need. That appreciation then becomes a magnet to attract more.

One of the symptoms of rejecting what you need is the formation of a new opposite desire. If you are rejecting the love you need, you may want the opposite. You will want others who cannot give you what you need to give it to you. If you eventually do succeed in getting what you need, you will reject it.

---

**If you reject what you need, you tend to
want what you do not need or can't have.**

---

Quite often, we reject the people who have what we need. We long to be loved by or to work with people who do not have what we need. By rejecting what we really need, we attract or create situations that mirror unresolved conditions of our childhood.

When we feel deprived of a need, we naturally feel jealousy

when we see someone else getting what we need. Jealousy is a very important emotion to bring us back to feeling what we really want and need. We often become envious of those who have something close to what we really want. If we do not feel, and then release our feelings of jealousy, we may end up rejecting what we deserve in life.

Many people are envious of the very rich. If you are envious sometimes, that is not a bad sign. It is sign that a part of you really wants to be rich. This is a hidden desire. By letting yourself feel the jealousy and feel your desire, you increase your power to get what you want. Unless you feel your earnest desire, you cannot create the abundance that you really want.

Once, when I bought a beautiful new car, someone saw it in a parking lot and keyed the side. By rejecting the car (and me, the owner), that person was not just rejecting me, but they were rejecting their inner desire for abundance.

When we reject some expression of outer abundance that represents what we really want, we may say things like: "Who wants that anyway? They are probably miserable and their kids hate them. Who needs that much money?" Instead, if we were to release our jealousy, we could say with an open heart, "That's for me, so what if they may be unhappy? I want it and I want to be happy as well."

Whenever you are envious, say, "That's for me." A positive sign that you are on your way to having what you want is being happy for the success of others and wishing to have it, too.

## 10. Withholding Only Holds You Back

One of the biggest blocks to getting in touch with your true desire to love and be loved is withholding love. When people hurt us, often our reaction is to withhold our love. Our motivation is either to punish or to protect ourselves from being hurt again. Either way, we are the ones who suffer. The greatest pain we can experience is holding back the love we feel in our hearts. When we withhold our love, we suppress and deny our heart's desire. We disconnect from our true selves. We cannot fully thrive in life until we learn to forgive and love again when our hearts are closed or we withhold the love we feel.

---

**The greatest pain we can experience is holding back the love we feel in our hearts.**

---

If we have been hurt by someone, we certainly need to make an adjustment so that we do not get hurt again. To protect ourselves in the future, we do not have to stop being loving. To love someone does not mean that we have to please that person or do what that person wants. It does not mean we have to do anything. It just means our hearts are open to that person. We can see the good in that person and we wish that person well.

If loving means that you have to sacrifice yourself for others or allow others to hurt you again, withholding would seem to be a good idea, but it is not. When the tendency to withhold exists, we need to be aware of it and then begin to let it go. Generally at those times we do not want to be loving. Sometimes the best way to release this tendency is to vent it.

To vent, write out all your feelings about the person or situation. After each sentence write, "I do not want to love you again." Each time you do this, begin to recognize that the only person you are hurting is you. In doing this exercise, some might be afraid that they are focusing on the negative too much. It is better to do it for ten minutes than withhold for ten years.

By writing it out, you will return to the awareness that ultimately you want that person to be happy, you do want to forgive or make up, or at least you wish that person well. Sometimes making up isn't possible or practical, because it involves spending more energy on someone who is not willing to make up with you. At least you can forgive and wish the person a good life.

## 11. Respond Rather Than React

Sometimes we are willing to do something for someone but the way that person asks for or demands more is such a turnoff that we "re-act" and change our minds. We righteously think, "If he had asked nicely, I would have said yes." Although we feel correct in this position, it is very limiting, and we suffer more.

When we mindlessly react, we let others determine what we are willing to do. Being generous is one of our soul's desires. If we are really willing to accommodate and help someone, we can't let that person's manners keep us from being true to ourselves.

When I began teaching workshops, some people complained afterward. Some would say I talked too much, while others would complain I did not talk enough. My inner reaction then was to mirror back. Inside, I would react and feel, "If you do not like me, then I do not like you. If you do not want to take my seminars, then I won't teach them anymore." Fortunately I was able to recognize my reactions and not act on them.

I have seen many sincere people, who were trying to help the world or do their best at work, become jaded by criticism. They stop wanting to help, because their efforts are not being appreciated. As a result, they gradually lose their power. To be powerful, we have to be able to overcome these challenges and not let them keep us from feeling and doing what we really want to do.

To transform my reactions to responses, I think, "If they had asked more nicely, what would I have done?" Then I do it. To keep your power, do not let others and their lack of manners or respect bring you down to their level. You sustain your grace, power, and position by not matching their energy and sending it back. You stay true to yourself by not reacting to their behavior. Instead of just reacting, you are choosing how you want to treat them. The soul always wants to be loving, respectful, compassionate, but also strong.

---

**You sustain your grace, power, and position
by not matching negative energy
and sending it back.**

---

When someone gets angry with us, we automatically become angry back. This is a reaction. We are just matching the emotion and sending it back. This reactive tendency is another reason we get caught in negativity and can't find our way out. When you send anger back out, others react to you with anger and negativity again. In this way, it goes on.

If you want your life to be different, you have to stop the endless cycle of reactions. If someone hurts you, you react and want to hurt back. This makes that person and others want to hurt you, which makes you more reactive. We live in the illusion that it works to react back.

Many people have a misguided sense of fairness exemplified by the old saying, "An eye for an eye." If you hurt me, then you deserve to be hurt. A better version of justice is: "You hurt me, so I deserve more. And I have the power to attract more." This attitude expresses a trust in your ability to attract what you want instead of making your happiness depend on hurting someone or reacting back. Our soul's desire is never to hurt someone. As people begin to experience their inner power to create the life they want, they do not get caught up in reactivity.

It is easy to get caught. This is why people get stuck in negativity and argue. When Mr. White shares his disappointment with Mr. Green, in reaction Mr. Green begins focusing on his disappointments with Mr. White. This focus on negativity only blocks them from finding any resolutions.

Most of the time, when we are experiencing negative emotions, it is best to keep them to ourselves. Be aware of them, learn from them, and then release them by coming back to a positive desire, and then act to communicate that desire. It can work sometimes to share our negative emotions if the listener is not the person to whom we are reacting blamed, attacked, or accused in any way.

To communicate a problem to someone in order to find a workable solution, you should first take some time to feel and release your negative emotions. Some may read this and say, "That's not possible." Well, it's not possible until you learn how. As you begin embracing your negative feelings, they quickly lose their power to control us. Our tendency to react rather than respond automatically lessens.

## 12. Making the Sacrifice of Love

When we love someone a lot, we are happy to make occasional sacrifices for that person. It feels good to show our love that way. Making sacrifices, however, is only an act of love when our love tanks are full. If we are not overflowing, we have no business making sacrifices in the name of love.

---

**If we are not overflowing, we have no business making sacrifices in the name of love.**

---

Since sacrifice is associated with loving, many loving people will keep sacrificing their own wants until they are completely empty and even sick. They are so used to making others happy and giving to others that they do not even know what they want. When asked, they even think what they want is to make people happy.

Making others happy is healthy and good, but it is just a part of what you want. To find your other desires, take time to ask yourself repeatedly what you want to be happy. One of the ways to start getting in touch with what you want when you are an overgiver is to pretend that you are selfish and give yourself permission to be temporarily angry and demanding. Make a list of the things you are angry about. Getting in touch with anger, frustration, and jealousy will lead you right back to a greater awareness of what you want.

## Getting Everything You Want

By learning to recognize the different ways you disconnect with your true desires, you can then make the necessary small adjustments to begin feeling what you want. By fully feeling your positive desires, you will begin to attract and create everything you want. The whole basis of outer success is positive, clear intention. When you passionately want it, when you believe that you can get it, when you put you full attention on it, you will find the power to make your dreams come true and live the life you were meant to live.

# CHAPTER 16

# *Removing the Twelve Blocks*

**W**HEN WE ARE NOT getting what we need, or we are not in touch with our true desires, we become stuck, unable to feel the positive feelings of our true selves. We become blocked from being able to connect with our true selves. At such times, we must first recognize our block and then use it to point the way toward getting what we need by using a variety of tools and processes to let go. It is not enough to feel what we feel and explore what we want.

When we are experiencing one of the twelve blocks to personal success, no matter how much we feel them, they do not go away. Feeling our blocks only makes them stronger. These twelve blocks are blame, depression, anxiety, indifference, judgment, indecision, procrastination, perfectionism, resentment, self-pity, confusion, and guilt. To remove these blocks, we must take a different approach.

Feeling blocks is different from feeling a negative emotion. There are twelve basically pure negative emotions (anger, sad-

ness, fear, sorrow, frustration, disappointment, worry, embarrassment, jealousy, hurt, panic, and shame). All other emotions stem
from these basic twelve. Feeling a few of these negative emotions
will allow us to come back to our true selves. Unlike these emotions, feeling the blocks will just keep us stuck. The major reason
we become blocked is that we haven't fully felt and released our
negative emotions.

---

**Although it works to feel negative emotions,
it does not help to feel these blocks.**

---

To remove a block we must do more than just feel it. For
example, sitting around and feeling blame will just make you
feel more like a victim, powerless to get what you need. Or sink-
ing into depression just reaffirms that you have no good reason
to be happy. Feeling a block does nothing to bring us back to
ourselves. This awareness of the twelve ways we block ourselves
is crucial.

With a clear awareness of how we are responsible and what
we can do, we are motivated to do what is required to remove
the block. We can recognize the blocks and shift our attention
in a way that works to bring us back to our true selves.

Dwelling on and feeling negativity only works when we are
feeling our negative emotions. Pure negative emotions help us
to find our way back to balance as we are moving away from the
true self. Blocks are different from negative emotions. Knowing
this distinction makes a world of difference.

Not understanding this distinction gives feelings a bad rep-
utation. People feel their blocks and just get worse. As a result,
many people are afraid of looking at their feelings, or they do
not see any value to it. When they have taken time to feel their
blocks they have gotten worse instead of getting better.

> Not understanding the distinction
> between blocks and emotions gives
> feelings a bad reputation.

The negative emotions let us know when we are off balance. They help us to remember what we really want and bring us back to being on track. Feeling the pure emotion always brings us back to what we want. Then as we come back into balance and connect with our true selves the negative emotion just goes away and we are left with positive feeling. Negative emotions let us know when we are off balance, but the blocks reveal that we have fallen over.

> Negative emotions let us know
> when we are off balance, but the blocks
> reveal that we have fallen over.

Once we have fallen over, we have to get back up and start riding again. The value in recognizing a block is to realize that we have fallen over and that we need to do something else if we want to get back up.

> When we feel our blocks,
> we just become more blocked.

Being aware of our blocks helps us to recognize how we are holding ourselves back and can then point us in the right direction if we know where to look. With new insight and practice, you can begin immediately to remove the blocks. Right away you will begin to feel more loving, happy, confident, and peaceful. Although most people have more of one block than another, everyone has a little of each. Sometimes after removing one block, you will discover that you have other ones.

Let's explore each of the twelve blocks and insights for releasing them. Before we can let go of a block emotionally, we must understand it intellectually. This chapter will expand our understanding of each of the blocks. In the next chapter, we will explore various emotional exercises to let them go.

## 1. Letting Go of Blame

When you blame others for your lack of happiness, you give up your ability to heal yourself from sickness and unhappiness. Blame prevents you from taking responsibility for your life and affirms that you are powerless. When you make others or circumstances beyond your control responsible for how you feel about your past, present, or future, you are unable to create the changes you would like. As long as someone else is responsible for how you feel, you forfeit the power to change your life. You lose your ability to trust in yourself and the world around you.

> **When you hold on to blame, you forfeit the power to change your life.**

It is not wrong to blame. We need to blame to determine the outer cause of our pain and to identify what we can do to get what we want. Once we have determined who and what caused our pain, we need to release the blame. As long I am holding on to the idea that you make me feel a certain way, I cannot find the power within me to heal or let go of my pain.

If you bruise my arm, it is appropriate to blame you for the bruise. You hit me and caused a bruise. But I have to let go of holding you responsible. I need to recognize that you bruised me, but now I have the power to right the wrong. I have the power to heal the bruise. I have the power to make things better. As long as I expect you to make it up to me, I am powerless to get better until you make it up to me. The bruise does not get better.

---

**As long as we depend on others, we are powerless to get better.**

---

If you stole money from me and it hurt my business, blame is helpful to recognize what happened in order to put me in the situation so that I can correct it and avoid its happening again. If I continue to blame you for my lack of success, I am holding on to the belief that I cannot create what I want because of you. This limited belief prevents me from being able to create my future. As long as I hold on to blame, I cannot fully connect with my ability to determine my destiny. I have put you in charge.

---

**When you hold on to blame, you cannot determine your destiny. Instead, you put someone else in charge.**

---

When we are in a blame mentality, this fact is hard to comprehend. It is easier if we shift out of this mentality for a moment. Imagine that you have achieved complete personal success. You have complete confidence that you always have everything you need available to you and you have realized your ability to get what you want. You know from experience that what you think and believe are what you get. You trust that you are in the process of getting everything you want. You know that ninety percent of what makes something happen is being your true loving self and passionately desiring what you want.

With this positive attitude of personal success, there is no reason or need to hold on to blaming others. Let's take another example. If you made one hundred thousand dollars a year and someone stole five dollars, you would not waste your energy holding on to blame. You would not go after the person or seek retribution in any way. Quite easily you would let go, saying, "So what? Who cares? There are more important things for me to focus my attention on."

If all you had was five dollars, you would feel a lot of blame, because that person had taken everything. You would get caught up in the false belief that the person who took your money was responsible for your well-being. In a similar way, when you get caught up in blame you are forgetting your net worth and your power to get what you want. You are believing that your net worth is five dollars and not one hundred thousand dollars. When someone steals or cheats you of five dollars, it is certainly okay to feel and release your negative emotions, but it is not healthy to hold on to blame. We need to move on and bless that person.

Forgiveness is letting go of the tendency to hold others responsible for our plight in this world. As long we make someone or any circumstance the reason we are not successful, we block our ability to create that success. Whenever you are pointing the finger of blame, three fingers point back to you. Three fingers pointing back remind you that you always have the power to make things right again. By forgiving, you once again regain your power to get what you need and want.

---

**Forgiveness is letting go of our tendency to hold others responsible for our plight in this world.**

---

When people feel powerless to get what they need, they remain stuck in blame. They feel, "If I forgive you, you will just do that to me again." They are afraid that forgiving will forfeit their power. This kind of power, the power to manipulate or punish people, is a false power. It depends on others rather than ourselves. As you experience your increasing power to create, you will be able to forgive more quickly. Even more important, as you forgive, your power to create will grow.

> As you learn to forgive more quickly, you will
> increase your power to create.

When hurt, some people want to punish or get even by with-holding their love. As we have already explored, this is never a true desire of the soul. It only takes us away from our power to create. The only person revenge really hurts is you.

Letting go of blame and finding forgiveness does not mean that you will treat the person the same. If someone hurts you, forgiveness means letting go of the hurt, it does not mean going back to get hurt again. To love someone does not mean that we should in any way allow that person to hurt us again. We must be practical in making any future decision to relate or work with this person.

> Finding forgiveness does not mean you will
> treat the person the same.

In some cases, you may forgive someone and want to con-tinue having a relationship or doing business with that person, but in other cases, you will wisely avoid the person. If this avoidance is done with the caring and wisdom of an open heart, you have found forgiveness. In most cases, when we get upset and choose not to open up, it is good to cool off, let go of blame, and reevaluate the relationship after feeling love again.

Jerry and Jack were good friends for many years. Then Jerry made a big mistake. He revealed publicly some things about Jack that hurt his friend very much. Jack's first reaction was to end their friendship. After Jack worked on finding for-giveness, he remembered once again the love and friendship he felt in his heart. By letting go of the incident, he was able to feel the love in his heart again.

An attitude of forgiveness opens your mind and heart to recognizing that all people makes mistakes but they are still worthy of love. Unacceptable behavior does not make a person unworthy of love. When you forgive, you release your tendency to withhold your love or to punish. Forgiveness allows you to come back to your loving nature, but alerts you to choose how you want to relate with this person in the future. To forgive does not in any way obligate you to do anything for the person, nor is the person obligated to you.

> **When you forgive, you release your tendency to withhold your love or to punish.**

One of the ways to release blame is to remember that whenever you are not getting what you need, you are looking in the wrong direction. If you blame your partner, make a shift and look to filling up another love tank. As you focus on getting what you need elsewhere, you are able to come back to your loving self and forgive your partner. When you are getting what you need and filling up a love tank, letting go of blame is almost automatic.

The negative belief associated with blame is: "Because of what happened I can't get what I need or want." By realizing this is not true, we are free to let go of blame and forgive the mistakes of others and ourselves. Instead of believing our past holds us back, we recognize that our past can serve us to find our way more clearly and strengthen our ability to love through forgiveness.

## 2. Letting Go of Depression

You become depressed when you have disconnected from your innate ability to recognize, appreciate, and enjoy the many blessings in your life. When your heart is not open to what you have received, you cannot anticipate a glorious future. With depression, you forfeit your ability to feel what you really want and lose your magnetic power to attract what you want in life.

You lose your natural ability to enjoy the little things in life.

The major cause of depression in women is feeling isolated. When a woman feels that she cannot get what she needs, she becomes increasingly depressed. If other tanks are empty she will feel a depression from not getting her other needs fulfilled. One of the major symptoms of depression is a feeling of emptiness and powerlessness. By shifting her focus to another love tank, she will begin to get what she needs, and the depression will lift. For many women, the practice of meditation will bring an immediate lift out of depression.

---

**The major cause of depression in women is feeling isolated.**

---

The major cause of depression in men is feeling unneeded. When a man is out of work or he does not feel appreciated in the office or in a relationship, he will become depressed. He will experience an immediate drop in his energy level, and he will start to feel his life is flat. Some men, because they are disconnected from their feeling selves, do not even know that they are depressed. One of the key symptoms of depression is·lack of motivation and a general feeling that nothing will make a difference no matter what they do.

---

**The major cause of depression in men is feeling unneeded.**

---

To overcome depression, we need to look in another direction to get what we need or to make a difference. What we have been doing has not worked because we have been looking for love, support, success, or happiness in the wrong direction. We can become unstuck as we begin getting a different need satisfied. What holds us back is that we reject the things that we need the most.

If you are depressed because you feel alone in a relationship, then look elsewhere for love. Do not get stuck in the limited belief that there is only one person who can make you happy. This does not necessarily mean you have to leave your partner; it means you have to look to another love tank for support.

If you are depressed in business because what you thought was going to happen didn't, realize that there are many other ways to achieve your goal eventually. We often become depressed when we think there is only one way to get what we need or achieve what we want. To get anywhere, there are always a hundred other options. By finding a love tank you can fill, as you get what you need, you will come back to the true self that has the confidence and wisdom to recognize another way to get what you want.

The negative belief associated with depression is that the love and support you need are not available to you. By understanding the ten love tanks, you have more options for finding what you need. The new insight is that whenever you feel you can't get what you need, you are looking in the wrong direction. What you need is always immediately available to you. The challenge of depression is understanding that you are attracted to finding love in one form and rejecting other opportunities for getting what you need.

## Bill and Susan

Bill was depressed because his wife, Susan, did not look the way he wanted his wife to look. He had a certain picture in his mind, and she never lived up to it. In the beginning, it did not matter, but he became depressed thinking he would never have the woman of his dreams. Bill's depression lifted when he shifted to love tank S (self-love).

Instead of feeling depressed about his marriage, he focused on doing things that he liked to do. After a time, he felt better and was able to come back to loving his wife again. When he was loving himself, he did not have to have his wife look a certain way to be fulfilled.

When we are depressed, we are always expecting life to look a certain way, and it does not. Being attached to the form prevents us from experiencing our success in getting what we need. When we let go of being attached to how something should look, we are then free to attract everything we need and want.

---

**Being attached to the form creates depression and prevents us from getting what we need.**

---

One easy way to let go of attachment is first to imagine getting what we need or want. Then imagine how that would make you feel. Relish those feelings. Realize what you really want is to feel that way. Then suppose that there are other ways to have that feeling. This attitude will open your mind and heart to attract what is possible.

## Carol's Attachments

Carol, age twenty-six, came for counseling because she was depressed. Using the techniques in the next chapter, we made great progress, and she was feeling much better. At the new year, she returned to counseling and was depressed again. I asked what had happened during the holidays.

She said, "I was so hurt. My own mother did not even invite me to share Christmas morning with the family. She invited my sister but she did not even invite me."

I asked her what she did on Christmas. She said her Aunt Ruth had called her and invited her over to celebrate. She described how wonderful it was, but she shifted to feeling even more hurt that her own mother would not give her what her aunt had.

I pointed out how she had made great progress. Although her mother had rejected her, she had healed her heart to receive the same kind of love from another source, her aunt. That moment of recognition was a big shift for Carol. She realized that it was true.

She had spent her life trying to get her mother to love her, and her mother just was not able to. By letting go of her blame and her need for her mother's love, Carol had attracted a perfect mother surrogate, who not only loved Carol but understood very intimately the challenges she faced growing up with her mother.

When Carol realized she was getting what she needed in a different form, she was able to let go of depression once again. When Carol faced her challenges in life, her reaction was often to be depressed. By remembering this direct experience of her power to get what she needed, she was able to face challenges with greater strength and without becoming depressed. For her, personal success was an experienced reality. She could now recognize that when she was starting to move toward depression she was not looking in the right direction for what she needed.

## 3. Letting Go of Anxiety

You experience anxiety when you have disconnected with your innate ability to trust that everything will work out and always does. When we have not healed certain events in our past, we experience anxiety in the present. Anxiety is almost always directly related to pain in our past that is still unresolved. In most cases, we block the creative energy that is wanting to flow through us when we are anxious. One day, the situations that make you nervous or anxious will instead make you feel excited, peaceful, and confident.

With anxiety, either you forfeit your ability to enjoy your life or you choose to avoid the discomfort of nervousness and live in your comfort zone. If you do not take risks, you cannot grow, and your life becomes flat. You deny your inner desires for more and limit your power. On the other hand, if you take risks because of the anxiety, you suffer. There is another option.

Take risks, let the feelings of nervousness come up, and then process your negative emotions.

---

### With anxiety, we forfeit our ability to take risks and enjoy life.

---

In my own life, I suffered tremendous anxiety about public speaking. At the beginning of the first talk I gave, twenty-eight years ago, my legs began to shake and I fainted. Everyone thought I had died, right before their eyes. My talk was entitled "Develop Your Full Mental Potential Through Meditation." When I came to, I continued the talk.

For years, I felt anxious and nervous before presentations. I was beginning to think that maybe this was not the right thing for me to do, but then I read an interview with John Lennon of the Beatles. He said he had stopped touring because he would become so nervous that he would vomit before each performance. At that point, I realized that if he experienced anxiety, then it wasn't a bad sign for me.

John Lennon's experience released me from the faulty belief that if I was nervous I must not have been any good. Gradually, as a counselor, I learned that there are millions of very competent and skilled professionals who still experience nervousness or anxiety. Anxiety in no way is a reflection of actual competence or events to come.

---

### Anxiety is in no way a reflection of actual competence or events to come.

---

I continued giving talks and feeling extreme anxiety for sixteen years until I discovered how to heal my past unresolved emotions. By learning to process past feelings, I was able to heal the pain of my past. At that point ninety-five percent of my anxiety disappeared forever. The five percent left comes and quickly goes when I do completely new things and there is a lot of pressure. After twenty minutes of processing my feelings, I am able to open the channels to feel the exhilaration of tremendous power. Where there was anxiety, there is now greater calm along with complete confidence.

## 4. Letting Go of Indifference

When you become indifferent, you are no longer able to feel your soul's desire. You have disconnected with your innate ability to know what is possible and what you want. You stop trusting that you can get what you want or you stop caring about what you really want. When trusting and caring are blocked, you will continue to deny or suppress your true desires.

When indifference sets in, you forfeit your natural motivation and power to change circumstances to get what you want. Life loses meaning and purpose and becomes devoid of love. Gradually numbness sets in, and you do not even know what you are missing. Feeling powerless to get what you want, you deny your true feelings and wants and thereby lose access to your intuitive knowledge of how to get what you want.

---

**When indifference sets in,
you forfeit your natural motivation and
power to change circumstances.**

---

Indifference is an automatic response to feeling powerless to get what we need. We assume that what we want is just not possible. Quite often, a man's first reaction will be just to shut down and stop caring. Without passion, he has no power or direction. To avoid the pain, he feels stuck in indifference and not caring. With his heart closed, life becomes a series of obligations and duties.

---

### When men feel indifferent,
### they shut down and stop caring.

---

When a woman begins to believe that she can't get what she needs, her first reaction tends to be mistrust. She has been hurt by depending on others or circumstances and she is not going to be hurt again. She does not let herself open up to avoid getting hurt again. By protecting herself, she remains safe, but she cannot grow in love and compassion for herself and others. She becomes cold, mistrusting, and detached. Unknowingly, she has closed the door to receiving what she needs.

---

### When a woman feels indifferent,
### she stops trusting.

---

The big problem with indifference is that we often do not realize that there is more to life. Feeling powerless to change things or make them better, we have settled. We rationalize our behaviors and our wants or lack of wants. We tell ourselves, "This is not what I want, but it is all I can get, so why bother about it?" In this way, we numb ourselves to our true feelings and desires.

---

### The big problem with indifference
### is that we often do not realize
### that there is more to life.

---

Even when there does not seem to be anything you can do, you can always process how you feel about a situation and feel better. You do not have to deny your wants and feelings. When people do not know how to release negative feelings, they believe that if they can't solve the problem the feelings must be pushed away. They do not know that they can heal the feelings.

No matter how bad things get, we can always process our negative emotions and come back to feeling much better. Even if the outer situation can't change, we can feel better. After we take this step to let go of negative feelings and come back to how we want to feel, outer circumstances always change for the better. This is a miracle that will always happen. Things will take a turn in a direction that you had never anticipated, but only after you let go of needing that change to find your positive feelings again.

---

**After letting go of indifference,
you will always experience at least
a little miracle in the outer world.**

---

Your greatest power is your power to release negative emotions and feel positive emotions along with strong desire. As little miracles begin to happen, your belief will grow stronger. Instead of becoming indifferent at times when you feel powerless to get what you need and want, you will be confident that somehow, some way, something is going to happen and things will be even better than you could have imagined.

---

**Indifference goes away
as we grow in confidence.**

---

When you experience indifference, it is a clear and definite sign that right under your nose there is a little miracle waiting to happen. By not giving in to indifference, but instead taking time to process your emotions and set your intentions after meditating, you will be happily surprised to discover you can get more and more.

Couples often end up feeling indifferent. They have been disappointed and misunderstood so many times that after a while they just give up. Without hope, the love they share becomes blocked and can't be felt. In this case, the first step, as with all the blocks, is to look elsewhere to fill up another love tank. After feeling better then we can shift back to our relationship and focus on releasing any blame.

It is generally when we hold on to blaming our partners that we feel powerless to get what we need. By processing the negative emotions linked with blame and finding forgiveness, we will find that ice blocks of indifference will begin to melt. In a relationship, indifference is always a sign that we have to look to another love tank first.

## 5. Letting Go of Judgment

You become judgmental when you disconnect from your ability to see the good in others and circumstances. Finding fault with others and situations is an important skill to make positive changes, but it is of little assistance if it prevents you from recognizing the good in a situation. When you are stuck in being judgmental, you feel annoyed and irritated by situations that you cannot change and overlook and miss the positive. Every cloud has a silver lining, but you are unable to find it.

We tend to judge and resist others when we are not looking at our inner feelings about something else. To process the feelings associated with judgment, we need to change the content. It is usually something else that is bothering us. While we may be frustrated with the person next to us, we are really worried and even embarrassed about something else.

---

**When we are frustrated
with the person next to us, we are really
worried about something else.**

---

If you are worried about your hair, it is often a displaced feeling. This means you are really worried about something else. If you are worried about a particular investment or business decision, you may instead feel that worry about something else and start feeling judgmental about your weight or your partner's. All you notice is fat. Whenever we fixate on something we can't change, there is always something else that is bothering us.

---

**A bad hair day means that
something else is bothering you.**

---

When we displace our feelings, we tend to resist situations that we cannot change. If we are able to look at the deeper feelings behind our judgments or charged reactions, we will always find that other things are bothering us. By looking at these emotions, we can release them and begin to correct the situation.

### Looking into the Mirror of Judgments

Many times, when we judge others, we are judging ourselves at some deeper level. We are looking in a mirror and not liking what we see. This realization is not clear right away. It takes practice. I used to judge others for being arrogant. I hated people who were full of themselves. Later on, I discovered that I felt that way because deep inside I was worried that others might see me as arrogant and reject me. Since I was not facing those inner fears, I was holding myself back from ever appearing arrogant in any way.

After I became aware of my underlying emotions and then processed them, two things happened. First, I stopped getting upset when I noticed someone who was arrogant. I realized that my judgments had only made me miserable and did not have any practical purpose. I could still not like someone or disagree with someone, but I did not have to pull back my love and acceptance. By releasing my judgments, I did not feel as if I had to criticize them, nor did I have to like them.

## Our judgments only make us miserable.

The second result I got was feeling free to acknowledge my own success and abilities. To market yourself, you have to let people know who you are and what you can do. You have to have confidence and put yourself out there without an attitude of "I am better than you." Instead, the attitude is more like: "Look at what I have done, you can trust me." By releasing my judgments about arrogance, I was able to put myself out in the world in a positive manner.

In the process of marketing myself and putting myself out there, I have made many mistakes and sometimes did behave in an arrogant manner. Since I had healed my judgments of others who were arrogant, I could forgive myself and make a necessary adjustment in my attitude and behavior.

When we have been holding ourselves back and then decide to come out, we are bound to make mistakes. If we cannot love ourselves, we will not be able to learn from those mistakes. Either we justify them, or we reject ourselves and give up trying.

## When we have been holding ourselves back and then decide to come out, we are bound to make mistakes.

With this insight, it becomes clear that holding on to judgments only holds you back. There is a fine line between arrogance and self-esteem. If we are judgmental of others, our self-esteem is tainted by arrogance. It takes practice not to cross that line. By letting go of judgments, we set ourselves free to experiment, make mistakes, learn a lesson, and get back up.

Many people who do not have a lot of money judge people with money. Some even judge money itself. Either of these attitudes just blocks them from receiving money in their lives. To open your heart and mind to receive abundance, it is important to root out any judgments. By becoming aware of those negative and limiting beliefs and judgments, you can gradually begin to let them go. Always under our judgments about money is the hidden embarrassment that we do not have more. By releasing that feeling, we are then free to want more and get it.

---

**Always under our judgments about money is the hidden embarrassment that we do not have more.**

---

When we judge others we are withholding our love for them. We withhold love because we believe if we were that way we would be unlovable. By looking at our judgments of others, we get a peek into the box that we keep ourselves in. Most people who are very judgmental are locked in a box of what is right or wrong and are unable to let go and be all that they can be. They are afraid of making mistakes, because they fear that they, too, will then be judged.

---

**By looking at our judgments of others, we get a peek into the box that we keep ourselves in.**

---

Judging others just reinforces the fear that if you do not meet certain standards you are not worthy of love. I was at a music concert and noticed that I was increasingly annoyed and judgmental of some people who were very wild but having a great time. As I watched myself being so judgmental, I looked a little deeper to a part of me that wished I could just let loose and be wild.

I thought about it a lot throughout the concert, but I just couldn't really let go and be free. After taking some time to process my feelings, I discovered that in my earlier years I did not feel safe to be wild and uninhibited. A part of me was afraid of being judged, ridiculed, and even punished.

I imagined going back in time, felt my fear, and then imagined others giving me the support I wanted and needed. By filling up my love tank for friends and fun, I was able to release my judgments of others who were having fun.

After doing this, I found many safe opportunities to express myself freely. My wild and spontaneous side got to come out, and I was not judged. After this experience, I became much less serious in my life and more playful. I became much more confident and even outrageous. So many times in the past I held myself back with the fear of what others would think. Now I can freely say, "So what? Who cares what they think?" This does not mean that I do not care about others. It means that I do not let their negative judgments hold me back or make me feel in some way bad or less.

---

**When someone judges you, say to yourself,
"So what? Who cares what they think?"**

---

By giving up judging others, we set ourselves free. We waste a tremendous amount of our power judging others. There is nothing wrong with being dissatisfied with others, but when we judge people we disconnect from the love in our heart. We often judge others because they do not think, feel, or react the way we would. As a result, we become impatient and frustrated. Our ability to love and have compassion goes straight out the window. Our judgments of others take us away from the patience of our true selves. This disconnection causes us to suffer, and we judge the other person even more.

When dissatisfied, we also judge others for their behavior. Though it is important to acknowledge what we want and what we think is right, it is not right to impose that on others. Everyone can't be the same. When people are different it does not make them wrong or less than us.

---

## What is best for one person
## is not best for all.

---

When we are judgmental, instead of finding ways to get what we need, we begin to focus on differences as the cause of our suffering. When we do not know our inner power to create, we mistakenly assume that it is the fault of the differences. We focus on judging the differences as if our way is the right way and theirs is wrong and bad. We become overly serious and negative.

It is amazing and wonderful how some people mellow out with age. They have been through life and discovered who they are. They are not so threatened by who other people are. You don't have to wait for the wisdom of a lifetime. As you learn to get what you need from the power within yourselves, you will be able to give up your judgments.

## 6. *Letting Go of Indecision*

You become stuck in indecision when you disconnect from your inner ability and strength to find your direction and persist. When stuck in indecision, you lose your ability to find your way in life or fully commit yourself to some task. You lose touch with your inner guidance and feel lost. You become too dependent on others to make up your mind or know what you want. Your will is too weak to make a decision. You forfeit your soul's power to follow through. You do not develop your inner power to make things happen by the power of giving your word or making a promise.

The major cause of indecision is discouragement and disappointments. When we are facing some of life's more difficult challenges, it is hard to make a decision and move forward. This often occurs because we have not successfully faced and dealt with the setbacks in our past. We still have lingering pain regarding mistakes or betrayals in our past. If we made a decision and the outcome was negative, naturally we will have difficulty making decisions in the future.

---

### Indecision means we have lingering pain regarding mistakes or betrayals in our past.

---

If we have trusted others and they have let us down, it becomes difficult to make a decision to trust others. If we have trusted ourselves in the past and gotten burned, when we feel something is really right and we want to make a strong commitment, we will suddenly back off and doubt our decision.

This tendency sabotages success enormously. Whenever we feel certain, we back off and can't make up our minds. If we are not sure, it is hard for others to depend on us as well. To avoid the possibility of failure, we choose to hold back.

In my own life, I decided at a certain point that I would rather experience a lot of failure than not to have tried. When I would hold myself back, I would feel bad anyway. Instead of passively feeling bad, I would just jump. I would make a decision, not because I was sure, but because a decision was needed for me to do something. Instead of being assured that I was doing the right thing, I was assured that if I wasn't doing the right thing I would find out and then know better what I did want to do.

---

### It is better to have failed than not to have tried.

---

To deal with a negative crowd, comedians will remind themselves that any show is rehearsal until you get on the *Tonight Show*. You do not know if something will work until you try. Gradually you know what works, and then you get a call from the *Tonight Show*. When I heard this in my thirties, it made a big difference to me. I decided that I did not care if everybody liked me or what I had to say. I followed my heart and learned from the feedback what worked and what did not.

As I developed and taught the *Men Are from Mars* ideas in the eighties, many people became upset with me. At times, I would start to doubt myself, but my persistence came back and gave me the strength to commit myself to the work I felt I was supposed to do.

For six years, people would get tremendous benefits from my ideas, but still relatively few people were coming to my seminars. Others wanted me to go back to teach what I was teaching before and not the new ideas contained in *Men Are from Mars.*

To overcome discouragement, I had to believe even more in my ideas. I gradually learned that before others would believe in me, I had to believe in me. When we get stuck in indecision, we become weak and others cannot rely on us or fully trust us.

---

**Before others will believe in you, you have to believe in yourself.**

---

As I kept experiencing that the insights from *Men Are from Mars* could actually save marriages, the ideas became accepted by millions. This is an example of how persistence and belief are fundamental to success. There are endless stories of other great successes that resulted from years of persistence and overcoming discouragement.

Without inner guidance, I would never have been able to persist. I felt the agony of not knowing and prayed to God to show me the way. Gradually it became clearer and clearer. With every new insight, I thanked God.

## Making Decisions

To be successful in the outer world requires making many decisions. Unless you can be comfortable making mistakes, it is very difficult. Besides accepting your mistakes, the next step is realizing that you do not have to figure everything out. In my company, I have to make many decisions every week. My simple way of handling them is first to hear them, think about what I want to do, and then forget it for a few days. Somehow it goes into the cosmic computer or intuition, and the answer comes out.

I have learned just to let go, and when it comes back, it is a go. Even then there are mistakes, but unless we make decisions and go for it we cannot grow and learn. The mistakes I make today may eventually lead to a solution down the road. It is foolish to think that we can figure out what to do all the time. Life is full of surprises. We need to put in the request and see how we feel a few days later.

---

### It is foolish to think we can always accurately predict the future.

---

If, however, you clearly do not know what to do, the best idea is not to do anything. Meanwhile, it is important to process all your feelings. As you process and release the stress around the difficult decision, the answer becomes obvious to you. Knowing what to do does not mean that you are absolutely sure of the outcome. Some people make the mistake of waiting until they are absolutely assured. This will slow you down tremendously. Making a decision means you know that your decision is the best you can come up with, and you are prepared to deal with the consequences.

---

### Knowing what to do does not mean you are absolutely sure of the outcome.

---

I am very careful about making decisions when it comes to committing myself to doing something. In most cases, when I say I will do something, I make sure to do it. This then strengthens the power of my word. One of the reason my books have been so helpful to others is that my word has power. Every word in my books is based on my personal experience. The insights in my books have worked for me and continue to work for me. There is nothing I have written that has not helped me and continued to be useful.

Once a woman approached Gandhi with a request. She asked him to tell her young son not to eat so much sugar. She believed that sugar was responsible for his hyperactivity and not good for him. Gandhi said he needed three months to prepare his statement.

In three months, the woman returned with her son. Gandhi told her son in very simple terms that eating too much sugar was not good for his health and that if he could stop he would be stronger and feel better. The boy agreed.

In private, the woman asked Gandhi why he needed three months to prepare such a simple response. Gandhi said before the suggestion would have any power he would have to experience its merit and believe it. By giving up sugar for three months, he was able to transfer the strength and confidence to the boy that he could do it as well.

When you live by your word, your word is stronger. When you always keep your promises, simply by giving your word you will draw in the power to manifest your word. When I get closer to a deadline, the clarity and power to make that deadline come.

---

### When you live by your word, your word is stronger.

---

This does not mean that we are weakening ourselves by not keeping our word. Sometimes we can't, and then we get another try. It is not that you "lose it all" because you do not fulfill a promise. It just means that you did not grow in power. Each time you succeed in keeping a promise, you will grow in the power to keep your word.

It is better to make a promise and break it than never to have made it. Some people are indecisive because they are afraid of disappointing others. This often stems from past experience of not being able to please a parent or from the fear of making a mistake and losing approval once it had been gained. Your soul has a chance to grow when you do your best to keep a promise. Sometimes you are not able to reach your goal. It is better to have tried and done your best.

---

**It is better to make a promise and break it
than never to have made it.**

---

If you make a decision and make a mistake, you can still process your feelings and come back to the self. By processing your feelings of discouragement and disappointment, you will gain power. If you stay on the fence and you do not commit or make a decision, you disconnect from your true self. Not only do you not gain power, but you actually become weaker.

The best time to change your word is while you are in the process of trying to keep it. Rather than hold back, make the jump. Then if you can't do it, change midstream. At least when you are moving toward what you think is right, you are connected to your inner self, which is strong, persistent, directed, and purposeful.

## 7. Letting Go of Procrastination

You procrastinate when you have disconnected from your innate ability to accomplish what you have decided to do. You are unable to get started until you have no choice. You put off or postpone action because you believe that you are not ready or prepared. With procrastination, you forfeit your ability to overcome life's challenges. Procrastination occurs when courage is weak.

---

**We put off or postpone action because we mistakenly believe that we are not ready.**

---

Courage is like a muscle. It cannot grow unless you face a challenge and then push into it. If you do your best, you will begin to experience that God's angels will always come to help. This is the rule: God helps those who help themselves. If you do not move, the energy that can help you to do what you have to do cannot begin to flow.

Nothing can get done if you do not begin. When you put will into action, power can begin to flow and your creative juices are once again realized. You cannot realize your inner powers if you do not exercise them. Courage grows by taking risks. When you postpone action, you not only suppress your inner powers, gifts, and talents, but you suffer.

---

**When you put will into action, power can begin to flow and your creative juices are once again realized.**

---

The two greatest causes of suffering in life are not loving and not doing what you want to do. When you do not push ahead to do what your heart is wanting you to do, it is like taking a knife and stabbing yourself again and again. The pain of failure you seek to avoid is always much less than the pain of not being true to yourself.

We procrastinate when we are worried about something. We generally feel helpless to do what we have said we are going to do. No matter what, we can't seem to do it. To break through this block, we need to realize that the answer lies in changing our feelings.

By turning inside and exploring your inner feelings, you will be able to release the negative emotions and feel what you want.

When you can fully feel your inner passion, procrastination goes away. By getting out of your head and coming from your passion, you can break through. One great phrase to remember is: "Don't think, just do it. Do it now." As you say this to yourself, push yourself into action.

---

**"Don't think, just do it. Do it now."**

---

Another tool that has helped me is setting my intentions. Rather than having to push at all, after each meditation, just keep visualizing yourself doing what you want to do. Imagine having the good feelings of relief and accomplishment. Through this process, you will experience the amazing organizing power of setting your intentions. In a few days, you realize that you are doing what you wanted to be doing.

Another reason some people put off going for what is important to them is that they believe they are not ready. They believe that if they were ready, they would have no fears, worries, and anxieties. This is not true. No matter how ready you are, you will always have fears. Your fears diminish and go away as you begin. If you wait for them to go away, you will never get started.

## 8. Letting Go of Perfectionism

When you disconnect from your innate ability to accept that life is not and can never be perfect, you get stuck in the desire to be perfect. As a result, you expect too much from yourself or others. Everything must be perfect, and it never is. When you expect perfection, you are never happy or content. You are too demanding and forfeit any grace in your life. Everything is measured and compared. When nothing is good enough, you cannot freely give and receive love.

> When things have to be perfect,
> you cannot rest and enjoy
> what you have or who you are.

The need to be perfect is a false need. It begins during childhood when we try to be perfect for our parents. We make the mistake of believing that we must be perfect to make our parents happy. Every child is born with the healthy desire and longing to please parents.

> The need to please others is healthy, but can
> easily become twisted and unhealthy.

When children are unable to succeed in pleasing their parents, the need to please turns into the need to be perfect. As children, we are so happy when are parents are happy with us, and we are so sad when we have disappointed them. To please them, we begin trying to adjust and correct ourselves in ways that deny who we are. The more we have to give up our true selves to please our parents, the more we feel we have to be perfect.

> When children are unable to succeed in
> pleasing their parents, the need to please
> turns into the need to be perfect.

As children, we commonly experience upsets at the most inconvenient times. As a result, we do not get the positive message that our feelings are okay. A child needs the freedom to feel and experience all the different levels of emotions and then gradually learn to manage them. If a parent does not approve of a particular emotion, then for sure the child will feel inadequate in some way for feeling that emotion. To win the parents' approval, they seek to suppress their feelings.

> ### As children we need to receive the message that our negative emotions are okay.

As children, we are supposed to make many mistakes to learn our lessons, but often we get the message that if we make mistakes something is wrong with us. As a result, we do not get the positive message that it is okay to make mistakes. When we feel as if we cannot make mistakes, we are well on the way to feeling that we have to be perfect.

> ### As children, we need to receive the message that making mistakes is okay.

If we happen to be gifted or talented in some special way, this can also lead to perfectionism. Since we are talented, we get special attention for being outstanding. We become accustomed to feeling this special praise for being so good. This makes it more difficult for us to risk doing things that we are not so good at.

We are used to pleasing our parents by being the best, so we cannot bear disappointing our parents by trying other things and not being the best. Unless we go through the process of struggling to achieve something and making mistakes, we do not get the important experience of failing and still being loved.

> ### It is essential that a child have the experience of failure to learn that it is okay to make mistakes.

The result of not feeling capable of pleasing our parents is a lasting feeling of inadequacy. Although perfectionists may be the most accomplished in their fields, they are rarely good enough for themselves. Rather than love what they have created, perfectionists sometimes don't like their work at all.

> **Although perfectionists may be the most accomplished in their fields, they are rarely good enough for themselves.**

To get a sense of the underlying feeling of inadequacy that determines many of your surface feelings and desires, make a recording of your voice in conversation. After hearing their voices, most people become very embarrassed and don't like it. Sometimes they can't even believe that is how they sound.

The reason this is such a powerful experience is that we have tremendous defenses inside to compensate for childhood feelings of inadequacy. We have built up an image of who we are in resistance to negative messages we may have received at different stages.

To hear ourselves because we sound different, brings up our early fears that we are not good enough and that we will be rejected. As a result, we feel tremendously embarrassed. It is hard to accept ourselves even though others who are listening think we sound wonderful.

> **To hear ourselves because we sound different, brings up our early fears that we are not good enough.**

If there are negative feelings lurking inside, listening to the tape will immediately bring them up. Listening to yourself in this way can be a great trigger to bringing up these feelings, and then you have the opportunity to go back in time to process them.

### Seeking Perfection

In most cases, we seek and demand perfection because we are deficient in vitamin G1. We need to fill up our spiritual love tank. When we are not feeling perfection in our lives because we are not spiritually connected, we look for that perfection in the outer world.

The outer world will never be perfect, but we can satisfy this need to be perfect by feeling our connection with God or a higher power. When we are connecting with more, we do not feel that we have to be more, do more, or have more to be satisfied. When we want what we have, we can feel our healthy desire to be, do, and have more without having to be perfect.

---

**It is healthy to want more,
but not healthy to expect perfection.**

---

This desire for perfection is only unhealthy when we look to ourselves to be perfect in the outer world. When we look inside for perfection, we are trying to discover more of our potential, and that is healthy. Although nothing is ever perfect, we can taste perfection in the process of perfecting or improving what we have. As we look within and draw in greater power, we feel that our lives, although not perfect, are unfolding perfectly.

## 9. Letting Go of Resentment

You become resentful when you disconnect from your ability to give your love and support. In most cases, you feel you have given more and not received what you deserve in return. You withhold your love because something happened that is not fair. Closing your heart in this way, you forfeit your power to create what you want and disconnect from your feelings of love and generosity.

---

**When resentment sets in,
we are not free to give our love.**

---

Although we complain that we were deprived, when we stop being willing to give our love, we close our hearts to receiving more. We can only receive more love when our hearts are open. Sometimes we are so resentful that we secretly will not let others give to us. Our hidden message to the world is: "You are too late. Nothing can make me happy now."

Since we tend to focus on what we did not get with resentment, we miss other opportunities to give and receive. By not forgiving, you continue to live in the past. You break the natural flow of give and take when you become too conditional with your love. Although you may seek to punish others, it is you who is punished. Building a wall of resentment around your heart, you may withhold your love, but you cannot let more love in.

---

**With resentment, we tend to focus on the negative and miss other opportunities to give and receive.**

---

Resentment makes us feel as if we have nothing left to give and stops us from giving more. Yet, if we do not give, we cannot receive. The way around this dilemma is to focus on another love tank. As you shift to filling up another love tank, you discover that you can give and receive love again.

Roseanne continued to resent her ex-husband for leaving her. She had given him the best years of her life, and he left her to marry a younger woman. She felt deprived of love and support throughout the marriage, but when she thought about his being happy in his new marriage, she felt resentful.

To heal her block, she took time for herself. She started filling up her love tank with vitamin S (self-love). Rather than dwell on what he was experiencing, she focused on doing what she wanted to do. In addition, she joined a support group of parents without partners. Just being with peers began to fill up her love tank for vitamin P2 (peer support). She then planned a vacation with some friends just for fun. In this way, she began filling up her love tank for vitamin F (family, friends, and fun).

She went on a cruise. One day, she got sick. When her friends looked in on her, she said she was fine and just needed to rest. For the rest of the day, while her friends were off having a good time, she suddenly felt really alone and hurt. Everything was getting better, but then she experienced a setback.

By using the feeling letter technique, Roseanne linked her feelings of hurt and deprivation back to her relationship with her mother. Growing up, she was the oldest and was expected to care for her five younger siblings. She even felt as if she had to take care of her mother as well. Her mother had difficulty breathing and was sick in bed most of the time, while her father was gone at work.

Her parents were very loving, but just not capable of giving Roseanne the time, attention, and help that she needed. She was too young to be a parent, but somebody had to do it. She felt responsible for everyone and was appreciated for that. She could push her feelings to the side and take care of everyone. She became strong and didn't even realize what she had missed.

That day, as she felt deprived of her friends' support, she was able to feel for the first time how deprived she would have felt as a child if someone had cared to ask her about her feelings. She discovered a Pandora's box of feelings and emotions.

She realized that she was jealous of other kids who got to have fun. She was hurt that nobody cared about how she felt, or what she needed. Her mother or her younger siblings got all the attention. As she explored these and other emotions, she was filling up her love tank for vitamin P1 (parents' love). Although she always knew her parents loved her, by doing the exercise, she could imagine her mother hearing her feelings with understanding, love, and compassion. She had missed that. She imagined her mother holding her and giving her that support and felt much better as a result.

In these different ways, Roseanne took all the right steps to fill her love tanks. Her resentment about her circumstances lessened and her life dramatically got better. She had more fun, made more friends, had several romantic flings, and then settled down with a very charming man who did not neglect her. Although she did not like the divorce, she was later grateful for the healing she got and the new, wonderful life she created.

To break the lock resentment puts on our hearts, we must recognize that we are doing it to ourselves. Yes, it may be that the world is unfair, but to respond by withholding your love does not make that any better. It only makes matters worse for you.

---

**Withholding your love does not make anything better.**

---

If you find yourself withholding your love, realize that you are creating the problem. Realize that when you resent you are now the problem. You not only send out negative energy to others, but that is what you will attract to yourself.

Ultimately, when we feel resentful, it is because we are not aware of our power to create what we want. The pain of deprivation that gives rise to resentment increases with the belief that we cannot get what we need. As we take back our power to create our lives, resentment drops away. Resentment is just another form of blame and judgment.

---

**Ultimately, when we feel resentful, it is because we are not aware of our power to create what we want.**

---

Resentment is a clear sign that you have been giving too much in the wrong direction. Rather than blame others for not giving back to you, take time to love yourself and fill up your other love tanks. By clearly recognizing your responsibility for giving too much, you are free to accept the problem without pointing fingers. This insight is important not only because it sends you in the right direction, but because it helps to release any guilt.

---

**Resentment is a clear sign that you have been giving too much in the wrong direction.**

---

Most people who give too much do it because they want to make others happy. They try to be perfect and end up giving too much. They expect others to do the same for them. The recognition that they are withholding their love makes them feel even worse.

To avoid feeling guilty, they have to justify why they feel resentful and need to withhold love. They keep reinforcing the idea that life is unfair, that they have been neglected and deprived. Although true, these justifications are limited beliefs. As we have seen in earlier chapters, if we apply the secrets of personal success, we can get what we need and create what we want. Life does not seem so unfair as we begin to experience our power to create.

## 10. Letting Go of Self-Pity

You experience self-pity when you have disconnected from your innate ability to appreciate and give thanks for the blessings and successes in your life. When you focus on what you are missing, you lose touch with your ability to appreciate what you have and do not recognize the many opportunities available to you. Although it is important to feel empathy and compassion for your setbacks and losses, you do not have to forfeit the inner joy that comes from an attitude of gratitude.

---

**When stuck in self-pity, you lose touch with
your ability to appreciate what you have.**

---

The cause of self-pity is often lack of attention. A child who is deprived of attention will often seek to get any kind of attention. Though every child needs to be heard and receive empathy, some children have a greater need than the parents can satisfy. As a result, these children learn to paint a bigger and more dramatic problem to get attention.

Often with dramatic or sensitive children, parents make the mistake of trying to ignore their children's negative feelings, hoping they will go away. Unfortunately these feelings do not go away, and in many cases, they become more intense. Such children get in the habit of painting a negative picture of their day so that they get attention.

---

**When our feelings are ignored, we tend to
make them bigger and more dramatic.**

---

If such children had a good day and everything went great, they would be ignored. To remedy this situation, people need to nurture their need to be heard, but also focus on giving and getting positive attention. They should take time to listen to their feelings and experience their sensitive hurts. Instead of feeling dependent on others to hear them, they need to take more responsibility. They should not expect others to hear their negative feelings until they have first written them out. By taking responsibility to hear their own pain, they will break their dependency on negative attention.

Another useful approach is to practice not complaining or sympathizing with other people's complaining for a whole day at a time. Notice how hard it is not to complain or say something negative about someone or some circumstance. Instead of speaking about your negativity, keep a journal and write it out. This will help to train your mind to recognize that you can get positive attention, and you can nurture your inner feelings yourself.

---

### Give up complaining for a day at a time.

---

Ultimately sensitive souls sense that they should have more in this world, and unless taught how to get it, will feel as if they are missing out. To release the feeling that we are being excluded from the party in some way, we have to arrive. Rather than feeling left out, we need to realize that what we were seeking outside ourselves is all within. When we take time to get what we need and feel our spiritual connection, our tendency to feel left out will be diminished.

By connecting with the source of fulfillment within, you do not have to get lost in the outer world, hungering for what is already inside. To let go of self-pity, we need to experience that what we think we are missing on the outside is already within ourselves. To rise out of the pit of self-pity, we need to remind ourselves again and again of the unlimited possibilities that await as we begin to turn inward.

One of the big problems with self-pity is that we not only miss opportunities for more, but we reject them as well. As if to justify our misery, we stay there. We believe that we have missed out, and nothing can make up for it. We feel sorry for ourselves, and we do not want anything to change that.

---

### One of the big problems with self-pity is that we not only miss opportunities for more, but we reject them as well.

---

We also miss the opportunity to help ourselves. Although we do not believe anyone can help us, another part of us believes that we can only be saved by someone else. We expect someone out there to make up for what we are missing and make us happy. As you begin to believe in yourself, this tendency will change. As you begin to feel your power to pull yourself back up, you will realize all along you had the power, and no one can do it but you.

Ultimately the tendency to self-pity is released when you are able to feel your anger with others who have rejected and excluded you and then forgive them. To feel that anger, you have to begin feeling other emotions besides hurt. By healing your inner feelings, you will begin to move back to your true self and trust that you can always get what you need and create what you want.

## 11. Letting Go of Confusion

You become confused when you have disconnected from your innate ability to see clearly, understand, or make sense of what life presents you. Every positive or negative experience has the potential to teach you something useful that you didn't know before and to reinforce and strengthen the positive qualities within.

In confusion, we assume that something important is missing. Instead of being open to finding the answer, we think that we have to have it now. When we think something is missing, we focus on feeling like a victim of circumstances. It is then easy to panic and assume the worst.

---

**When we do not understand what is going on, it is easy to panic and assume the worst.**

---

By looking for and expecting clear and definite answers right away, we miss the bigger picture that life is an unfolding process of learning to be all that we can be. We forfeit our inner confidence that we are doing the right thing when we require clear and definite answers to our questions.

---

**To let go of confusion,
we need to learn to live with a question
and not require answers right away.**

---

Life will always present us with challenges and changes that will push us to our limit to understand. Particularly when bad or tragic things happen or seem to be happening, we do not understand why they are happening to us. Without a clear understanding that life presents challenges and obstacles to "good" people as well as "bad" people, we begin to think we are bad. We often stay confused to avoid feeling bad or responsible in some way.

When bad or painful things happen, we cannot understand why they are happening or what good could come from them. I remember when my first marriage failed. I was so devastated. I cried to God, "How could you let this happen? Nothing good will ever come from this."

## Learning from Divorce

Little did I know then that because my first wife and I divorced, I would reunite with my soul mate, Bonnie, and we would get married. Bonnie and I had dated years before. I had loved her, but I was not ready to get married. If my first marriage had not failed, I would never have reunited with her and created the wonderful life and family we have today. Although the failure of my first marriage was painful, I am incredibly grateful for the new life it gave me.

In addition, I am grateful for lessons learned from analyzing why that marriage failed. Although at the time I felt like a victim, in retrospect I can see so many gifts that came from healing from that experience. Possibly the most important is that after my failure, I reevaluated everything I knew about relationships and began to realize my mistakes. A friend approached me and said, "You know a lot about relationships, but you still do not recognize men and women are different."

Well, because I was so devastated, I was open to looking at my mistakes. I took that message in and gradually developed all the ideas in *Men Are from Mars, Women Are from Venus*. Not only was this one of the best career shifts I have experienced, but it gave me the insight to make my marriage work today. All this came from the struggle I went through to heal my heart after a painful breakup.

---

**When we are devastated, we are usually more open to learning new things.**

---

Now when setbacks occur and I do not know why or what to do, I am much more assured that something good will come of it. It always does. This does not mean that I sit back and let it happen. It is just the opposite. I can be fully engaged in the process of actively looking for the answers.

When we become confused, it is often because we are not able to accept what is right before us and trust that things will get better even if we do not know how. The wisdom of age tells us that everything always works out, often in ways that are far better than we could ever imagine.

---

**When we are confused, things always seem worse and more urgent than they are.**

---

To be free of confusion, take some time to reflect on the many times when you thought things were really urgent or something terrible was going to happen and it did not. So much positive energy is wasted feeling confused rather than trusting that things will work out.

## Life Lessons

All setbacks and unexpected obstacles will always present life's lessons to be learned. Although you may be doing everything right, you cannot avoid the challenges. Once you have begun to grow from life's challenges, you understand how they have helped to mold you into what you have become.

One of the ways to begin looking at your life lessons is to imagine that you have achieved all your goals. As you feel grateful for the support you have received, go back and appreciate all the challenges that made you grow and become stronger. As you cultivate an attitude of gratitude for all the lessons learned from life's challenges, you will become free of confusion and experience great wisdom.

---

**Practice giving thanks for the lessons learned
from your past.**

---

You cannot stop the world from upsetting you at times, but you can learn how to use every upset or setback to bring you back to the wisdom of your true self. You can learn to use every negative experience to strengthen and empower you. Every challenging experience can assist you in discovering your inner gifts and powers.

---

**You can use every negative experience to
strengthen and empower you.**

---

When you go to the gym, you do not work out by lifting easy weights within your comfort zone. Your muscles need to be challenged if they are to grow stronger. To build muscle, you must push beyond your comfort zone, break down your muscles, and then, after you give them some rest, they will grow back stronger. Likewise, to grow in personal success you need to be challenged. As you meet each challenge by coming back to the wisdom of your true self, you will grow in your ability to achieve personal success.

Even your bones need to be stressed if they are to remain strong. When astronauts go into space and experience no gravity, their bones will seriously weaken and even break within a few days unless they continue to put stress on them. In a similar way, setbacks in life serve an important role in making us strong, but only if we know how to handle them.

Before a butterfly emerges from its cocoon, it goes through a great struggle to break free. If a compassionate observer was to cut open the cocoon to free the struggling butterfly, the struggle would be quickly finished but the butterfly would experience certain consequences. It would soon die, because it would be unable to fly. What the helpful observer did not know was that the struggle was necessary for the butterfly to strengthen its wings in order to fly. Without the struggle, the butterfly will be weak and die.

---

**Unless a butterfly struggles to break free, it will never fly.**

---

In life, we think our challenge is to change the outer world. We think the enemy is on the outside. Our true battlefield is within ourselves. Whenever we are stuck in any of the twelve blocks to personal success, our real challenge is within. By winning our inner battle and overcoming our blocks, we are able to come back to our true selves. Each time we win this battle, we increase our ability to experience love, joy, power, and peace.

---

**Life will never be free of challenges, but our ability to meet these challenges will continue to grow.**

---

This important recognition frees you to shift your focus from what is wrong to what you can learn. Instead of panicking when we are confused, we are able to pose the question and then confidently look for the answer.

## 12. Letting Go of Guilt

You become stuck in guilt when you have disconnected from your innate ability to love yourself and forgive your mistakes. Feeling different degrees of shame after making a mistake is a good thing, but it is not good when the shame does not go away after you recognize and learn from your mistake. Lingering guilt robs you of your natural state of innocence and keeps you from feeling a healthy sense of worthiness and entitlement.

---

**Lingering guilt robs you
of your natural state of innocence.**

---

Instead of knowing and acting from what you want, you act too much for others, you accommodate too much, and you do not feel comfortable asking for or asserting your wants and needs. You are a good and nice person, but you have a hard time saying no to others. You care too much about what others think about you. You forfeit your self-esteem each time you deny your needs to please others.

Paula had it all. She had the house, the car, the education, the husband, the kids, and the great job with flexible hours. On the outside, she had it all, but on the inside she was not happy. Something was missing. When she took a personal success workshop, she realized her block. She felt guilty that she wasn't happy. She felt guilty that having it all just wasn't enough.

She discovered that to have it all, she had given up who she was. She had become someone else. She was always happy to make others happy, but had never really looked at what she wanted. She had done all the right things to make her parents proud and her husband and kids happy, but she wasn't aware of what she really wanted.

The thought of saying no to others or disappointing them was practically unbearable. She hated to disappoint others and would worry all the time about what other people thought about her. These were all symptoms of being stuck in guilt. When she took some time to process her feelings of anger about her life along with her guilt, her fears started to disappear.

---

### Guilt makes us overly giving and nice to others.

---

Larry was also stuck in guilt. He felt guilt because he was convicted of robbery. He had hurt others, and now he was serving time. He experienced another kind of guilt: the guilt we feel when we really do something wrong to others. In a healing workshop at his prison, he was able first to feel his remorse and then to cleanse his soul of guilt. Although he was guilty of the crime, having felt remorse, he had to release his pain and love himself again.

Being stuck in guilt keeps us from loving ourselves. Either we turn off our feelings because it is too painful, or the guilt just eats at us day by day. Fortunately there is a healing alternative. Larry learned to feel the pain of his unworthiness and self-blame and eventually forgave himself. He was able to give himself another chance. He spent his sentence preparing to create a better life for himself and felt grateful for the opportunity to give back what he had taken unfairly.

Feeling guilty of a crime is the first step, if we are guilty. The next step is to forgive ourselves and to try to make amends if possible. Most people who feel guilt can't shake it. It grips hold and does not let go. The reason many criminals go back out and commit more crimes is that they have not learned to feel and release their guilt.

Rather than feel the pain of their shame for making a mistake, they suppress their feelings altogether and disconnect from their inner conscience, which knows the difference between good and bad, right and wrong. Without a connection to their inner feelings, they justify future crimes by the suffering they had to endure in prison.

## Why We Get Stuck in Guilt

Whether we are guilty of a crime or just overly responsible for others, we can easily get caught in guilt. Some people carry guilty feelings an entire lifetime for stealing bubble gum at the drugstore, or for saying something mean and hurting in grade school. Little mistakes can haunt us for a lifetime, when we don't know how to get unstuck from guilt.

The tendency to feel guilty increases when negative things happen to us before the age of eighteen. The younger we are, the more vulnerable we are to feeling bad. Particularly up to about nine years old, children will feel guilty for any abuse they experience or even witness. Children feel that when negative things happen they are in some way responsible and therefore unworthy of good things. Though they are not responsible, they feel unworthy and guilty. Parents can heal the unworthiness children feel by taking responsibility for what happens to the children.

---

**Children will feel guilty for any abuse they experience or even witness.**

---

When parents argue or fight or are just generally disappointed and unhappy, a sensitive child will absorb their negative feelings and feel responsible. To the extent that our parents did not take responsibility to get what they needed to be happy, as children we begin to shoulder that burden.

Some parents even actively reinforce this guilt. The child is made to feel bad or responsible for how the parents feel. These sorts of messages are confusing enough for adults and much more so for kids. The way a child grows up with a healthy sense of innocence is to be surrounded by the positive message of parents' taking responsibility for their own feelings and not blaming their children.

To free ourselves from guilt, we must understand innocence. Innocence means that we are worthy of love. All children are innocent, even when they make mistakes, because they do not know better. They may make trouble, but the wise parent knows they are just children and they are doing their best. This seems obvious.

---

**Innocence means that we are worthy of love.**

---

As we get older, we need to realize that we still deserve to be loved even though we make mistakes. To acknowledge a mistake and then correct ourselves, we do not need to hold on to guilt or shame. We just need to feel it, and then come back to a sincere desire to learn from and grow from our mistake.

We need to recognize that even though we make mistakes and are guilty of the mistakes, who we are is really innocent. Being stuck in guilt is really the inability to forgive ourselves. By releasing our feelings of shame, we get back to feeling innocent and responsible for our mistakes.

When we recognize that we made a mistake, we naturally feel ashamed that we did not know better. Although we may think we should have known better, we did not. Ultimately people always do what they think is the best thing to do. No one really goes around thinking, "How can I make a bunch of stupid mistakes?"

---

**Ultimately people always do what they think is the best thing to do.**

---

Self-forgiveness is the recognition that we are still innocent deep inside, and we are worthy of love. Innocence is a part of who we truly are. The place we come back to when we release shame is innocence. When we are able to forgive ourselves, once again we feel worthy of good things.

To achieve success in life, we must feel worthy. Without self-love and a sense of worthiness, we can never let our dreams out. If we feel unworthy, as soon as we begin to feel our true wants, we begin to suppress them with the belief that we are not deserving. When we feel stuck in guilt, we tend to sacrifice too much for the people we care about and do not think enough about ourselves.

## Letting Go of Your Blocks

Overcoming the twelve blocks to personal success will not only allow you to enjoy your outer success, but will also help you to connect to your true self. When you learn to experience inner peace, love, joy, and power, you will most effectively be able to attract and create what you want in your life. Without giving up who you are and by doing what you love, you will be able to get what you really want.

Although these insights are simple to understand, they are not so easy to master. Just as outer success requires time, energy, and commitment, so does personal success. We must not only change our thinking and look within ourselves, but we must seek out and heal the hidden feelings behind each of these blocks.

In the next chapter, you will learn practical and spiritual insights, methods, and practices for getting back to your true self, and then getting what you need to remove your blocks. By practicing the different exercises and meditations for removing the blocks, you will create the fertile ground to plant the seeds of your true desires. As you learn to remove each of the blocks, you will immediately experience your inner power to attract and create what you want.

# CHAPTER 17

# *Practices and Healing Meditations*

W
ITH A DEEPER understanding that you are responsible for your blocks, you are then ready to dive into
a variety of practices and healing meditations to
remove the twelve blocks. For each block, there is a process
to help you feel and release the negative emotions as you
come back to connecting with your true self. In addition, a
special meditation prayer when practiced regularly will begin
to open the channels for God's grace to help you remove
your blocks.

## *The Iceberg Effect*

The basic technique for removing blocks is to feel the underlying emotions associated with the block. Imagine an iceberg.
Only ten percent is above water and the rest is below. By simply feeling the block, you will stay on the surface. By looking

for the feelings, emotions, and wants under the surface, you will remove the block. When you are blocked, you are upset about many things at once, and most of your feelings are hidden.

---

**When you are blocked, you are upset about many things at once.**

---

Let's say I bump a particular man by mistake, and he becomes very angry with me. He may think he is just angry with me, but he is also angry about other things. If at that time everything was great in his life, he would not have felt so angry. Let's look at the other feelings he may be having just under the surface of his conscious awareness.

He is angry about my mistake, but he is also angry that he lost his job.

Under his anger is sadness that he doesn't have steady income.

Under his sadness is fear. He is afraid that he will not get a job or ever solve his problems. He is afraid that his wife will not love him.

Under his fear is sorrow. He is sorry that he can't find his way to be a success.

On the surface, he may be blaming me for bumping him, but underneath the tip of the iceberg are many feelings. When a person has a big reason to be upset, like losing a job, it is easy to understand the deeper levels of emotions, and we can be very understanding of his pain.

## *Create a Big Reason to Be Upset*

If we create a big reason to be upset, we, too, will easily be able to understand the deeper levels and be understanding and compassionate. Although this is a simple idea, it is the fundamental method for letting go of blocks.

---

**If we create a big reason to be upset,
it is easier to feel and to understand
the deeper levels.**

---

When you feel a block, create a big reason to be upset. Imagine going back in time and feeling the emotions that are associated with the block. If you need to fill the love tank for vitamin P1, imagine yourself interacting with a parent. If you need to fill the love tank for vitamin F, imagine yourself interacting with a family member or friend.

To process a block, turn back the clock. Imagine yourself at a time in your past when you were vulnerable and able to feel more intensely. It is always easier to process feelings in the past. Even if you feel fine now about your past, go back and experience what you felt before you felt fine.

---

**To process a block, turn back the clock.**

---

If you are blocked, you are not fully feeling your emotions. This means that you are not connected to the emotional part of you. To find that part, you must become like a child again. You must feel the tender and vulnerable emotions that are childlike. By imagining yourself to be like a child, you can easily create a big reason to feel upset.

---

**To heal emotional blocks, you must feel
childlike emotions.**

---

If you can't recall an incident, you have to invent a story and pretend that it happened. Most people can remember at least a few painful or difficult moments from childhood. All it takes is one event to be able to connect with the painful feelings you felt as a child.

## How to Process Your Past

It is easy to process your past. With a little practice, you will have discovered your inner power to remove all the blocks. There are four basic steps:

1. Identify your block and link it to the past.
2. Write a feeling letter.
3. Write a response letter.
4. Write a connection letter.

When you learn to process your past and let go of your blocks, your history will lose its power to hold you back and instead give you important support to create the future you wish. Let's explore each of these steps in greater detail.

## The Feeling Letter

The feeling letter format is a little different for each of the twelve blocks. By using the following chart, you can determine which emotions will provide the best release and in what sequence. This chart is particularly helpful in the beginning. After a while, when you gain emotional fluency, you will not need to use it.

# THE FEELINGS CHART

| Block | General Feeling | Healing Emotions |
|---|---|---|
| 1. Blame | Betrayed | Angry |
| 2. Depression | Abandoned | Sad |
| 3. Anxiety | Uncertain | Afraid |
| 4. Indifference | Powerless | Sorry |
| 5. Judgment | Dissatisfied | Frustrated |
| 6. Indecision | Discouraged | Disappointed |
| 7. Procrastination | Helpless | Worried |
| 8. Perfectionism | Inadequate | Embarrassed |
| 9. Resentment | Deprived | Envious |
| 10. Self-pity | Excluded | Hurt |
| 11. Confusion | Hopeless | Scared |
| 12. Guilt | Unworthiness | Ashamed |

Using the chart, you can create the appropriate feeling letter by exploring the emotion linked to the block and then the next three emotions on the chart.

For example, to release block one (blame), you would recall a time you felt betrayed and then explore the four emotions of anger, sadness, fear, and sorrow. Or to release block twelve (guilt), you would recall a time you felt unworthy and then explore the four emotions of shame, anger, sadness, and fear.

## Twelve Feeling Letter Formats

Every time you write a feeling letter to remove a block, it generally takes four different emotions in succession to create a complete release. Sometimes it may be necessary to skip around the feeling chart to discover your unexpressed emotions, but usually the suggested format will suffice. Each of the twelve feeling letter formats will assist you in finding the key emotions which need to be felt. The twelve feeling letter formats are:

1. For blame: recall a time when you felt betrayed, and then explore anger, sadness, fear, and sorrow.

2. For depression: recall a time when you felt abandoned, and then explore sadness, fear, sorrow, and frustration.

3. For anxiety: recall a time when you felt uncertain, and then explore fear, sorrow, frustration, and disappointment.

4. For indifference: recall a time when you felt powerless, and then explore sorrow, frustration, disappointment, and worry.

5. For judgment: recall a time when you felt dissatisfied, and then explore frustration, disappointment, worry, and embarrassment.

6. For indecision: recall a time when you felt discouraged, and then explore disappointment, worry, embarrassment, and jealousy.

7. For procrastination: recall a time when you felt helpless, and then explore worry, embarrassment, jealousy, and hurt.

8. For perfectionism: recall a time when you felt

inadequate, and then explore embarrassment, jealousy, hurt, and panic.

9. For resentment: recall a time when you felt deprived, and then explore jealousy, hurt, panic, and shame.

10. For self-pity: recall a time when you felt excluded, and then explore hurt, panic, shame, and anger.

11. For confusion: recall a time when you felt hopeless, and then explore panic, shame, anger; and sadness.

12. For guilt: recall a time when you felt unworthy, and then explore shame, anger, sadness, and fear.

## *Writing a Feeling Letter*

Once you have selected the four appropriate emotions, decide to whom you want to address your letter. Generally, when you address a feeling letter to your parents, you are able to release the deepest feelings. Even if you did not know a parent, you have a relationship with your mother or father in your mind and heart. You can always imagine talking to them. You may also choose to write a feeling letter to anyone who has bothered you or to anyone to whom you feel a connection and whose support you would like.

It is fine to write your letter to a parent sharing the upset feelings you have about other things. To write a feeling letter to a parent doesn't mean you have to blame them. In some cases, people do not want to blame a parent, because they think that would mean they did not love the parent. This is clearly an indication of suppressed emotion that needs to be expressed. If we cannot feel angry, it is a sign that early on in life we learned that it was not loving and that our parents did not deserve it.

To be angry does not mean that your parents were bad or unloving. They did the best they could, but no one can give a child everything the child needs. Getting angry and being upset is an important part of growing up. Learning to manage and release anger, rather than suppress it with reasons why you shouldn't get angry, is essential.

Sometimes people don't write letters because they have let it go. It is water under the bridge. They may feel that everything is fine now or they really don't care. In this case, remember how you felt before you patched things up or stopped caring. Go back to when you had the feelings and relive that moment, giving yourself the ability to write out your feelings.

Once you have determined to whom you are going to write the letter, a feeling letter looks like this:

## THE FEELING LETTER FORMAT

*Dear ———,*
  1. *"I feel betrayed when . . . "*
  2. *"I am angry that . . . "*
  3. *"I am sad that . . . "*
  4. *"I am afraid that . . . "*
  5. *"I am sorry that . . . "*
  6. *"I want . . . "*

After selecting the appropriate feeling and emotions for a block, use the lead-in phrases to assist you in expressing them. At the end of your letters, express what you want. For each of the levels, write for at least two to three minutes. In this way, after ten to fifteen minutes, you will have completed the letter.

This feeling letter is for your own healing. It is not necessary to send it to someone. Sharing your feelings from a more resolved and loving perspective when you believe your feelings will be heard is always a good idea.

## Writing the Response Letter

After writing out your feelings and wants, imagine getting the ideal response. For example, if the person to whom you are writing upset you in some way, write out the response that would make you feel heard, understood, and more forgiving. If you were disappointed or betrayed in any way, have that person make promises to make you feel better. Reflect on what that person could do to make you feel better. Maybe you primarily need encouragement or reassurance that you are loved and special. Write whatever you need to hear. As you write out the response you want to hear, imagine how it would make you feel and let those feelings come up.

Even if the person in real life would not say those positive words and follow up with supportive action, write them anyway. Say the things you deserved to hear, and you will experience the positive feelings you missed out on. By generating positive feelings in this way, you will be reconnecting to the part of your true self from which you disconnected at that time. Even though that person is not really giving you the support you need, by writing out the response you would have wanted to hear, you are giving yourself that love and support.

Imagination is very powerful. Most of the time, when we are upset, we are imagining things to be worse than they are. Think about all the times you thought things were worse than they were. If you are not achieving personal success, some part of you is not fully connected to your true self. By giving yourself the responses from the world that you didn't get, you will discover your inner connection.

The response letter format is always the same for each of

the feeling letters. It is useful because while we are in our feelings, it is sometimes hard to know what we need. The lead-in phrase will pull out the loving messages you need to hear.

Use each of the following lead-in phrases to write a response that would make you feel heard and supported. Feel free to add any additional comments that would make you feel better.

## THE RESPONSE LETTER FORMAT

*Dear* ——:
1. *"I apologize . . . "*
2. *"Please forgive me . . . "*
3. *"I understand . . . "*
4. *"I promise . . .*
5. *"I love . . . " "You are . . . " "You deserve . . . "*
                        *With love,*

## *Writing the Connection Letter*

After writing out the response that you want, imagine how you would feel if you got that response and write it out. By taking this important time to express the positive feelings you have generated, you will become more centered and connected to your true self. By taking a negative experience and then generating positive feelings from it, you will no longer resist looking at your past.

When you are able to heal, learn from, and grow from your past, you are no longer attracted to situations that repeat the past. You are free to create whatever you want. By linking current negative feelings to your past and generating positive feelings, you hold the power to remove the blocks and move on to create whatever you want.

These seven lead-in phrases will assist you in drawing up and generating positive feelings to assist you in finding and staying connected to your true self.

## THE CONNECTION LETTER FORMAT

*Dear* ————:
1. *"Your love makes me feel . . . "*
2. *"I now understand . . . "*
3. *"I forgive . . . "*
4. *"I am happy that . . . "*
5. *"I love . . . "*
6. *"I feel confident that . . . "*
7. *"I feel grateful for . . . "*

*With love,*

By taking the time to express the positive feelings, you are filling up the emptiness left by feeling the negative emotions. Even if you feel better by writing out your negative feelings, take a few extra minutes to hear and write positive feelings as well. This will help solidify your connection to your true self.

### *Practicing the Four Steps*

Here is an example of practicing each of the four steps to release a block. Carl felt stuck in blame. He was always blaming his job for his unhappiness. He put in long hours, but he was not getting the money he wanted. He was not interested anymore. He could sit down and write out what was bothering him, but it just did not bring relief. He decided to let go of his block by processing his past.

He felt anger that his job was not what he thought it was going to be. He felt betrayed inside. Yet he did choose the job, so he could not get very upset about it. To get into his deeper emotions, he linked his anger to an earlier time when he felt betrayed.

He remembered a time, when he was around eight years old, when his dad promised to take him fishing. He sat waiting for his dad all day long. When his dad came home, instead of apologizing, he criticized Carl for not using that time to do his homework.

To process his past, Carl turned back the clock and imagined himself after his father rejected him and criticized him. He then proceeded to express the four emotions linked to blame. This is his feeling letter:

## CARL'S FEELING LETTER

*Dear Dad,*

   *1. Betrayal: I feel betrayed when you don't keep your promises or take time to be with me.*

   *2. Anger: I am angry that you are being critical of me. I am angry that you are mean and selfish. I am angry that you only think about yourself, and you don't think about me. You promised to take me fishing and you didn't. It is not fair. I am angry that you didn't keep your promise.*

   *3. Sadness: I am sad that you didn't come to pick me up. I am sad that other things were more important. I am sad that we didn't get to have a fun Saturday. I am sad that you work so hard. I am sad that you don't want to spend more time with me. I am sad that you didn't even apologize. I am sad that I spent all day alone by myself. I am sad that I didn't have a fun day.*

*4. Fear: I am afraid that I can't trust you. I am afraid that you will misunderstand my feelings. I am afraid that you will yell at me. I am afraid that I am being too demanding. I am afraid that I am missing out on having a fun childhood. I am afraid everyone else is having a good time when I am not. I am afraid that I am not important to you. I am afraid that you don't like me and that I am not good enough.*

*5. Sorrow: I am sorry that we didn't go fishing. I am sorry that I didn't do my homework. I am sorry that I wasted my day waiting for you. I am sorry that we are not closer. I am sorry that we don't do fun things together. I am sorry that you work so hard and that you are gone most of the time. I am sorry that I don't make better grades. I am sorry that I am not as good as my brothers.*

*6. Desire: I love you, and I want to spend more time with you. I want you to understand how I feel. I want to have fun. I want to enjoy growing up. I don't want to sit around and wait for you. I want you to call and let me know what is happening. I want to feel like an important part of your life. I want you to be proud of me. I want to feel good and happy. I want to feel free and innocent and not always afraid of your disapproval. I want you to spend time with me. I love you and miss you.*

After writing a feeling letter, Carl then did step two and imagined getting what he wanted. He wrote out the response he would have wanted from his father. Even though his father would never have given this response in real life, the process still works.

By writing out the ideal response, Carl is in effect giving to himself what he didn't get. More important, he is generating positive feelings to balance the negative feelings he just expressed. This is his response letter.

## CARL'S RESPONSE LETTER

*Dear Carl,*

*1. Apology: I apologize for being late. I am very sorry that you didn't get to go fishing with me. I am sorry that I have disappointed you again. I made a mistake by not calling.*

*2. Asking for forgiveness: Please forgive me for not being there for you. Please forgive me for not taking you fishing and doing other fun things together. Please forgive me for neglecting you.*

*3. Understanding: I understand that you are upset with me. You have a right to be angry with me. I understand that you are afraid to talk with me, I have been so critical. I understand why you are so sad. This is your childhood and it feels like you are missing out. I understand that I promised to take you fishing, and I let you down. I am so sorry, and I want to make it up.*

*4. Promises: I want you to be happy and have lots of fun. I want to take you fishing. This time I will do it. Next Saturday we will go fishing and have a lot of fun.*

*5. Love: I want you to know that I love you, and from now on things will be different. You are so special to me, I love you so much.*

*Love, Dad*

The third step in processing is to imagine and express how it feels to get what you want. This is called a connection letter, because it expresses the feelings of connecting with the support you need and want.

# CARL'S CONNECTION LETTER

*Dear Dad,*

*1. "Your love makes me feel . . . ": Your love makes
me feel better. You make me feel good inside. You make me
feel hope that I can be happy, that we can spend time
together and have a good time.*

*2. "I now understand . . . ": I now understand that
you do love me. I understand that you made a mistake and
not me. I am not bad. I know you love me, and I love you,
Dad.*

*3. "I forgive . . . ": I forgive you. I forgive you for
not being there for me. I forgive you for being inconsiderate
and critical. I forgive you for keeping me waiting*

*4. "I am happy that . . . ": I am happy that you care.
I am happy that I can talk with you. I am happy that we
can be close and have fun. I am happy that I can trust and
rely on you. I am happy that you love me, and you heard
me.*

*5. "I love . . . ": I love going fishing. I love feeling
free to be me. I love feeling that we are close. I love
knowing that we will do more things together. I love feeling
safe to be me.*

*6. "I feel confident . . . ": I feel confident that I can
have a happy life. I feel confident that you love me and that
I am important. I feel confident that I can make you happy.
I feel confident that I am good enough the way I am.*

*7. "I feel grateful for . . . ": I feel grateful for your
love and Mother's. I feel grateful that you want to spend
more time with me. I feel grateful for the nice teachers I
have at school. I feel grateful for my neat room. I feel
grateful to God for giving me such great parents.*

After doing the connection letter, Carl felt so much better that he wanted to do more. This time he imagined going on that fishing trip with his dad and generated more positive feelings of support.

## ANOTHER CONNECTION LETTER

*1. "Your love makes me feel . . . ": Right now I feel so good to be fishing with my dad. I have just caught a fish and he is so proud of me. I feel peaceful and content. It is just a nice thing to do together. I am so glad to have my father. He loves me so much, and I love him. We are having a grand time.*

*2. "I now understand . . . ": I now know how wonderful it is to go fishing and have a good time with my dad.*

*3. "I forgive . . . ": I forgive my dad for all the times he didn't come through.*

*4. "I am happy . . . ": I am happy that he drove me here. I am happy that it is a really nice day. I feel happy that we can just be together without much to do. I feel happy that today I can do no wrong. I feel really happy that I caught a fish. I feel happy we are having a good time together.*

*5. "I love . . . ": I love being with Dad and doing things together. I love having a good time. I love hanging out in the boat. I love getting better and better at this. I love driving around in the pickup truck. I love going to new places and doing new things. I love going on adventures.*

*6. "I feel confident . . . ": I feel confident that I can be me and have a good time. I don't have to be perfect. I can relax and everything will work out. I can trust my dad.*

*He really loves me, and is there for me. I can trust that he understands me, and I am important to him.*

*7. "I feel so grateful . . . ": I feel so grateful for this fishing trip. We have had such a good time. I feel grateful for the fish that I caught. I feel grateful for the terrific weather. I feel grateful that my dad took the time to do this. I know he is busy. I feel so grateful that I am not alone in the world and that he loves me. I feel so grateful that we could have fun together.*

With this attitude of gratitude Carl brought his awareness back into present time and felt much better. Although he didn't do anything that differently, he started to like his job more. In addition, he started taking more time for himself and for his kids.

## Healing Feelings with the Help of a Parent

Sometimes, when writing a letter to a parent, you may be upset with your mother or father. Sometimes you are just writing the letter to your parent to receive support, but you are upset about another matter. Let's take a short example.

Lucy was upset that she didn't win a skating contest. She fell in the finals. For months, she was depressed. To let go of her depression, she first linked it to her past. She remembered a time when she wasn't invited to a birthday party in seventh grade. It had hurt her feelings a lot. This is a short version of her feeling letter:

*Dear Mom,*

*1. I feel abandoned when the kids at school don't like me.*

*2. I am so sad that I wasn't invited to the party. No*

*one likes me. I don't know what is wrong with me. I do my best but I keep getting rejected.*

*3. I am afraid that I will never be accepted. No one loves me. I can't do anything right. The other day, when I answered a question in class, everyone laughed at me. At lunch, when I go up to kids, they run away.*

*4. I am sorry that I couldn't go to the party. I am sorry that I can't make friends. I am sorry that I can't be one of the popular girls. I feel sorry that I can't figure out what to do.*

*5. I feel frustrated that I am not invited. I feel frustrated that no one cares about me. I feel frustrated that the kids at my school are so mean. I feel frustrated that I have to be like them to be accepted.*

*6. I want to be myself and have lots of friends. I want to have lots of fun. I want to wake up in the morning excited to go to school. I want to be invited to parties and feel special. I want to do really well at school. I want others to want to be my friend.*

*Love, Lucy*

Then for the response letter, Lucy wrote the response she wanted to hear from her friends.

*Dear Lucy,*

*1. I apologize for being mean to you. I am sorry that I didn't invite you to my party. I was being mean. I invited everyone else but you.*

*2. Please forgive me for excluding you. Please forgive me for making jokes about you and putting you down. I am sorry.*

*3. I understand I have hurt you. I understand that you don't deserve to be treated this way. I understand that you are frustrated with me.*

*4. I will be more respectful in the future. I will stop being mean and try to be nice.*

*5. I would like to be your friend. I think you are really a wonderful person and lots of fun. I would like you to come over to my house, and we can do homework together.*

To complete the exercise, Lucy imagined receiving the response and then expressed her positive feelings.

*1. Your friendship makes me feel so good. I just want to be part of the group, but I don't want to give up being me. I like you.*

*2. I now understand that I am liked, and I don't have to give up who I am to be liked by others.*

*3. I forgive you for not inviting me to your party.*

*4. I am happy that we are having so much fun together now. I am happy that I am popular at school. I am happy that I have so many friends.*

*5. I love my life. I love my friends. I love going to school and having fun on the weekends.*

*6. I feel so grateful that I have so many friends and so much fun at school. I feel grateful that my friends want to spend time with me, and they miss me when I am gone.*

## Writing Feeling Letters to God

When I begin to feel any of the blocks like blame, resentment, or judgment, I will often write out my feelings to God. In this case, I don't really need to link them to my past. When talking to God, I always feel smaller and vulnerable, like a child. This is really what most prayers are. They are a means to communicate your feelings to God and express your wants and needs.

By using the feeling letter, response letter, and connection letter formats you can deepen your connection with God and fill up your vitamin G1 love tank. Some people believe in God, but feel betrayed by God. When this is the case, it is even okay to blame God. If anyone can hear your blame without feeling hurt or defensive, it is God. By forgiving God, you will be free to fill up your vitamin G1 love tank.

## The Four Steps to Process a Block

With practice, it gets easier to process your feelings. In the beginning, you will feel relieved, but sometimes a little drained. This is just because you are not in shape. A little drained is much better than blocked. After a time, just like with healthy exercise, you will not feel drained afterward. In summary, to get unstuck and remove a block, follow these four easy steps:

1. Become aware of your block and link the corresponding negative feeling to your past.
2. As you imagine yourself in the past, write a feeling letter to express the four levels of emotions that are linked to your block. Complete the letter by getting in touch with and expressing what you want.
3. As you imagine yourself in the past, write a response letter and say the things you would want to hear in response to your letter.
4. As you imagine yourself in the past and getting what you want, write a connection letter to express the positive feelings linked to getting what you need and want.

## Using Feelings to Find Emotions

As you explore the four emotions linked to each block, if you cannot feel one of the emotions, take some time to explore the negative feeling at that level. When you are blocked at any one level, the general feeling linked to that level will assist you in finding the pure emotion. Usually that will release the block and the emotion will begin to come up.

Let's say you are releasing perfectionism and you recall a time when you felt inadequate. To process feeling inadequate, you proceed to feel and express embarrassment. Then the next level down is jealousy. You may be blocked and unable to feel jealousy. To make this shift, you may first need to reflect on what makes you feel deprived, and then jealous feelings can begin to come up. Deprivation is the feeling linked to the emotion of jealousy. Refer to level nine on the feelings chart.

One of the major reasons we remain blocked is that we have suppressed certain emotions for years. Sometimes the emotion we need to feel and release is an emotion that we don't give ourselves permission to feel. Someone may be very good at anger but not good at sadness. He may easily feel sorry but not jealous. She may feel scared but unable to feel anger. To release a block, we must give ourselves permission to feel all twelve of the pure negative emotions. Remember, all twelve negative emotions are healing and natural. They are just messengers telling us we are moving away from our center. They are important signals to help us find balance. By feeling pure emotions, you come back to yourself, but by feeling blocks you disconnect from your true self.

## Finding Sarah's Jealousy

Let's look at an example. Sarah was a perfectionist. She recalled a time when she was criticized by her dad. He expected her to sing perfectly, and she could never measure up. She was a great singer, but inside she did not feel good enough.

To process her block, she first remembered a time when she felt inadequate and began to write out her feeling of embarrassment. When she was in a play, her voice was off-key. She went back to that time and wrote her dad a feeling letter starting with embarrassment. The next emotion was jealousy. She didn't think she had any jealousy. So to find it she had to shift back to the negative feeling of deprivation associated with jealousy. By looking at her feelings of deprivation, she began to discover her supressed jealousy.

Sarah felt that other kids were being loved and supported, but her dad was overdemanding. Other kids were out playing and having a good time, but she was inside practicing all the time or taking care of her younger siblings. Now she could feel jealous. After giving herself permission to feel jealous, the next two emotions were easy for her to find. In most cases, the one emotion that is difficult to find is the one you need to feel the most to remove a block.

## Linking Feelings to Your Past

To link feelings to your past, it does not mean that you had to have a terrible childhood. Everyone has challenges growing up, and some of us just had more support in dealing with those challenges. Each of the twelve blocks is linked to a variety of painful circumstances. In each of these circumstances, your parents could have been involved, or others could have been involved. If it is difficult to link your present feelings with past feelings, use these questions. They will point you in the direction of some of the common circumstances that generate negative feelings.

1. To link present feelings of betrayal to your past, use any of the following suggestions:

Recall a time when you felt betrayed in some way.

Recall a time when someone mistreated you.

Recall a time when someone lied to you.

Recall a time when someone disappointed you.

Recall a time when someone opposed you.

Recall a time when someone tricked you.

Recall a time when someone ganged up against you.

Recall a time when someone defeated you.

Recall a time when someone turned on you.

Recall a time when someone excluded you.

Recall a time when someone rejected you.

Recall a time when someone misunderstood you.

Recall a time when someone criticized you.

Recall a time when someone didn't keep a promise.

Recall a time when someone talked about you.

**2.** To link present feelings of abandonment to your past, use any of the following suggestions:

Recall a time when you felt abandoned in some way.

Recall a time when you were left behind.

Recall a time when you were unhappy.

Recall a time when you were left alone.

Recall a time when you were lost.

Recall a time when you were rejected.

Recall a time when you were left out.

Recall a time when you were not picked.

Recall a time when you were not missed.

Recall a time when you were forgotten.

Recall a time when someone was late.

Recall a time when someone left.

Recall a time when someone else got all the attention.

Recall a time when you were less popular.

Recall a time when someone disappointed you.

Recall a time when you experienced failure or defeat.

**3.** To link present feelings of uncertainty to your past, use any of the following suggestions:

Recall a time when you felt uncertain in some way.

Recall a time when you didn't know what to say.

Recall a time when you didn't know what would happen.

Recall a time when you were waiting a long time.

Recall a time when you were held back.

Recall a time when you were lost.

Recall a time when you didn't know the time.

Recall a time when you couldn't get home.

Recall a time when you couldn't get water or food.

Recall a time when you couldn't find your way.

Recall a time when you ran away from danger.

Recall a time when you needed help.

Recall a time when you were waiting to find out a punishment.

Recall a time when you didn't know what you did wrong.

Recall a time when you didn't know how to protect yourself.

Recall a time when you didn't know how to solve a problem.

**4.** To link present feelings of powerlessness to your past, use any of the following suggestions:

Recall a time when you felt powerless in some way.

Recall a time when you couldn't get what you needed.

Recall a time when you couldn't please someone.

Recall a time when you couldn't fix something you broke.

Recall a time when you made a mistake.

Recall a time when you couldn't undo a mistake.

Recall a time when you couldn't do better.

Recall a time when you didn't meet your expectations.

Recall a time when you couldn't go somewhere.

Recall a time when you could not do something.

Recall a time when you were not accepted by others.

**5.** To link present feelings of dissatisfaction to your past, use any of the following suggestions:

Recall a time when you felt dissatisfied in some way.

Recall a time when you didn't get what you wanted.

Recall a time when what you received was not what you wanted.

Recall a time when others didn't measure up to your expectations.

Recall a time when you didn't win something.

Recall a time when you didn't do well.

Recall a time when someone let you down.

Recall a time when you were not progressing fast enough.

Recall a time when you had to wait for someone.

Recall a time when you didn't like someone.

Recall a time when you didn't like a situation.

Recall a time when you heard bad news.

**6.** To link present feelings of discouragement to your past, use any of the following suggestions:

Recall a time when you felt discouraged in some way.

Recall a time when you were disappointed.

Recall a time when you didn't hear what you expected to hear.

Recall a time when you didn't get to do what you wanted to do.

Recall a time when you were going to do something and it was canceled.

Recall a time when you were not as good as you thought.

Recall a time when you were less than others.

Recall a time when you had less than others.

Recall a time when you got less than others.

Recall a time when you made a decision and it didn't turn out well.

Recall a time when you made a choice and ended up missing out in some way.

Recall a time when you were held back.

Recall a time when you were grounded.

Recall a time when you were a disappointment to others.

Recall a time when you got in trouble.

**7.** To link present feelings of helplessness to your past, use any of the following suggestions:

Recall a time when you felt helpless in some way.

Recall a time when you were little and needed help.

Recall a time when you were lost and asked for help.

Recall a time when you didn't know how to get home.

Recall a time when you were new and didn't know how things worked.

Recall a time when you couldn't make something work.

Recall a time when you couldn't do what was expected of you.

Recall a time when you felt pressured.

Recall a time when you were late.

Recall a time when you waited until the last minute.

Recall a time when you finally got help.

Recall a time when you eventually achieved a goal.

Recall a time when you struggled to get out.

Recall a time when you were physically held back in some way.

Recall a time when you didn't know whom you could trust.

**8.** To link present feelings of inadequacy to your past, use any of the following suggestions:

Recall a time when you felt inadequate in some way.

Recall a time when you disappointed a parent or someone else whom you loved.

Recall a time when others laughed at you.

Recall a time when you said the wrong thing.

Recall a time when you got into trouble.

Recall a time when someone else got into trouble and you felt bad.

Recall a time when you couldn't stop someone else from doing the wrong thing.

Recall a time when you witnessed violence or abuse.

Recall a time when you had more than others.

Recall a time when your zipper was down.

Recall a time when you publicly embarrassed yourself.

Recall a time when you were someplace and you didn't know anyone.

Recall a time when you were not picked.

Recall a time when you were rejected.

Recall a time when you failed.

Recall a time when you had a big pimple on your nose.

9. To link present feelings of deprivation to your past, use any of the following suggestions:

Recall a time when you felt deprived in some way.

Recall a time when you had less than others.

Recall a time when you didn't get what you wanted.

Recall a time when someone else got what you wanted.

Recall a time when your sibling got more than you.

Recall a time when you were ignored.

Recall a time when you were neglected.

Recall a time when you were not forgiven.

Recall a time when you were punished.

Recall a time when you didn't get to go.

Recall a time when life was unfair.

Recall a time when you did something nice and were then mistreated.

Recall a time when something was taken from you.

Recall a time when you didn't get to have your turn.

Recall a time when someone had more than you.

Recall a time when someone did better by cheating.

Recall a time when someone cut in front of you.

Recall a time when you got in trouble and it wasn't your fault.

**10.** To link present feelings of being excluded to your past, use any of the following suggestions:

Recall a time when you felt excluded in some way.

Recall a time when you were left behind.

Recall a time when you were rejected.

Recall a time when you didn't get to go.

Recall a time when you were left out.

Recall a time when you were not invited.

Recall a time when you were laughed at.

Recall a time when you were mistreated.

Recall a time when you missed out.

Recall a time when you didn't get somewhere on time.

Recall a time when others had a good time and you didn't.

Recall a time when you were misunderstood.

Recall a time when you were ignored.

Recall a time when you were not allowed in.

Recall a time when you were not dressed appropriately.

Recall a time when you were different.

Recall a time when you were judged by your skin color, size, sex, or family.

Recall a time when you did poorly on a test.

Recall a time when others were jealous of you.


**11.** To link present feelings of hopelessness to your past, use any of the following suggestions:

Recall a time when you felt hopeless in some way.

Recall a time when you felt you didn't know what to do.

Recall a time when you were late.

Recall a time when someone you needed left or died.

Recall a time when you were unable to do something.

Recall a time when you didn't do something well.

Recall a time when you were not as good as others.

Recall a time when you couldn't make up your mind.

Recall a time when you didn't have enough information.

Recall a time when you didn't have enough help.

Recall a time when you got mixed messages.

Recall a time when you didn't know why you were punished.

Recall a time when you didn't know why you were hurt in some way.

Recall a time when you didn't know how to get out of something.

Recall a time when you were chased.

**12.** To link present feelings of unworthiness to your past, use any of the following suggestions:

Recall a time when you felt unworthy in some way.

Recall a time when you were misbehaving.

Recall a time when you were not helpful.

Recall a time when you were not what others thought about you.

Recall a time when you were not good enough in some way.

Recall a time when you let others down.

Recall a time when your body was not big enough or was too big.

Recall a time when you realized something about your body was flawed or imperfect.

Recall a time when something happened that had to be kept secret.

Recall a time when you couldn't talk about something.

Recall a time when you couldn't tell your mother.

Recall a time when you couldn't tell your father.

Recall a time when you couldn't stop something.

Recall a time when you didn't measure up to someone's expectations.

Recall a time when you couldn't tell the truth.

Recall a time when you were inappropriate.

Recall a time when you made a mistake.

Recall a time when you upset someone.

Recall a time when felt you had more than others.

Recall a time when you kept someone waiting.

Recall a time when you felt different.

When you are processing a block and you can't remember a time in your past when you had similar feelings, these different suggestions are very helpful. You may wish to use them on an ongoing basis to look back at your past and discover any hidden blocks you have.

If you cannot remember anything from your past and you are still blocked, this may not be the right way for you. Quite often, being in a workshop setting will provide the right stimulation. In other cases private therapy is very helpful. Sometimes the blocks go away without looking into your past. Sometimes the best way to remove a block is with one of the following twelve special healing meditations.

## Twelve Healing Meditations

These healing meditations are powerful for anyone stuck in a block or for anyone with a chronic sickness. In most cases, when we have pushed our feelings down, our body takes on a sickness. Some people respond to healing treatments and others don't, depending on how stuck they are in a block. To facilitate the healing of any disease, use any of these healing meditations twice a day for a minimum of fifteen minutes each time. These meditations open our hearts to receive God's blessing.

**1:** Healing Meditation for Letting Go of Blame
"Oh God, oh merciful Father, your heart is full of kindness. Your love is boundless and always present. I need your help. I feel so betrayed. My heart is closed. I cannot forgive. Help me to love again. Heal my heart, heal my heart."

**2:** Healing Meditation for Letting Go of Depression
"Oh God, oh nurturing Mother, my heart is open for you. Please come into my heart. I feel so abandoned. Make me happy. Please come into my heart. Make me happy. Oh Mother, my heart is open for you, open for you. My heart is open for you, open for you."

**3:** Healing Meditation for Letting Go of Anxiety
"Oh radiant and glorious God, oh divine light, I feel so uncertain. I am lost in the darkness. I am blind. I can't see my way. Bring your light to my heart. Remove the darkness, remove the darkness. Give me peace."

**4:** Healing Meditation for Letting Go of Indifference
"Oh heavenly Father, the whole creation is in your hands. I feel so powerless. I am tired, really tired. I need your help. Please come into my heart. Fill me up, fill me up. Remove my pain, remove my pain."

**5:** Healing Meditation for Letting Go of Judgments
"Oh God, oh holy Mother, all of creation is your garden. I am like a bee attracted to the flowers. Let me taste the sweet honey of your love. I feel so dissatisfied. Nurture my soul with peace and kindness, nurture my soul with peace and kindness."

**6:** Healing Meditation for Letting Go of Indecision
"Oh Holy Spirit, my life is in your hands. I feel so
discouraged. I have lost my way. Guide me on the right
path. I am your child. Don't let go. Hold my hand. Don't
let go. Hold my hand. Show me the right path, show me
the right path."

**7:** Healing Meditation for Letting Go of Procrastination
"Oh God, oh divine energy, the source of all creation, the
infinite power that sustains all life, please help me. I feel so
helpless. Lift my burdens. Carry my load. Lift my burdens.
Carry my load. Don't forget me, don't forget me."

**8:** Healing Meditation for Letting Go of Perfectionism
"Oh holy Mother, your heart is always full. I am so thirsty
for your divine milk. I long for the comfort of your love
and the kindness of your touch. Please help me. I feel so
inadequate. Release my pain, release my pain."

**9:** Healing Meditation for Letting Go of Resentment
"Oh God, oh holy Father, thank you for your ever-present
kindness and generosity. Hear my soul's desire. I feel so
deprived. Remove all obstacles. Take away my fears. Make
me confident, make me confident."

**10:** Healing Meditation for Letting Go of Self-Pity
"Oh God, oh divine spirit, Mother and Father of all
creation, my heart is hurting. I feel left out. I am alone.
Don't forget me, don't forget me. Help me, help me. Heal
me, heal me."

**11:** Healing Meditation for Letting Go of Confusion
"Oh heavenly Father, by your blessings I came to earth.
Please look at me. Don't forget me. I feel so hopeless.

Please come to me. I really, really want your help. Please look at me. Don't forget me. Please come to me. My heart is open for you, my heart is open for you."

**12:** Healing Meditation for Letting Go of Guilt
"Oh God, oh divine Mother, your love is without limit. Your creation is most beautiful. Please help me. I am in a desert. I can't see your beauty. My life is empty. Fill me with your love, fill me with your love."

## Twelve Meditations to Achieve Greater Success

The following meditations are designed for people who feel healthy and content, but wish to experience greater outer success. The twelve healing meditations heal the blocks in our heart to attract what we need. These twelve success meditations help remove the blocks to creating what we want. They help to open our minds to our unlimited potential.

**1:** Success Meditation for Removing Blame
"Oh God, I feel so betrayed. Give me love. Help me to forgive. Remove this blame. Take away my anger. Help me to feel pleased with my life and others."

**2:** Success Meditation for Removing Depression
"Oh God, I feel so abandoned. Give me joy. Help me to reach out. Remove this depression. Take away my sadness. Help me to be happy with what I have."

**3:** Success Meditation for Removing Anxiety
"Oh God, I feel so uncertain. Give me faith. Help me to have trust. Remove this anxiety. Take away my doubts. Help me to feel excited. Help me to believe."

**4: Success Meditation for Removing Indifference**
"Oh God, I feel so powerless. Give me compassion. My heart is closed. Remove this indifference. Take away my sorrow. Lift my spirit. Help me to feel gladness. Give me purpose and direction."

**5: Success Meditation for Removing Judgments**
"Oh God, I feel so dissatisfied. Give me patience. Help me to find loving acceptance. Remove these judgments. Take away my frustration. Help me to be satisfied with what I have."

**6: Success Meditation for Removing Indecision**
"Oh God, I feel so discouraged. Give me persistence. Help me know what to do. Remove this indecision. Take away my disappointment. Help me to feel encouraged."

**7: Success Meditation for Removing Procrastination**
"Oh God, I feel so helpless. Give me courage. Help me to be strong. Remove this procrastination. Take away my worries. Help me to feel assured that I can do what I am here to do."

**8: Success Meditation for Removing Perfectionism**
"Oh God, I feel so inadequate. Give me humility. Help me to love myself just the way I am. Take away this need to be perfect. Take away my embarrassment. Help me to feel good about myself."

**9: Success Meditation for Removing Resentment**
"Oh God, I feel so deprived. Give me abundance. Help me to feel my generous nature. Take away this resentment. Take away my jealousy. Help me to feel content with what I have and confident that I can get what I want."

**10:** Success Meditation for Removing Self-Pity
"Oh God, I feel so left out. Give me gratitude. Help me to open my heart to appreciate and receive your many blessings. Remove this self-pity. Take away my hurt. Help me give thanks for all that I have and the many opportunities I have for more."

**11:** Success Meditation for Removing Confusion
"O God, I feel so hopeless. Give me wisdom. Help me to see clearly. Show me the way. Remove this confusion. Take away my panic. Help me to feel confident."

**12:** Success Meditation for Removing Guilt
"Oh God, I feel so unworthy. Help me to open my heart to receive your blessings. Set me free to feel worthy. Remove this guilt and restore my innocence. Take away my shame. Help me to feel delighted with myself and others."

## Six Weeks to Personal Success

To remove a block by practicing one of the twenty-four special meditations, plan on spending at least six weeks. First, take a few days to memorize the prayer. Then, with your fingertips above your shoulders, repeat the meditation ten times out loud and then quietly for fifteen minutes. At the end, take a few minutes to feel your wants. Imagine getting what you want. Explore the positive feelings of getting what you need and want. Generally speaking, it takes six weeks to change a habit and the way we think and act. By practicing these meditations for that amount of time, you will reap the benefits.

When you generate these positive feelings every day, your inner and outer life will begin to improve each day. Sometimes overnight you will experience great benefit. After time, your particular meditation will be automatic and spontaneous. You will be able to access inner support, and the grip of lifelong patterns will lose their power over you.

---

**After time your particular meditation will be automatic and spontaneous.**

---

After clearing one block, you may find that another comes up. At this point, you will not be troubled, because you will have experienced within yourself the power to create what you want. Besides doing the practices of personal success to sustain your clear intention in the right direction, make sure to read again and again the ideas and insights that support you in that direction.

# CHAPTER 18

# A Brief History of Personal Success

I N EVERY GENERATION, there have always been a few people who have achieved great personal success. They were ordinary people but seemed extraordinary simply because they were ahead of their time. They were born with the ability to comprehend certain insights that the rest of the world did not have. Although powerless to communicate these insights, they were able to point mankind in a helpful direction until the day their insights became more accessible to others.

> Wise men and women have pointed people of
> their generation in a direction that was
> helpful for that time.

Now we are at a time in history when we are ready to grow up. It is a time when we can look directly within for the guidance we need to experience greater personal success. We are now capable of looking within to find our connection to God. As more and more people are making this shift to finding their connection to God within themselves, many have left their religions. There are empty churches and temples everywhere. This trend is changing, though, as many people are returning to their religions with greater insight and appreciation.

---

**We are now capable of looking within to find our connection to God.**

---

Many people wonder if religion will survive these changes. The answer is yes. Finding the power to hear our inner guidance does not in any way mean that we are beyond the need for religion or other forms of organized spirituality. As people grow up and leave their parents, they continue to need and depend on their parents' love, support, and guidance if they have a good relationship. Our level of dependence changes.

When we leave our parents, we experience the freedom to know what is true from within ourselves. Likewise, as we open our hearts through love and connect with our true selves and God, we begin to see the underlying truth in all religions. We recognize what is good in all paths and don't get caught up focusing on the differences.

This is the time for us to outgrow our dependence on one way and realize that the ways of truth are many. If there is "one way," then it is the one way for you, and that can only be known in your heart. The day has come when people of all faiths can join together and recognize goodness and Godliness in everyone. We do not all have to think, feel, and believe the same things to live together in harmony and peace.

---

**This is the time for us to outgrow our dependence on one way and realize that the ways of truth are many.**

---

Today we see around us thousands of people who have achieved outer success and inner fulfillment. Although the tabloids are often full of tragic stories of the rich and famous, there are many people who have it all. They may not all be super-rich and famous, but they have learned to get what they want, and they continue to want it. They have both inner and outer success. You, too, can have it all.

We see this good life in the movies and on TV, and we wonder why we don't have it. While we get to see what is possible in the movies, we don't know how to make it happen. Either we become discouraged and think it is only for a few, which was certainly true in the past, or we feel excited, expecting that one day it will happen for us.

That long-awaited day has come. It's time now to wake up from our slumber. The long night is over. Achieving personal success is no longer for a select few, nor is it ahead of our time. It is no longer extraordinary. It is within the reach of every person, because now its secrets can be understood.

---

**Achieving personal success is no longer for a select few, nor is it ahead of our time.**

---

The ideas of personal success are simple and easy to understand, and can be put into practice immediately. They are new, and yet they are a collection of age-old ideas put in a new arrangement. What is most different is that now everyone can understand them and put the techniques into practice.

You have the potential to create your destiny, but you must find it. No longer do you need someone to direct you. That wisdom can now be found within.

Let these ideas of personal success help awaken you to who you truly are and assist you in claiming your inner power. Let this book be a set of jumper cables to charge up your battery. You can be all that you are and fulfill all your true desires. The seeds of desire would not be in your heart if you did not have the special potential to create your future.

When you are true to yourself and in touch with your authentic feelings, wishes, and desires, you are connecting to your true self. The true self or natural state of every person is joy, love, confidence, and peace. These attributes are already present inside you. When you are unhappy, anxious, feeling bad, or experiencing any of the twelve blocks, you are just temporarily disconnected from your true self.

---

**Whenever you are not getting what you want, you are disconnected from your natural state in some way.**

---

In a very real sense, the world you live in is a reflection of your inner state. You cannot change everything in the world, because it is a reflection of the inner state of others as well. How you experience the world and the situations you attract or are attracted to are mirrors of your inner world. As you take back the power to determine how you experience your world, the way the world touches you changes. When you come from unconditional love, joy, confidence, and peace, the world is fertile ground to sow the seeds of your desires.

---

**Your experience of the world continues to reflect your inner state.**

---

Whether you are aware that you are stuck in your blocks or you just can't seem to get what you want, by reconnecting with your natural state you can and will begin to create the life you want. To release the twelve blocks, you must take back your power by recognizing that you have the ability to change your feelings. No one else can do it for you. When life is pulling you down, it is only because you have disconnected from your natural state.

Although someone or some circumstance may upset you, you still hold the power to bounce back and feel good again.

---

**You have the power to change, and no one else can do it for you.**

---

You have the power to change how you feel, regardless of circumstances in the outer world. To do this, you must remember again and again that although it seems like the outer world is making you unhappy, it is an illusion. By looking within and finding love, joy, confidence, and peace, you gain the power to attract and create in your life what you want.

If you get punched on your arm, you may get bruised, but you still hold the power to heal yourself and then plan ways to protect yourself in the future. By acknowledging that you are stuck in any of the twelve blocks, you are clearly recognizing your responsibility for how you feel. You are taking back your power.

With this positive and powerful attitude you are saying:

"Right now, I am responsible for how I feel, therefore outer conditions cannot keep me from experiencing my positive feelings."

"Right now, if I have disconnected from my true self, I have the power to find my way back."

By taking responsibility for your blocks, you open the door to reconnect with your true self. Each time you come back to your true self, you strengthen your ability to tap into the full power and potential that are your birthright.

## *Preparing for Your Journey*

With these various processes, practices, and special meditations, you are now well prepared for your journey in this world.

You have the necessary tools and insights to remove all the obstacles to achieving personal success. Each of these tools has helped me and thousands of others in our journeys. I hope that you cherish and rely on these insights as much as I do. I hope they open doors for you that you never imagined were possible.

May you always grow in greater love and success. You deserve it, and so does everyone else. You can make your dreams come true. You have what it takes. By removing the twelve blocks, you will be well on your way.

This is a very special time to be born. You have access to many more opportunities than any other generation. Make use of your opportunities, and each day take a step closer to your goals. Always remember that you are not alone and that you are needed in this world. You are loved, and you do make a difference. God bless you.

# If you like what you just read and want to learn more...

Call our representatives, Mars-Venus Institute, twenty-four hours a day, seven days a week, toll free, at 1-888-INFO-MVI (1-888-463-6684) or visit John Gray's website at www.marsvenus.com for information on the following subjects:

## MARS-VENUS SPEAKERS BUREAU

More than 500,000 individuals and couples around the world have already benefited from John Gray's relationship seminars. We invite and encourage you to share with John this safe, insightful and healing experience. Because of the popularity of his seminars and talks, Dr. Gray has developed programs for presentations by individuals he has personally trained. These seminars are available for both the general public as well as private corporate functions. Please call for current schedules and booking information.

## MARS-VENUS WORKSHOPS

The Mars-Venus Institute offers workshops that bring information to local communities around the world and trains those interested in presenting these workshops. These exciting workshops features John's favorite video segments and exercises presented by trained facilitators that have completed an in-depth course of study. Participants take home positive, practical experience that allows them to use Dr. Gray's suggestions comfortably and naturally. You can call the Mars-Venus Institute toll-free at 1-888-INFO-MVI (1-888-463-6684). If you are out of the USA, call 415-389-6857 or look for us on our website at www.mars-venus-institute.com.

## MARS & VENUS COUNSELING CENTERS

In response to the thousands of requests we have received for licensed professionals that use the Mars/Venus principles in their practice, John Gray has established the Mars & Venus Counseling Centers and Counselor Training. Participants in this program have completed a rigorous study of John's work and have demonstrated a commitment to his valuable concepts. If you are interested in a referral to a counselor in you area call 1-800-649-4155. If you seek information about training as a Mars & Venus counselor or establishing a Mars & Venus Counseling Center, please call 1-800-735-6052.

## Videos, Audiotapes and Books by John Gray

For further explorations of the wonderful world of Mars and Venus, see the descriptions that follow and call us to place an order for additional information.

Mars-Venus Institute
20 Sunnyside Avenue, A-130
Mill Valley, CA 94941
1-888-INFO-MVI (1-888-463-6684)

## VIDEOS

### Men Are from Mars, Women Are from Venus
#### Twelve VHS cassettes

This is a complete collection of John Gray's work on video. In this series, Dr. Gray shares the insights and tools necessary for understanding, accepting, and loving our differences. In a positive and uplifting way, couples and singles learn to improve communication and enjoy healthy, happy relationships without sacrifice.

### Mars and Venus on a Date
#### Seven VHS cassettes

After years of focusing on couples, Dr. Gray finally answers the thousands of singles and dating partners who asked him, "What about me?" John examines his five stages of dating: attraction, uncertainty, exclusivity, intimacy, and engagement. Find out why women need reassurance and men need encouragement. Increase your understanding of male/female differences and women's most asked question, "Why don't men commit?"

## Men Are from Mars, Women Are from Venus—
## Children Are from Heaven

### Two VHS cassettes

Dr. Gray lends his insights to parents trying to understand their little Martians and Venusians. In these cassettes you'll learn the five most important messages to give your children: It's Okay to Be Different; It's Okay to Make Mistakes; It's Okay to Have Feelings; It's Okay to Ask for What You Want; It's Okay to Say No, But Mom and Dad Are the Boss.

## AUDIOTAPES

### Secrets of Successful Relationships

#### Twelve 45-minute audiocassettes

This audio series was taped live at Dr. Gray's two-and-a-half-day seminars and features three themes: The Secrets of Communication; Getting the Love You Deserve; and The Secrets of Intimacy and Passions.

## BOOKS

### What You Feel, You Can Heal

An enjoyable guide to understanding and enriching your own personal growth. Learn to heal and forgive past hurts and resentments, increase your self-confidence when dealing with the opposite sex, and enjoy clear communication in a loving relationship. Dr. Gray teaches you: The Ultimate Healing Technique–The Love Letter; How to Transform the Inner Circle; How to Heal the Past; and The Power of Forgiveness.

Paperback, Heart Publishing 0-931269-01-6 $12.95

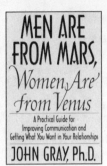
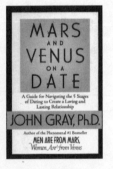
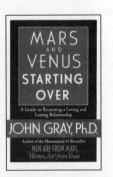

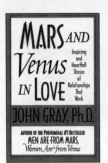

## True Stories from Couples!

### MARS AND VENUS IN LOVE

Inspiring and Heartfelt Stories of
Relationships That Work

Hardcover
0-06-017471-4 $18.00
Two audiocassettes
0-694-51713-5 $18.00

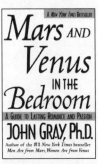

## Keep Passion Alive!

### MARS AND VENUS IN THE BEDROOM

A Guide to Lasting
Romance and Passion

Hardcover
0-06-017212-6 $24.00
Trade paperback
0-06-092793-3 $13.00
Two audiocassettes
1-55994-883-3 $18.00

Also available in Spanish:

### MARTE Y VENUS EN EL DORMITORIO

Trade paperback
0-06-095180-X $11.00
Two audiocassettes
0-694-51676-7 $18.00

## The Keys to Making Love Last!

### MARS AND VENUS TOGETHER FOREVER

Relationship Skills for
Lasting Intimacy

Trade paperback
0-06-092661-9 $13.00
Mass market paperback
0-06-104457-1 $6.99

Also available in Spanish:

### MARTE Y VENUS JUNTOS PARA SIEMPRE

Trade paperback
0-06-095236-9 $11.00

## ALSO AVAILABLE:

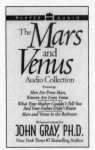

### THE MARS AND VENUS AUDIO COLLECTION

Contains one of each cassette:
*Men Are from Mars, Women Are
from Venus; What Your Mother
Couldn't Tell You and Your Father
Didn't Know;* and
*Mars and Venus in the Bedroom.*

Three audiocassettes
0-694-51589-2 $39.00

### MEN, WOMEN AND RELATIONSHIPS

Making Peace with the Opposite Sex
Mass market paperback
0-06-101070-7 $6.99
One audiocassette
0-694-51534-5 $12.00

### WHAT YOU FEEL YOU CAN HEAL

A Guide for Enriching Relationships
Two audiocassettes
0-694-51613-9 $18.00

Visit our website at http://www.harpercollins.com